ONE WEEK

Narratives and Narrators

Narratives and Narrators

A Philosophy of Stories

Gregory Currie

OXFORD
UNIVERSITY PRESS

OXFORD

UNIVERSITY PRESS

Great Clarendon Street, Oxford OX2 6DP

Oxford University Press is a department of the University of Oxford.
It furthers the University's objective of excellence in research, scholarship,
and education by publishing worldwide in

Oxford New York

Auckland Cape Town Dar es Salaam Hong Kong Karachi
Kuala Lumpur Madrid Melbourne Mexico City Nairobi
New Delhi Shanghai Taipei Toronto

With offices in

Argentina Austria Brazil Chile Czech Republic France Greece
Guatemala Hungary Italy Japan Poland Portugal Singapore
South Korea Switzerland Thailand Turkey Ukraine Vietnam

Oxford is a registered trade mark of Oxford University Press
in the UK and in certain other countries

Published in the United States
by Oxford University Press Inc., New York

British Library Cataloguing in Publication Data
Data available

Library of Congress Cataloging in Publication Data
Data available

Typeset by Laserwords Private Limited, Chennai, India
Printed in Great Britain
on acid-free paper by
MPG Books Group, Bodmin and King's Lynn

ISBN 978–0–19–928260–9

10 9 8 7 6 5 4 3

Preface

Claims that this or that capacity is unique to humans have been controversial. Toolmaking of an elementary sort turns out to be quite common among our relatives. Perhaps even language skills are reproducible, albeit at very low levels, in some other creatures. There may be no basic cognitive capacity which separates us absolutely from all the other animals. It is what we do with the whole package that is so distinctive. In our ability to change the world we live in, no other creature comes close. The results, for good and ill, are all about us. They are all, in one way or another, testimony to our mental and behavioural flexibility—our imagination, in the broadest sense of that notion. One such result, undramatic compared with our technology but absolutely pervasive, is our storytelling, something I am pretty confident no other species goes in for. With stories we are released from the here and now, even if the story is a dull recounting of yesterday's journey. Stories turn the experiences of one into the knowledge of all; they make vivid what may have happened, what might have but did not; what we hope for or fear. Not that the news is wholly good; a lying story may become the false opinion of all; I address this issue in appendices to Chapters 2, 5, and 11.

Tellers of stories have found ways to open other doors to the merely possible, by crafting their stories in ways which encourage us to respond to them from unexplored, sometimes exciting, sometimes disturbing, perspectives. Stories give us alternatives to reality, and alternative ways of responding to these alternatives. This depends on another capacity which, if not absolutely unique to humans, is vastly more powerful with us: I will call it shared emotional attention. We share emotions, not simply in the sense of sometimes happening to be in the same emotional state, but in the sense of experiencing, and valuing, our emotional states as shared. Narrative before the days of writing and the privatization of experience was a communal activity and its power to generate shared emotions would have been very evident; I draw attention later on to a remnant of this communal past in carer–child storytelling. Writing makes the bond between storymaker and audience less obvious but it does not destroy it; written as well as filmic and theatrical narratives have available to them refinements of technique which create perspectival effects of the subtlest kind, inducing in the audience a sense of sharing with an absent but complex and sometimes ambivalent personality. We share emotions, of course, with the characters of a narrative, and this has been the focus of the recent debate over empathy and its role in storytelling. I don't ignore this, but my primary focus is on the complexities that emerge when we examine something briefly noted by Hume as a barrier to the maintenance of a standard of taste: that 'we choose our favourite author as we do our friend, from a conformity of humour and disposition'. I will suggest that, while we are capable of reaching beyond mere conformity of disposition when we look for an engaging author, a sense of shared engagement with the story is immensely important for understanding the pleasures and the values of narrative.

This emphasis on the duality of storytelling—the duality of story told and mode of telling—makes clear how unfortunately ambiguous 'story' is, since it can mean either. One remedy is to distinguish between the story told—the characters and events—and the vehicle of telling, the narrative. That's the tradition I will follow, and in these terms this is a book which, despite its subtitle, is first of all about narratives and only secondarily about stories. But it is about both; it is about how narratives convey stories. It is also about how narratives shape the responses of their audiences to the stories they tell.

Such a project has antecedents with frightening scholarly credentials. Eric Auerbach was able to write his book on mimesis only when separated from all those texts which, had they been within reach, would have paralysed the enterprise by the weight of their authority. Gerard Genette cites a similar genesis for some of his work on narrative, though this may be more of an affectionate tribute to his predecessor than serious personal history. Writing with all the resources of the electronic age, I have no such excuse. Everything unread, unacknowledged, unexplored is my fault. This is a very small book on a big subject. If much of what is written about narrative is true, the subject is vast. What is written about it certainly is. Searching under 'narrative' brings up a list that stretches off into cavernous spaces marked history, fiction, the literary, language, communication, memory, personhood, psychiatry.

I aimed to write a brief account of the approach to narrative which I favour; to orient it according to philosophical ways of thinking; to avoid the history of narrative and the history of reflection on narrative, yet to engage, briefly, with real narratives of influence and distinction; to include discussion of non-literary forms. Mostly, I have held to this plan. It was never likely that I would produce an excess of literary or historical scholarship. I chose examples based on casual reading and because they seemed vivid rather than representative of narrative as a whole—and being representative is impossible, given that at least nine-tenths and probably a great deal more of the history of narrative is inaccessible to us now. Most of my illustrations, it turns out, are boringly canonical, but that should not worry us; the only relevant question is whether they do in fact illustrate the claims made, and their familiarity will make them less of a distraction from the general argument. I have occasionally engaged with a few leading aspects of narrative theory in the literary and filmic tradition, but only where it suited the direction of the argument. In one place it seemed especially appropriate. I make a good deal of use of the idea of a point of view. Theorists of narrative have expressed dissatisfaction with the term—and, though less clearly, with the concept—and have tried to substitute less familiar notions such as 'focalization'. I care hardly at all what terms we use, and rather more about what we manage to explain by using them. I hope I have managed to rehabilitate point of view by showing how, when linked to the right other notions, it plays its part in an explanatory enterprise.

One early ambition did not survive. I had wanted to embed the account of narrative in a thoroughly worked out theory of communication that would (I imagined) be a judicious weighing of Gricean, relevance theoretic, and other pragmatically oriented approaches. It did not take long to see that this would be a disastrous policy: very injurious, first of all, to the cause of pragmatics and, secondly, not very illuminating of at least many of the specific aspects of narrative I wanted to discuss. Occasional references to these ideas survive in material on the explicit/implicit distinction, irony, and (of course) authorial intention. But such issues as the exact nature of the mechanisms of implicature that operate in narrative, and the difference (if any) between fictional and non-fictional cases in this regard will have to be treated of on a better occasion.

That is one (possible) difference between fiction and non-fiction I don't take up. But while the book is about narrative in general, and so emphasizes commonalities between the two, it is not blind to the distinction, nor is its discussion evenly balanced between the two cases. I say more about fictional cases, and this is not merely (though it may be in part) because prior work makes me more at home in this region. There are non-fictional narratives, but there are non-fictional other things: theories, recipes, descriptions of legal systems, driving manuals, etiquette books, musings on the natural world such as we find with Gilbert White. Narrative and non-fiction are not connected in any special way. When we turn to fiction, the case is different. While virtually everyone consumes fictional narratives, no one, to my knowledge, has an interest in fictional theories. There are science fiction novels, but there is no fictional science.[1] Cooks do not relax by reading recipes for imaginary cakes made from non-existent ingredients, nor barristers by reading the hypothesized legal system of Neptune. We sometimes get hypothetical laws, natural and social, in fiction, but in the service of filling out the details of narratives of characters and incidents on which those laws have some bearing. The universal response to the suggestion that we might take an interest in fictional jurisprudence or fictional cookery is 'why bother?' Such a response to the idea of taking an interest in fictional narratives would be regarded as very odd.

What about the depictive arts? Surely we are engaged by fictional portraits and sculptures. I won't argue that such things are narratives, though we do speak sometimes of narrative painting. But they do have some of those features I will later emphasize as significant marks of narrative: the representation of the particularity of an individual thing, and (sometimes) its location in a causal nexus. Depictive works have other interests: formal features, qualities of balance and beauty, display of skill or sensitivity, or it may be that they are merely representations of beautiful or otherwise interesting things. Narratives don't quite exhaust the field of what we regard as the legitimate domain of fiction, but they occupy a vastly greater portion of that territory than they do of the non-fictional. And there is another reason behind the lack of balance in this book. By and large, it is fictional narratives that show the most developed, most imaginative

---

[1] As Paul Smith points out to me, there is a genre of science writing which takes its theme from science fiction. Thus, Krauss examines the extent to which *Star Trek* violates known laws and mechanisms, providing some physics instruction along the way (Krauss 2007). There are also serious scientific inquiries into the consequences of setting physical constants at counterfactual values, from which we have learned something about the surprisingly narrow range of values that support life. What I am claiming we do not find is avowedly false scientific theorizing divorced from any narrative context and yet offered as material to engage the imagination.

resources with which to portray character and personality, point of view, motive, and action. These things justify a leaning towards, though not an exclusive concentration on, the fictional.

The intended (or hoped-for) audience for this book consists of graduate students and professionals in philosophy, along with scholars of anthropology, drama, history, literature, film, linguistics, psychology, and psychiatry who have a little familiarity and much patience with philosophical ideas. General readers willing to give it a go are very welcome.

G.C.
Epperstone

Acknowledgements

A very large number of people have commented on versions of these chapters, and I am not able with confidence to recall all their contributions. A few of those whose comments have been especially helpful are Lanier Anderson, Michael Bristol, Noël Carroll, Pascal Engel, John Ferrari, Peter Goldie, Paul Harris, David Hills, Jon Jurideini, Andrew Kania, Peter Lamarque, Josh Landy, Jerry Levinson, Patrizia Lombardo, Kevin Mulligan, Jenefer Robinson, Blakey Vermeule, Kendall Walton, and Deirdre Wilson. The suggestions of two anonymous readers were very helpful. As on previous occasions, I have benefited from the advice and encouragement of Peter Momtchiloff.

Versions of some of the chapters were given as colloquium talks and conference papers at the Universities of Barcelona, Durham, East Anglia, Geneva, Hertfordshire, Maryland, Nevada (Las Vegas), Nancy, Nottingham, Otago, Sheffield, Stockholm, Sussex, Texas (Austin), Warwick, at Stanford University, Victoria University, Wellington, the École des hautes études en sciences sociales, and the Sorbonne. Thanks to the audiences on all these occasions.

Sam Guttenplan and I organized a conference on narrative at Cumberland Lodge, Windsor Park in June 2003; a selection of the papers was published in *Mind and Language* in 2004. My thanks to Sam, to Gerard O'Brian, and to all the speakers and participants who helped to shape my thinking about narrative. A decade ago, Jon Jureidini and I worked on a project on narrative and psychopathology. My thanks to Jon for all that I learned from him, a little of which has made its way into this book.

The work was supported, at various times, by generous grants from the Arts and Humanities Research Council, UK, the Australian Research Council, and, most recently, by the provision of a Senior Research Fellowship funded jointly by The British Academy and the Leverhulme Foundation.

My greatest debt is, once again, to Gabriel, Martha, and Penny.

Some of these chapters have their origins in papers previously published. Chapter 8 contains material from 'Why Irony is Pretence', in Shaun Nichols (ed.) *The Architecture of the Imagination: New Essays on Pretence, Possibility, and Fiction* (Oxford University Press, 2006). Chapters 10 and 11 contain material from 'Narrative and the Psychology of Character', *Journal of Aesthetics and Art Criticism*, 67 (2009), 61–71. Elsewhere in the book I draw, unsystematically and with many changes, on material from: 'Point of View', in G. Hagberg and W. Jost (eds) *The Blackwell Companion to the Philosophy of Literature* (Blackwell, 2009); 'Both Sides of the Story: Explaining Events in a Narrative', *Philosophical Studies*, 135 (2007), 49–63; 'Narrative Representation of Causes', *Journal of Aesthetics and Art Criticism*, 62 (2006), 119–28; 'Narrative Frameworks', in D. Hutto (ed.) *Narrative and Understanding Persons*, Royal Institute of Philosophy Supplement, 60 (Cambridge University Press, 2007), 17–42. Thanks to the editors and publishers of all these journals and volumes for their kind permissions.

Untitled Film Still #6 © 1997 Cindy Sherman is used courtesy of the artist and Metro Pictures.

Contents

1. **Representation**   1

   1.1. Artefactual Functions   1

   1.2. Narrative and Story Content   7

   1.3. Implicit and Explicit   12

   1.4. Nature's Narratives?   21

   1.5. Implied Authors   25

   1.6. Looking Ahead   26

2. **The Content of Narrative**   27

   2.1. Causes   27

   2.2. Narrativity   33

   2.3. Weighing Factors   36

   2.4. Causal History   39

   2.5. Coincidence and Humean Cause   41

   2.6. Salient Possibilities   42

   Appendix: Cheap Talk and Costly Signals   43

3. **Two Ways of Looking at a Narrative**   49

   3.1. Limits to the Content Approach to Narrative   50

   3.2. Telling the Time in *Marienbad*   52

   3.3. Possibility, Probability, Evidence   54

   3.4. Representational Correspondence   58

4. **Authors and Narrators**   65

   4.1. A Distinction without a Difference?   65

   4.2. Implied and Second Authors   69

   4.3. A Concession   73

   4.4. A Note on Non-fiction   74

   4.5. Should there be a Presumption in Favour of the
         Internal Narrator?   76

5. Expression and Imitation   86

   5.1. The Framing Effect of Point of View   87
   5.2. Conversation, Framing, and Joint Attention   93
   5.3. Joint Attending and Guided Attending   97
   5.4. Imitation   100
   5.5. Imitating the Unreal   101
   5.6. The Standard Model   106
   Appendix: Expression and the Reliability of Signalling   107

6. Resistance   109

   6.1. Kinds of Resistance   109
   6.2. Abilities   114
   6.3. The Evolution of Resistance   115
   6.4. Confusing Framework and Content   117
   6.5. Conclusion   121

7. Character-focused Narration   123

   7.1. Genette's Distinction   124
   7.2. The Knowledge Criterion   127
   7.3. Expression   129
   7.4. Focalization   136
   7.5. Context Shifting   139
   7.6. Empathy   144
   7.7. Conclusion   146

8. Irony: A Pretended Point of View   148

   8.1. Ironic Situations   148
   8.2. Representational Irony   150
   8.3. Points of View   155
   8.4. Responding to Criticism   158
   8.5. Pretence of Manner   161
   8.6. Ironic Narration   164

9. Dis-interpretation   167
    9.1.   Irony in Pictures   168
    9.2.   Point of View Shots   169
    9.3.   Ironic Narration   171
    9.4.   The Birds and the Psyche: Internal vs External
           Perspective   175
    9.5.   Irony and Horror: The Tradition   182
    9.6.   Science and the Supernatural   184

10. Narrative and Character   186
    10.1.   Preliminaries   187
    10.2.   Some Claims about Character   188
    10.3.   What Narrative does for Character   190
    10.4.   What Character does for Narrative   192
    10.5.   Character and the Critic   195

11. Character Scepticism   199
    11.1.   The Case against Character   199
    11.2.   Response   204
    11.3.   Simplifying the Problem   208
    11.4.   The Role of Character in Narrative   211
    11.5.   Reflections   213
    Appendix: Character and the Costs of Deception   216

12. In Conclusion   219

Bibliography   221
Index   239

Analytical contents

CHAPTER ONE

Narratives are *intentional-communicative artefacts*; intentionally fashioned devices of representation that work by manifesting the communicative intentions of their makers. The representational *content* of a narrative is the story it has to tell, and we can provide a notion of representational content which fits both fictional and non-fictional narratives. Occasionally we play with the idea of non-artefactual narratives, but this notion, like many in the realm of magical thinking, does not require us to drop the artefactuality condition for narratives; we need only acknowledge it as one way in which sensible ideas get extended into the realm of the incoherent. Nor should we think of memories or dreams or lives as non-artefactual narratives.

CHAPTER TWO

To distinguish narratives from other representational vehicles we need to say something about what distinguishes the contents of narratives from the contents of other things: theories, lists, annals, rambling conversational remarks, instruction manuals. I don't seek to define narrative, choosing instead to focus on the graded notion of *narrativity*. We can then think of things high in narrativity as combining certain features which make for the detailed representation of particulars, especially agents, in their causal and temporal relations. While it needs careful handling, I find this idea defensible against recent criticism. I speculate on the evolutionary background which makes representations of just these kinds so very important to us.

CHAPTER THREE

We may think of a narrative as a door-way into the world of its story. But we are never far from conscious awareness of the narrative's artefactual status, where facts about the motives of its maker, and the constraints on the maker's situation, inform our expectations of the story's events. Many judgements we make about a work derive from a combination or superposition of these two perspectives, internal and external. Sometimes a question about narrative requires an answer from one or other perspective. Often it's self evident which perspective is the right one; sometimes the choice between them is more difficult; occasionally a narrative will engineer the appearance of a collapse of the perspectives, but this is only ever an appearance.

CHAPTER FOUR

Narratives have *authors*; theorists of narrative, however, have concentrated mostly on the *narrator*, a role which they distinguish from that of author. I argue that this is a mistake. In virtually all cases, the arguments that identify some or other persona as a narrator, real or imagined, identify that same person as an author. But we do need to distinguish (at least) two kinds of narrator/authors: the real one responsible for the story and—sometimes—an *internal* one who lives within the story itself. Arguments have been given for thinking that we either always need to postulate an internal narrator, or that the assumption that there is one is the default position. I argue against both these propositions.

CHAPTER FIVE

Authors create stories for us. In the process of doing so they often provide a *framework* within which to respond to the story. How do authors create these structures? I argue that they do so by *expressing a point of view*. I suggest that this activity of framing is a common yet important feature of all kinds of interpersonal exchanges, and that we are highly tuned, by evolution and by development, to their occurrence. I suggest that narrative framing occurs by a process of *guided attention*—a notion which generalizes the psychologically crucial concept of joint attention; it is linked to powerful mechanisms of *imitation*. This helps me to define the *standard mode of engagement* with narrative.

CHAPTER SIX

Sometimes we are *resistant* to the framing that narratives offer us. I note a broad range of circumstances where this occurs: in some we seek to overcome the resistance, while in others we are grateful for its protection. I connect this phenomenon with the widely discussed puzzle(s) of *imaginative* resistance, and suggest that there is an interesting intersection with resistance to framing. I look for an evolutionary explanation for resistance to framing, and examine a couple of cases where the distinction between framework and story-content is not clear, and where clarifying the distinction helps to identify worries one may have about aspects of these narratives.

CHAPTER SEVEN

Stories are narrated from a point of view, but occasionally the narrator, of whatever kind, modulates the style of narration to take account of the point of view of some other character. I call this *character-focused narration*. I argue that this phenomenon has been misunderstood, notably by Genette, whose account has led down the blind alley of *focalization*. Character-focused narration is best explained by invoking the mechanisms used to explain framing: expression and imitation. I show how a variety of stylistic and grammatical devices, including *free indirect discourse*, aid character-focused narration.

CHAPTER EIGHT

Narrators occasionally help themselves to pretended points of view. Such points of view are crucial to understanding one kind of irony, sometimes called 'verbal irony' but better termed *representational* irony. An ironic performance is, I suggest, the pretended adoption of a point of view—a defective one—and so there are natural ways in which narrators are led to ironize their characters' points of view, and sometimes their own. Criticisms of the idea that irony is pretence are rebutted. I introduce a notion that will be important later on: *narration from an ironic point of view*. I also discuss the relation between *representational* and *situational* irony.

CHAPTER NINE

I examine an example of narration from an ironic point of view: Hitchcock's *The Birds*. I consider the roles of various devices in the expression of this point of view: the use of *point of view shots*, *sound* which is only ambiguously diegetic, careful placement of dialogue and action. From there I launch an attack on some of the ways in which this film has been interpreted. I also note differences between the capacities of *language-based* and *picture-based* media for the expression of ironic points of view.

CHAPTER TEN

I examine the relation between narrative and the psychological notion of *Character*. Narratives often focus on more than simply the intentions that determine a particular action; they postulate more or less settled Characters for the people who perform those actions. I argue that there is a natural connection between narrative and Character which makes the latter the natural mode of representation for the former, and gives Character a stabilizing and clarifying role in narrative. The twentieth century has seen literary theorists turn against character and I argue that the literary case against Character is very weak indeed.

CHAPTER ELEVEN

But there is another case to answer, deriving from social psychology, according to which the very idea of Character is simply a *cognitive illusion*. I summarize the argument: an argument that's strong enough to warrant serious consideration. I suggest that even if the sceptical case can be made out, we can see a positive role for Character in narrative, though I note at the end a worry about this claim.

1

Representation

Narratives are the product of agency; they are the means by which someone communicates a story to someone else. Narratives represent their stories, and do so in a special way characteristic of communication between agents. This first chapter provides an overview of the relations between narrative, agency, representation, and communication. Its concerns are largely methodological, providing background to later, more substantial claims. Impatient readers will probably not lose much if they delay reading it until they get a sense, from later material, of what is at stake.

1.1. Artefactual Functions

George, a sensitive and attentive reader, reads *War and Peace* with enjoyment and understanding. He follows the plot, and is able to summarize it; he can tell us about the book's ideas on character, history, and morality. Alice, a paleo-anthropologist, examines a stone implement. She forms beliefs about how it was made (by striking against other objects), its age (about a million years), the beings who made it (a probable ancestor species of ours), the use to which it was put, and the use for which it was intended. Against the background of her knowledge in the area, she finds in this artefact a good deal of information about the minds of these creatures, and in particular the intentions they had in making it.

These two activities and their outcomes are certainly different. Language plays a central role in George's project, but not in Alice's. The makers of the stone tool probably had no articulated language, and if they did Alice knows nothing of it. Alice depends on specialized knowledge: theories about the course of evolution in which she has limited confidence. George draws, apart from a few facts about Russian history, only on an understanding of human beings and their social arrangements which he would find difficult to state and does not actively question.

There are also similarities. The book and the stone implement are both things which emerge from a creative process; they come to be the things they are—a narrative, a cutting tool—by being intentionally shaped. The properties, or a large number of them, which make them those things are intentionally imposed. There is a good deal in common between the interpretive activities of George and Alice. Both hope for an understanding of *artefactual* function; the function an object was intended to perform and in virtue of which it was shaped.[1] *War and Peace* was made in order, among other things, to tell a certain story. With that aim in mind the author chose certain words and sentences suitable for getting that story across. George, having access to those words and sentences, is in a good position to understand what that story is, though he might not get it right in every detail. The best account of what story the narrative was intended to tell is the best account of how its internal organization—the structure of words and sentences that make up its text—enables it to fulfil its artefactual function.

The stone tool has an artefactual function: a different one. It was made, let us suppose, to aid in the stripping of meat from a carcass. With that aim in mind its maker chose to shape it in a certain way, skilfully hammering flakes away to create a cutting edge. Alice, having access to the resulting shape, is in a good position to understand what that aim was, together with a good deal about the details of the intentions that guided its shaping.[2]

---

[1] See Thomasson 2007. For a different approach to the functions of artefacts, see Parsons and Carlson 2008. Empirical studies support the idea that the common understanding of artefact privileges intended use over actual use; see Kelemen and Carey 2007 for review, and for discussion of the development of the 'design stance', which they tentatively locate at 4–6 years of age. Frank Keil, the developmental psychologist, famous for his work on children's understanding of natural kinds, says that 'social conventions such as driving on the right side of the road [are artefacts]' (Keil, Greif, and Kerner 2007: 233). This confuses a thing's status as a social object with its status as an artefact. To be an artefact a thing has to be not merely made by us but shaped by us. It has to have some properties (perhaps not many) which it has in virtue of intentional activity directed towards giving the object those very properties.

[2] Thomas Wynn says 'The directed action of stone knapping preserves something of the cognition of the knapper. Even in the simplest example, the knapper must make a decision about where to place a blow and how much force to use. These decisions are preserved in the products themselves' (2002: 392). Actually there is some uncertainty about the artefactual functions of these stone tools. It has even been suggested, though not many share this view, that they were a kind of frisbee, good for throwing at game (Calvin 2002). Bear in mind that there are occasionally radical disagreements about what story a narrative has to tell; consider those debates about whether the narrator is reliable or not.

Once again, the best guide to how exactly it was intended to fulfil this artefactual function is the best account of how its organization—its shape, dimensions, and material—enables it to fulfil that function.

Are there similarities in the ways that George and Alice acquire their knowledge of artefactual function? It is tempting to say that George's understanding of *War and Peace* is mostly intuitive, while Alice's understanding of the stone tool is theoretical. Perhaps theoretical processes require inference, while intuitive ones are more like perception, giving us knowledge directly—as we know, without inference, that something is red by looking at it. Is that the difference between understanding *War and Peace* and understanding the stone tool? Understanding *War and Peace* involves both inference and immediacy. On the model of language understanding I adopt here, we understand communicative uses of language by doing two things. First, we understand the words uttered in a non-inferential way—a way that makes it sensible to say that we see or hear their meanings.[3] Even when your utterance is so ambiguous, complex, or gnomic that I fail to understand what you mean by it, I hear or see the meanings of the words you speak or write; I do not infer those meanings from the perceived sounds or shapes. But understanding communication always involves more than this: it involves *pragmatic* inference. We must infer the communicative intentions of the speaker/writer from the linguistic meaning together with surrounding context, though most of the inferring is done quickly and with little awareness.[4] In the case of the gnomic utterance, what goes wrong is not my understanding of the language, but my grasp of the communicative intention behind its production.

Is Alice's work with the stone all theoretical? Not all of it is, since she has a direct grasp of its shape and other appearance qualities. Plausibly, she also sees in it strong clues as to its intended function.[5] She perceives not merely a piece of stone with a certain shape, but an object with a potential for

---

[3] I put it like this because I am not insisting that we do, literally, see or hear meanings; I am claiming only that language processing is so like these other processes that only philosophical scruples would trouble us at this point.

[4] One way to put this is to say, with Fodor (1984), that understanding language is modular—the province of a fast, dedicated, and encapsulated mechanism—while understanding the use to which a piece of language is being put is the province of general purpose reasoning. This would not suit those linguists who think that pragmatic inference has its own module (though not, perhaps, a module with all the Fodorian features: see Sperber and Wilson 2002).

[5] The same reservation applies here as in n. 3 above.

use—certain affordances, as Gibson called them.[6] Alice perceives, and does not infer, the graspability of the stone. Alice needs to test any hypothesis she comes up with about the intended use of the stone against evidence, and this evidence can come from just about anywhere. But some of the evidence comes from her direct awareness of the possibilities of engagement with the object.

For those impatient with this comparison, I agree that we think of the stone axe as an artefact much more readily than we think of *War and Peace* as one. The obvious examples of artefacts are inanimate, concrete objects like tools and computers. But, as Dan Sperber has argued, there are good grounds for classing even biological entities such as bulldogs as artefacts; their features are to a large extent explained by the intentions of agents who intervened in the reproductive process in ways intended to produce certain results. We can distinguish sub-kinds of artefacts, but axes, novels, and bulldogs are all good examples of the general kind.[7]

If we think of narratives as artefacts, should we think of the characters in them as artefacts as well? Not, presumably, in the case of undeceptive, reliable histories, which tell us only about the activities of real people, referred to in the ordinary way by means of proper names and descriptions. The view that fictional characters are artefacts has some defenders.[8] But we need to keep hold of the thought that fictional characters like Sherlock Holmes simply do not exist. A response has it that while there is nothing that is a person, a detective, a resident of Baker Street, etc.—nothing which *exemplifies* those properties—there is something (not a person but an artefact) which *encodes* those properties. On that view, statements like 'Holmes lived in Baker Street' are ambiguous. As it occurs in the larger context, 'It is fictional that Holmes lived in Baker Street', we have

---

[6] See Gibson 1979. For a defence of the idea of affordance and a reinterpretation of Gibson's difficult notion of the 'ambient optic array', see Noë 2004: sect. 3.9: 'Gibson's theory . . . is that we don't see the flatness and then interpret it as suitable for climbing upon. To see it as flat is to see it as making available possibilities for movement' (ibid. 104). One can accept this view while rejecting Noë's own primary claim that perception is 'an activity of exploring the environment' (see Block 2005, for criticism). Recent work in neuroscience has suggested mechanisms of affordance-detection in the shape of canonical neurons. These neurons fire when the agent undertakes a grasping action on a perceived object; they also fire when the agent merely sees a graspable object. These neural processes constitute, it is suggested, implicit or simulated acts of grasping.

[7] See Sperber 2007. Sperber asks why it is that biological and abstract entities do not come readily to mind when we are asked for examples of artefacts; he guesses it is due to the long evolutionary history during which middle-sized physical objects—stones are the ones we know about—were the only artefacts there were.   [8] See esp. Thomasson 2003.

something correctly heard as a case of exemplification, since what is so according to the story is that Holmes exemplifies living in Baker Street, just in the way a real human resident of that street would. As it occurs in my assertion about the story, 'Holmes lived in Baker Street', we have something correctly heard as a case of encoding. Objections to this include the accusation that there is no intuitive support for this postulated and, it turns out, quite complex ambiguity.[9] But suppose we accept that fictional characters are created by the authors of the stories they appear in; it is still not settled that they should have the status of artefacts. It seems to me better to say that story-makers make stories, and that their characters come in to existence as a result of that story-making; they are entities that supervene on the making of artefacts rather than being artefacts themselves.

One difference between the book and the axe is significant. The book, like other vehicles of narration, is a representational artefact; it is something made for the purpose of telling a story, and it does so by being a representation of the story's events and characters. The axe, though it may carry information about its maker and his or her community, does not represent anything.[10] Narratives tell us things by providing representations of them: of people and actions, of objects and occurrence. Often, much of what they tell us is not true, and may not be, as with fictional narratives, presented as true. Still, we can say, for any intelligible narrative, roughly what that narrative represents by way of actions and occurrences: if we cannot, we surely have no idea what story the narrative tells.

In general, the fact that something is an artefact and the fact that it is a representation are independent. Being a representation requires intentional activity on someone's part, but not the activity of making. A fallen tree bough may be pressed into service as a representation of the tree's age; then it is a representation because it is *used* to represent, but it is no artefact. Even if the bough was intentionally lopped, it might not count as a representational artefact. It might have been lopped and shaped for use in chair making, discarded, and later used as an indicator of the tree's age. It would then be an artefact and a representation, but not a

---

[9] See Sainsbury 2009: chap. 5.
[10] Or so, I think, it is fair to assume. There is no evidence for 'symbolic' culture at the time these objects were made. I follow Dretske (1988) in distinguishing between something being an indicator and something being a representation. Both the axe and the book are indicators, but only the book is a representation.

representational artefact. Using something in a certain way will often make it a representation, whatever its prior history, but use alone never makes something an artefact; that requires an act of making.[11] A narrative may come to fill some representational role that it was not intended to fill; it might be used as an indicator of some psychopathology suffered by the author, which manifests itself in strange constructions of grammar. Such a narrative plays more than one representational role. In telling its story it fulfils its artefactual function; in telling us about its author's psychopathology it fulfils another function.

There is another difference between the hand axe and the book that is worth our attention. The function of a narrative is to tell a story, and a story may be told—rather than accidentally conveyed—only through a process of making which aims at communication. We may come across the manuscript of an intelligible story, and have good reason to think that its author did not intend anyone to read it; perhaps they very much wanted it not to be read. But this is irrelevant to the question whether the author had a communicative intention. If the manuscript was intentionally fashioned in such a way that it would, if read, be the vehicle of an intelligible story—fashioned, that is, with regard to the requirements of communication—then the author counts as having a communicative intention. Success in narrative communication is a matter of enabling an audience to know the artefactual function of that narrative. I have said that we come to know what that artefactual function is when we know what story the narrative has been constructed to tell. We can now say that narratives are intentional-communicative artefacts: artefacts that have as their function the communication of a story, which function they have by virtue of their makers' intentions.[12] The rest of this chapter is concerned with how our understanding of intention guides us in recovery of the story from the narrative.

Being an intentional-communicative artefact, *War and Peace* was made with the purpose that its story be understood. Alice's stone axe almost certainly was not made with the intention that its artefactual function be understood. It was made with a purpose, and that purpose shaped its making, but it was not made with a communicative purpose, and

---

[11] On representation as a functional notion, see again Dretske 1988: chap. 3.

[12] Ray Gibbs uses 'communicative artefact' in a somewhat different way to mean an object intended to 'cause a belief' about another object (Gibbs 1999: 53).

so it is not an intentional-communicative artefact. When someone does something intending it to be understood, he or she pays attention to how the doing of it may facilitate understanding. If things go right, even approximately so, understanding the result is easier than it would otherwise be. This is one reason why George's task is easier than Alice's, for Alice is trying to understand the function of an artefact which was not designed to facilitate understanding, and she has no living exponents of the tradition to turn to.[13] If you want to do something that will be understood, it is best to do something that signals the intention to be understood. Using language is a good way (but not the only way) to do that.[14] Language has the great advantage that, when we see that someone is using language, we generally conclude that they are doing something which they intend will be understood.[15] And we can conclude that much even without knowing the language they are speaking; we sometimes understand what people say to us without understanding the words and sentences they utter, having nothing more to go on than the fact that they are using language—perhaps one we happen not to understand. The fact that they are using language encourages us to look closely at behaviour, expression, and context for clues to what they want to communicate; sometimes we find them.

1.2. Narrative and Story Content

Narratives represent things as existing, and circumstances as being so. Lots of things other than narratives do that: they all belong to a wider class

[13] See Carston 2002: chap. 1. It is possible that intelligibility of a kind played a role in shaping Alice's stone artefact. Successful tools—the ones that get replicated by other makers—were probably those which best facilitated imitation. Imitation does not mean copying the behavioural routine of someone you see doing something; successful imitation may require the learner to abstract from the details of the teacher's performance, many of which will be accidental, and to see the point of the action. Certain kinds of activity, leading to certain kinds of shaped materials, may be easier to imitate than others, because they are more intelligible. The most easily understood techniques of making will, other things being equal, be those that spread most successfully, and so the successful tools will be those shaped by the forces of intelligibility. It does not follow that individual stone toolmakers intended their products to be intelligible.

[14] Sperber and Wilson compare communication to fire-lighting. Having matches makes fire-lighting much easier, but there is no conceptual connection between the two. Language makes communication much easier, but there is no conceptual connection between the two (Sperber and Wilson 1995: 27–8).

[15] There is the odd exception—someone is practising their English. But in most cases the inference is good.

of things which David Lewis calls *corpora*. His examples are 'someone's system of beliefs, a data bank or almanac or encyclopaedia or textbook, a theory or a system of mythology, or even a work of fiction' (Lewis 1982: 435). A corpus is a body of representations, emanating from a more or less unified source—a single individual, a team of experts, a tradition—and in which we may have a more or less systematic interest. Some corpora, like narratives, are artefacts; some, like belief-systems, are not.

Corpora are things according to which something or other is true; it may not be raining in actuality, but it may be raining according to someone's belief, according to the bulletin from the weather bureau, according to a story, fictional or non-fictional. When something is true according to a corpus, the agents from which it emanates are not always committed to its truth; that will be so for belief systems and historical texts, it may be so for weather reports, it is not so for fictional stories. Representing-as-true and being-committed-to-truth are different. The representations in a corpus have this much in common: they are all representations-as-true-according-to-that-corpus. Often, the representations in a corpus have more connections, one to another, than this. While only an extreme monomaniac has beliefs all on a common theme, we do expect a well-run belief system to maintain a reasonable level of internal coherence. The ravings of a madman may provide a much less structured corpus, with little regard for coherence, and a book of interesting facts for boys will have virtually no thematic unity. Narratives are generally highly organized corpora and, below a certain degree of organization, we cease to count the corpus as a narrative at all.

What sorts of internal structure are characteristic of narrative? Some of the things we look for in narrative we also look for in belief systems and other corpora, such as rich relations of *consequence*. If P is part of a well-organized belief system, and P has certain manifest and salient consequences—logically, or causally, or conventionally—we expect those consequences to belong to it also; we expect people to extend their beliefs outwards in ways which track the ramifications of things they already believe. There are limits to this; we cannot have, and do not need, belief systems that endlessly ramify, though in particular cases we may end up wishing that our beliefs had extended outwards just a little further, enabling us to see that crucial unpredicted consequence. With narratives also, we expect rich but bounded relations of consequence between items within the corpus, partly to keep the quantity of information manageable, but also because we are looking for thematic unity, and long chains of consequence threaten to take us away from our theme. Narratives and belief systems are alike as well in that content is not always explicit content. Lots of our beliefs are ones that have never occurred to us, and much—most—of the content of a narrative is not written down or otherwise explicit. Explicitness is a difficult notion, and I will return to it in the next section.

Consequence is especially an issue for inconsistent narratives. Classically, any inconsistency licenses inference to everything, but we do not say that everything is automatically so according to an inconsistent story. In some narratives we take the contradiction to be a mistake, as with the conflicting information Doyle provides concerning the location of Watson's wound from the Afghan campaign. How do we resolve the mistake? We make judgements about the maker's intentions. We assume that, had he realized the problem, Doyle would have opted for one location or the other. We may believe that it makes no difference to the story which of the mentioned locations is chosen, since the consequences of the choice of one location are not significantly different, from the point of view of the story, from the consequence of the other. In that case what we otherwise assume about the intended content of the narrative is unaffected by the choice, so it makes no difference which one he would have chosen, and we think no more about it.[16] If the wound's placement actually makes some difference—suppose that Watson is said to be a strong runner—then we would go for maximizing coherence with the rest of the story, understanding the story so as to place the wound in the arm and not the leg. In that case again we would be guided by our best estimate of the author's intention; when an author makes much of his character's running ability, he is less likely to have intended that character to be wounded in the leg than to have intended him to be wounded in the arm.[17]

Is it the same with a non-fictional narrative? Suppose a confused historian manages to say both that Nelson's (one) wound at Tenerife was in the arm and, further on, that it was in the leg. If something significant elsewhere in the narrative hangs on its being placed, say, in the leg, then we have

[16] This procedure corresponds roughly to that urged by Lewis for this case and other 'venially impossible fictions', though Lewis does not present his proposal as justified by its respect for authorial intention (see Lewis 1978).   [17] Throughout this section I am indebted to Byrne 1993.

grounds for thinking that the right revision places it there; the overall weight of textual evidence suggests, via assumptions about the coherence of people's plans, that that's where the author believed it to be, and we are entitled to assume that he intended his belief to be reflected in what is so according to his story. Thus far, the fictional and non-fictional cases are alike. But suppose that coherence with the rest of the historian's narrative does not tell in either direction. Then, one might say, charity requires us to understand the narrative to place it in the arm, since that is where in fact it was. I do not favour that resolution, since I am too much of the opinion that intention rather than truth should be our guide to the content of narrative. But my view comes to much the same thing in practice, for the following reason. Just as in the fictional case, I think we should ask ourselves, 'what would the author have done, had the problem been pointed out?' We will usually answer that the author, in accordance with her intention to say something true, would have checked the record and revised in accordance with the facts, placing it in the arm. In that case, and in most cases, the way of intention gives the same answer as the way of truth.

We can say this: our approach to inconsistency is guided by what we conclude about authorial intention; if we think the inconsistency a mistake we revise the narrative in accordance with what the evidence suggests was the author's intention; if there is no evidence that favours one particular resolution, we simply note that various resolutions are possible, no one of which is preferable to the others, and leave it at that; we assume it resolved, without choosing any particular resolution. If we think the inconsistency intended, or think that the author's intentions were such that, had he known of the inconsistency, he would have tolerated it, we should retain it, and infer no more from it than we think we are intended to infer.[18]

---

[18] Some will complain that vague appeals to intention are not sufficient; we need a story about the inferential mechanisms involved. This is not the place to provide detail, but here, in brief, is a hint: suppose that entailed propositions can also be conversational implicatures. (Grice denied this, holding that implicatures are 'cancellable', but see Carston 2002: sect. 2.3.3; on the distinction between what is said and what is implicated, see below, n. 25 and text.) We might then work up a theory according to which an entailed proposition is allowable as story-content just in case it counts as an implicature, thus allowing stories to have contradictory content without needing a paraconsistentist logic to quarantine the effects of contradictions (something urged on us by Priest; his 1997 is especially relevant here). Logic—classical logic—gives us an account of the closure conditions for truth; implicature (I do not say yet exactly how specified) gives us the closure conditions for story content. But we should stop thinking of stories as 'worlds' and of narratives as descriptions of worlds (see ibid. moral 5). Worlds

We expect specificity in belief systems, as well as coherence. People have general beliefs, as well as existential ones; they believe that whales are mammals and that someone, God knows who, keeps the power running. But it would be a useless belief system that said nothing about particular things, since we are constantly called upon to deal with particulars. With narrative, the emphasis on particularity is strong; we expect narratives to track the histories of individual things. Usually the things are human or human-like; in exceptional cases, we may have a narrative of the evolution of a species or the formation of a planet. Particularity will come up again, in Chapter 2; so also will something else I mentioned in passing: thematic unity.

Throughout this chapter, I have emphasized the artefactual status of narratives, their dependence on an act of making, and the ways in which recognition of the makers' intentions guide our understanding of them. These are important points, and most of what follows will be informed by them. But we ought not to elevate this into a rigid set of rules for the comprehension of narratives. There are times when a narrative's audience will strike out in its own direction, pursuing a line of inquiry about a character or situation just because that line of inquiry looks interesting and rewarding and without finding, or seeking, any direct sanction for that line of inquiry from what can be understood of the maker's intentions, and perhaps in defiance of what can be known or guessed of those intentions. I briefly discuss our inclinations in this direction concerning Richardson's *Pamela* in Chapter 3.[19] The extent to which this is appropriate in any particular case is a matter for nice judgement, but there ought not to be any general rule that prohibits it absolutely. My point is that any appropriate act of narrative engagement will be strongly guided, but not always and in detail determined, by a sense of the agency behind the story.[20]

are (or correspond to) maximal, consistent sets of propositions. There are many other kinds of sets of propositions, some of them very disorderly. Some of the more orderly ones, but never maximal and sometimes inconsistent, are (or correspond to) stories. Logic governs worlds; the hypothesis on the table is that implicature governs stories. Of course, if P is part of the story's content, then it will be part of story content that P is true. Does that mean that, so far as story content is concerned, entailment is non-classical? No. Suppose that P entails Q. It may be part of the story's content that (i) truth is closed under classical entailment, and (ii) P, without it being part of the story's content that Q; for that we need an implicature from story content so far encountered to Q. See also text to n. 24 below.

[19] See Chap. 3, sect. 4.

[20] This sort of 'partial intentionalism', as Paisley Livingston calls it, has been defended by other writers: by Iseminger (Iseminger 1992) and, in considerable detail, by Livingston himself (Livingston 2005: esp. chap. 6).

To end this section, two housekeeping issues. First, what I am calling a narrative's content is often, when applied to fiction, described as 'what is true in the story'.[21] But I treat fictional and non-fictional narratives alike as corpora, and talk of what is true in the story can badly mislead us in the non-fictional case; 'What is true in Plumb's history, *The First Four Georges*?' sounds like an inquiry about how much truth there is in the book, and that's not what we are interested in. Instead of saying that something is true in *Emma* or in *The First Four Georges*, I will say that this or that is part of the story content of *Emma*, or of *The First Four Georges*.[22] Sometimes, meaning the same thing, I will say that this or that is so according to *Emma*, or so according to *The First Four Georges*. The difference between the cases, fiction and non-fiction, is that we are crucially interested in whether what is so according to *The First Four Georges* is true, and we are not comparably interested in the question whether what is so according to *Emma* is true.

Secondly, thinking about story content naturally leads us to problems about non-existence. Some of the things that narratives represent do not exist. Fictional narratives often tell us about non-existent people and about non-actual events. Non-fictional narratives sometimes do the same, either by error or through intended deception. This is not a book on the semantics of fictional names, and I am not going to address formal or philosophical problems to do with existence here.[23] Anyway, representations of all kinds—narratives, theories, devotional tracts—may represent the non-existent, so the problem is not peculiar to narrative. I will assume that narratives represent characters and events, existing or not, and I refuse to inquire further into the metaphysics of non-existence.

1.3. Implicit and Explicit

Earlier I contrasted the explicit content of a narrative with its implicit or inferred content. That distinction needs careful handling; indeed, it can mislead us badly. It suggests a division between content that is unambiguous—written into the text, visible on the stage or screen, etc.—and

---

[21] See e.g. Lewis 1984 and Currie 1990.
[22] I adopted this terminology, unannounced, in n. 18 above.
[23] I have had my say on this in Currie 1990: chap. 4.

content which is a matter of interpretation. In fact, it is all a matter of interpretation. As David Lewis remarked, it is merely implicit in the Holmes stories that Holmes is a human being, the author making no explicit statement on this topic (Lewis 1978). But if it is written into the story that Watson, the narrator, declares 'by this time I had had breakfast', what is explicit? That at some point in his life Watson had had breakfast? That would be to adopt a very restricted sense of 'what is made explicit'. A more reasonable sense would allow us to say that Watson made it explicit that he had had breakfast *that morning*, something we could contrast with such merely implicit content to his statement as that he was now happy to leave with Holmes and energetically pursue the case. And suppose the stories did contain some such statement as 'Holmes did not always succeed in solving his cases; after all, he was a human being', would that make it any more certain than it otherwise was that Holmes was human? It might have the opposite effect: an ironical clue to the crypto-supernaturalism of the stories, perhaps. A statement that made us doubt whether Holmes was human could hardly be said to make it explicit that he was.

For these reasons, when we talk about the explicit content of a story we generally do not mean 'that which is literally encoded in the text'. We mean something like this: P is explicit story content when we can find some statement or set of statements in the text, S, which meets two conditions: (1) S is naturally interpretable in such a way as to convey directly, rather than merely to implicate, the thought that P, and (2) an overall best interpretation of the text is one which treats S as reliable.[24] On this reading of 'explicit', we may count it as explicit in the story that Watson had breakfast on the day in question (and not merely at some time in his life) if we read in the text 'by now I had eaten breakfast', without having to count it as explicit that Watson had eaten a snake that morning if the text contained the words 'by now I had eaten snake'. And we shall count it as *not* explicit in the story that Smith is a moral hero, despite reading in the text 'Smith was a moral hero' if we reckon that statement to be an example of unreliable narration.[25] On this

---

[24] The ideas of the various kinds of implicatures which may belong to what is meant by an utterance distinct from what is said, and the specially important class of conversational implicatures which are inferred by a hearer on the assumption that conversational principles are being observed, were outlined by Grice in his William James Lectures of 1967 (see Grice 1989).

[25] This is consistent with our also holding it as part of the story that the narrator explicitly says that Smith is a moral hero; what is explicitly said by a narrator and what is explicit content of the story are sometimes different things.

account, pragmatic inference—inference to the intended meaning behind
the words—intrudes even into the determination of the explicit content
of the story, as with Watson's statement about having had breakfast, which
pragmatic inference allows us to enrich to the point where we understand
the announcement to refer to breakfast *that day*.

How often do we need pragmatic inference? Very occasionally, language
functions simply as *code* and without our needing to engage in pragmatic
inference.[26] A thermometer may be attached to a mechanical device which
every so often reliably produces a written or spoken message such as
'fifteen degrees centigrade'. The information from the thermometer is
encoded into language, and understanding that information requires only
the ability to understand the combination of spoken or written words—to
decode the linguistic signal—and the rule that the number thus encoded
corresponds to the current ambient temperature measured in centigrade.
Perhaps someone, the machine's maker, intended that this be the rule, but
that is irrelevant; what matters to the user is just that there is a reliable
association between the numbers encoded by the words the machine
produces and the ambient temperature. Cases like that are rare, especially
when we are considering how language conveys narrative. Almost always,
language functions as a clue to what people want to communicate. The
historian who writes 'the city was empty' means, but does not encode
in words, that the city had no (or perhaps very few) living people in it,
not that there was literally nothing within its boundaries; the adventure
novelist whose verbal account of an episode is confined to the words 'his
wounds took time to heal' encodes a near triviality—since all processes
take time—but means something more substantial: that the character's
recovery took a time which, by the standard for time intervals set by the
context of the narrative itself, was considerable.[27] The historian and the

---

[26] On code models of language use, see Sperber and Wilson 1995: sect. 1.1.

[27] The notion of what is said is itself a complex and disputed one, and there are those who hold
to a very narrow view of what is said according to which what is said in the two examples above is
just that the city was empty and that the wounds took time to heal; what is understood—that there
were few people left, that healing took significant time—is then said to be a matter of *impliciture* (as
distinct from implicature) (Bach 1994). Thus, instead of simply distinguishing what is said from what
is implicated, Bach requires us to distinguish between what is said on the one hand and, on the other,
the implicitures and the implicatures of what is said. See also Recanati's distinction between m-literal
and p-literal meaning (Recanati 2001). There are other taxonomies. These disputes about how to cut
the cake need not bother us here.

novelist do this because they, like the rest of us, know that there is no need to encode their remarks to any greater degree of specificity or coincidence with intended meaning. They know that their intended meaning, or some approximation to it that will do in the circumstances, will, with high probability, be inferred by their readers; these inferences are pragmatic ones, from the words used to the actions that produced them. And the lesson is not that we should all try harder to be explicit; greater explicitness would often make it *less* likely that intended meaning will be understood; unusual precision in speech is often an indication of irony, and an ironic speaker is generally understood as not asserting the proposition her words would naturally be taken to express. Greater explicitness would lead us down the garden path.[28]

None of this is problematic, nor should it be surprising. Human beings have an immensely developed capacity to undertake pragmatic inference on the basis of slender clues; the co-evolution of language and mind-reading has, in all probability, kept our tendency to be explicit in our communications well below what it would be if we were much poorer mind-readers.[29] And, shifting the burden of communication from language to pragmatic inference helps to overcome a design fault in the communication system that humans have evolved. Our speech-production runs at a slow rate, much slower than the cognitive processes that enable us to think and draw inferences from our thoughts and from what we see and hear; taking short-cuts in speech is therefore highly advantageous from the point of view of efficient communication.[30]

Someone unwilling to grant much room in literary interpretation to pragmatic inference might urge two further points: (1) that cases where there is a mismatch between the purely linguistically encoded meaning and the meaning inferred by a suitably attentive audience are exceptional, or not the norm, or (as a last-ditch stand) that there are at least some cases where there is no such mismatch, and (2) that where there is no mismatch there is no need for pragmatic inference because the audience needs only

---

[28] On the revolution in linguistics which took us from 'encoded meaning with a few inferential additions where necessary, to pro-active pragmatic inferencing constrained by bits of encoding', see Carston 2002: chap. 2, sect. 8.

[29] See ibid. chap. 1 for an elegant and comprehensive account of these kinds of mismatch.

[30] See Levinson 2000: sect. 1.3; I am here indebted to Bach 2000, which drew my attention to Levinson's hypothesis.

to understand the linguistically encoded meaning. In response to (1), I say that an examination of the circumstances in which there is a mismatch shows that mismatching is at least very common.[31] These circumstances are very varied, and include cases of ambiguity, cases where the reference of an indexical requires us to understand which individual the speaker intended to refer to, cases where something in the sentence is missing (I haven't had dinner (*today*)), cases where a component is weaker or stronger than what is intended (I am tired (*too tired to answer your question*)); (the meal was inedible (*would have been unpleasant to eat*)). Indeed, it has been suggested that, given basic assumptions about human psychology and language, we never do, and never could, express exactly what we mean in words.[32] But I need not appeal to this extreme formulation to defend the idea that pragmatic inference is ubiquitous in the comprehension of narrative. All I need—as a response to (2)—is the principle that, even when a speaker does speak literally, *that is so only in virtue of the speaker's intentions*. Speaking literally, if there is such a thing, is a matter of having your intended meaning coincide with your verbal meaning. So knowing whether someone is speaking literally requires pragmatic inference to their intended meaning.[33]

In sum, to understand the words and sentences of a narrative is one thing and to understand the narrative those words and sentences convey is another. The latter depends, as do most forms of linguistic communication, on pragmatic inference—inference to the maker's/utterer's intentions.

Pragmatic inference, partly because of the seminal role of Grice's *Logic and Conversation* in our thinking about it, is closely associated with conversational exchange—something rather different from narrative utterance, wherein a (usually) single voice occupies a significant stretch of our attention to convey a story. A narrative may provoke a conversation, but it is not one. Are we wrong then to put so much emphasis on pragmatic inference in understanding narratives, particularly when they are of aesthetic or

---

[31] Carston argues for mismatch between verbal production and what is said largely on the grounds that the semantic content of the sentence uttered underdetermines the proposition communicated.

[32] Carston 'inclines towards the view' that 'no sentence ever fully encodes the thought or proposition it is used to express' (Carston 2002: 29).

[33] As Kent Bach puts it: 'no sentence has to be used in accordance with its semantic content. *Any* sentence can be used in a nonliteral or indirect way . . . That [the speaker] is attempting to communicate something, and what that is, is a matter of his communicative intention, if indeed he has one. If he is speaking literally, and means precisely what his words mean, even that fact depends on his communicative intention' (Bach 2005: 27; emphasis in the original).

artistic interest? Peter Lamarque thinks we are. He identifies a 'subtle form of linguistic reductionism', which takes literary works to be

contextualised utterances akin to utterances in any form of communicative exchange . . . On this view there is no difference *in principle* between writing a novel, writing a letter, or making a political speech. All manifest the same desire to convey meaning. All invite the same goal of understanding and success is judged on whether the meaning is conveyed. It is no wonder that the debate about intentions is so prominent among philosophers who start with this premise about literature. The primary questions become what kind of meaning is conveyed and what are the constraints in grasping that meaning: is it the explicitly intended meaning of the author, is it the contextualised meaning of the words used, is it the meaning of an utterance combining intention and convention, and so forth? I suggest that this framework is utterly misconceived.   (Lamarque 2007: 34)

Whatever is wrong with the view Lamarque rejects, it should not be described as a case of *linguistic* reductionism; the point of the assimilation of narrative to communicative utterance is to show that language alone will not get us to understanding—we need large doses of mind reading also. What is wrong with that view?

Quoting from Spenser's *Epithalamion*, Lamarque asks us to see that, with such a work, we may need information about the meanings of words in the Elizabethan age, but we go from there straight to such matters as the highly personal tone of the poem—since the wedding celebrated is Spenser's own—an issue 'some distance from a search for utterance or conversational meaning'. Suppose we agree that literary criticism needs to move beyond pragmatics. That does not make pragmatics dispensable, or even unimportant. Consider Spenser's line (from elsewhere in the poem) 'Make feast therefore now all this live-long day'. Is the instruction, then, to be eating at every moment of the twenty-four hours? Obviously not; we know that the poem's speaker communicates something to us distinct from the literal sense of the words uttered, and we know this by the ordinary pragmatic inference procedures we apply when a conversation partner tells us he spent the whole day eating. Similarly, we infer that Spenser's use of the expression 'the world's light-giving lamp' is an intended reference to the sun and not to any lamp; that 'truest turtle dove' is intended to refer to no dove but to Spenser's bride. If we did not know these things we could not understand the poem, and could not wonder about its tone. Pragmatic inference may not be everything but it is, even in so literary a case as *Epithalamion*, indispensable.

Lamarque might agree that pragmatics is indispensable as a kind of heavy-lifting, foundation-digging enterprise, while literary analysis is an elite activity, more like interior design. For my purposes that would be enough of a concession on his part. But why is Lamarque so confident that when we turn from 'what the poem means' to 'how the poem works, how its effects are achieved' we move into a realm disjoint from that of pragmatic inference? One of the interesting suggestions of relevance theory is that 'poetic effects' such as style 'result from accessing a large array of very weak implicatures in the . . . pursuit of relevance'.[34] I will grant that we do not know whether or to what extent this claim is true, but it ought not to be simply assumed, without detailed treatment of cases, that pragmatics has nothing to tell us about how literary and other high-end narratives work.[35] I am not going to try to settle that issue here—it would take us too far from the core concerns of this book—but until it is settled Lamarque cannot have even the more modest conclusion his argument suggests.

What about cases where a narrative is conveyed by, say, film? I will say more later about narrative and the film medium, and Chapter 9 is a case study in just this connection. But there are fundamental differences between language and the medium of film, and these differences may make us wonder whether pragmatic inference plays much of a role in the filmic case. Here is one way the filmic medium is special: that what a film image is *of* does not depend on anyone's intentions but on causal facts about what happened to be in front of the camera at the time. Does that make film narratives more like thermometers than they are like novels? No. We have seen that in the linguistic case there is a distinction to be made between the meanings of the words and sentences of the text and the

---

[34] Sperber and Wilson 1995: 224. On weak implicatures, see ibid. sect. 4.4 and, for applications to the literary, Pilkington 2000; Fabb 2002, esp. chap. 3; see also Gibbs 1999. For scepticism about the literary/conversational distinction from the point of view of cognitive science, see Gibbs 1994. The best account of relevance theory—Sperber and Wilson's psychologically oriented approach to the pragmatics of communication much indebted to the work of Grice but opposed to his dependence on knowledge of conversational principles—is Carston 2002.

[35] Another view, with which both Lamarque and I could agree without resolving the present dispute, is that we move beyond pragmatics when we seek, as we must, the '*significance* of the fictional worlds the text brings to view. The search for literary meaning is in large part the struggle to render explicit the import, the consequence, of the worlds that literary works bring to view' (Gibson 2007: 11).

communicative use to which those words and sentences are put. The use to which those words and sentences are put is *telling a story*, and identifying that story requires plausible inference from the meanings those words and sentences have to the communicative content of the narrative. The filmic case parallels this in such a way that we can say, for film as well as for narrative in language, that we arrive at the story by pragmatic inference. The starting-point is a distinction, for both film and still photography, between two kinds of representational contents: *representation by origin* and *representation by use*. We will hear more about representation by use in a moment.

Photography depends on representation-by-origin, because the process that goes into making a photograph involves the leaving of a visible trace on a surface by exposure of that surface to light emitted or reflected from the source; the source is then what the photograph represents-by-origin. Does that mean that a photograph can represent only its source? If that were so a photograph could never represent a fictional character such as King Arthur, for Arthur is not available to be a source. But if a photograph cannot represent King Arthur, it is hard to see how a cinematic image could represent him, since cinematography uses a basically photographic method. Even video and other more recent technologies of image-making are source-based in the way that photography is; the process of making images by means of these technologies results in an image of the source. Don't these things ever give us representations of King Arthur? I think it is evident that they do.[36]

We make progress when we see that a photograph, or movie, or video image can represent in more ways than one, representing one thing by origin and something else by use. We regularly press things into representational service simply by using them to represent, as a pepper pot may represent a regiment by being so used in the course of my explaining the battle to you.[37] And, something which is a representation-by-origin of one thing may also be a representation-by-use of something else. A small plastic figure

---

[36] Here I ignore, as I said I would, issues of existence. The scrupulous may prefer talk of Arthur-representations rather than of representations of Arthur.

[37] Strictly speaking, the categories of representation-by-origin and representation-by-use are not disjoint; something which represents by convention might have a process of making which is, in effect, a process of establishing its use as a convention. Here I am concerned with the distinction between things which represent-by-origin and things which represent-*merely*-by-use—i.e. things which do not get their use as part of their process of making.

made to represent Napoleon might be used to represent his army in my tabletop explanation of the battle.

So a photograph or film image may represent one thing by origin—Cary Grant for instance—while representing something else because of the use of that image in a project of narrative communication. Thus, the images in Hitchcock's *Notorious*, which represent-by-origin Cary Grant, get to represent-by-use Devlin the American agent, because it is part of the narrative project to convey to us facts—make-believe facts—about Devlin and his activities. In practice, cinematic images do this much more effectively than still photographic images do, because a moving image can itself be the means by which the narrative is conveyed, whereas a still image is apt to be used merely as an illustration of a narrative presented in other ways, as with Julia Margaret Cameron's photographic illustrations intended to go with an edition of Tennyson's *Idylls of the King*.[38] When the image is the means of conveying the narrative it is imaginatively engaging in ways which raise the salience of what is represented merely by use, something which tends to be swamped, in the photographic case, by what is represented by origin. It is difficult to see Cameron's photographs as anything other than representations of people dressed up to look like Arthurian characters, whereas there is no difficulty in seeing Devlin and the other fictional characters in Hitchcock's film images.[39]

Does this analysis apply to a documentary, wherein there is no distinction between the characters of the story told and the people we see on screen?[40] Even in a documentary film, the bare facts concerning what the film images are of do not determine the content of the narrative; that has to be inferred from such things as editing, commentary, and other intention-manifesting interventions. A film counts as a documentary exactly when there is a relation of *harmony* between the photographically determined contents of its images and its story; the people and events recorded by the camera have to be the people and events which are the contents of the narrative.[41] But harmony is not identity; the story which the auditory and visual images of the film represent is never identical with the sum of

---

[38] See Cameron 1875.

[39] Or, for that matter, seeing Errol Flynn as Robin Hood. See Currie 2008 for elaboration of the limitations on such representation in still photography.

[40] I have in mind here something that approximates to a 'pure' documentary, without recourse to dramatic reconstruction.   [41] See Currie 2004: chap. 4.

what those images are images of. In photography and the various screen media, fictional and non-fictional, we need a distinction between a basic, given meaning, meaning-by-origin, and an inferred, narrative meaning, meaning-by-use.

1.4. Nature's Narratives?

I said that a narrative *must* be an artefact. Some other kinds of things, such as hammers and cars, do not have this strong requirement. Hammers can be made, but an unmodified stone might do as a hammer. It is improbable, but not impossible on conceptual grounds, that we should find something lying around that would do as a car though it was not made for that purpose. But to think that narratives are like hammers or cars in this respect is to confuse narrative—something essentially artefactual—with the source of narrative, which need not be artefactual. The earth's strata may be the material from which a geological narrative can be constructed, but they do not themselves constitute a narrative. I have said that narrative-making need not involve writing or speech, since there are narratives in other media. Indeed, the maker need not make any physical thing; it may be enough for the detective to point meaningfully and in a certain order to items at the crime scene in order to communicate a narrative of the crime to her assistant. But, until those items are linked in this intentional way, we have no narrative.

We seem occasionally to recognize a category of what I will call magical narratives. I do not mean by this that we believe in them, but rather that we take them in our stride when they occur in the realm of the imagination. In one of M. R. James's ghost stories, a dolls' house provides its owner with a narrative of horrid goings-on, coming to life in a theatrical or cinematic way.[42] We might perhaps think of the dolls' house as providing access to those very events and hence as a sort of time machine rather than a representation. A more natural reading has the dolls' house *represent* events that took place in the house of which it is a copy. This is so also in another of James' stories, where a narrative is conveyed by

---

[42] 'The Haunted Dolls' House', *The Collected Ghost Stories of M. R. James* (London: Edward Arnold, 1931).

means of a mezzotint which changes between the occasions on which its possessor looks at it. On one occasion it shows nothing more than a house and grounds; later on there is a figure; later still the figure is doing some unpleasant things. James is unspecific about the mechanisms in these cases, but there is not much encouragement to think of the dolls' house or picture narratives as being told by an agent—even by an agent with magical powers. With these stories and many others that involve magic, it is as if certain causal pathways are naturally sensitive to meaning.[43] These causal pathways select a certain sequence of events to replay in narrativized form, because the narrative form preserves the moral and psychological import of those events.

We often think of magical phenomena as the result of intentional agency on the part of supernatural beings, able to implement their intentions directly, merely willing the world to behave in certain ways. On such a view, magic really is just agency writ large: we might call this the reductive view of magic. According to the picture I described one paragraph back, magic is irreducible to agency. Narratives which are the product of magic reducible to agency, even of a supernatural kind, are no threat to the idea that narratives are artefacts: supernatural agents merely have better, more-direct ways of making artefacts than we do. The threat, if there is one, comes from irreducible magic.

How much of a threat is there here? We get the notion of irreducible magic by taking ideas which have their natural home within a theory of agency, wrenching them from the context in which they make proper sense, and imagining them, somehow, to be features of the world. There is something emotionally appealing about the idea of a world in which things happen just as if they were the product of an agent, but without their being such a product; a world which, of its own nature, carries meaning. I doubt that this is any more coherent than the idea of a world of beautiful things—but beautiful in some absolute sense, unrelated to the responses of any group or individual. Giving an account of narrative for the cases outside the domain of the irreducibly magic will not be easy; if we can do

---

[43] The existence of such pathways is suggested even in ghost stories where there are supernatural agents. Another story by James, 'Oh, Whistle, and I'll Come to You, My Lad' has a hapless academic holidaying in East Anglia summon a supernatural agent (though not a very powerful one) by blowing on an ancient whistle that he finds. The causal pathway from the blowing to the summoning of the agent is one of these magically meaning-preserving ones, but that part of the causal process is not mediated by the activity of any other supernatural being.

that you ought not to complain that we have not also covered a kind of case that is of doubtful coherence.

What of those dreams and episodic memories which have, or seem to have, a narrative structure? Should we think of these as nature's narratives? The evidence is hard to interpret; it is far from clear that the memories and dreams have narrative structure themselves, rather than being the materials out of which we, persons, make narratives of the past or the fantastic. Let us grant that they do have a kind of intrinsic narrative-like structure. Then I think we should say that this exemplifies a more general state of affairs, which is that there are non-artefactual things which have some of the features of artefacts. And in this case the non-artefactual things—the memories and dreams—lie as far apart from narratives as natural meanings lie from non-natural meanings. Clouds may mean rain and spots may mean measles, but these are things of a wholly different kind from the communicative acts which belong to Grice's category of non-natural meanings (Grice 1957). We might, on the basis of whatever narrative structuring that memories and dreams have, label them 'narratives'. Then we would need some other term with which to label the intentional-communicative artefacts which I intend to focus on here. Actually, 'narrative' seems as good a term as any for this purpose. And, while some non-artefacts, such as bits of stone, may become hammers by being used in certain ways, no memory or dream can become the kind of communicative artefact which I am labelling 'narrative'; dreams and memories are at best the materials around which to build such a communicative artefact.

None of this should prevent us seeing affinities, important ones, between narratives and the kinds of non-agent-based corpora just described. We could add in here the mechanical thermometer which records, over the day, the ambient temperature at a place; as a record of causally connected particular occurrences at a particular place, it is certainly narrative-like but not, according to me, a narrative.[44] Within this larger class, there is a category of things which includes novels, histories, biographies, and other, similarly structured, intentional-communicative artefacts. These are the things which discussion of narrative has traditionally been about and there are important connections to be teased out between what they represent—the stories they tell—and their origins in intentional action.

---

[44] See Chap. 2 for more on the role of causal connection in narrative representation.

These are the things, whatever we call them, which this book is about. I choose to call them narratives.

What, finally, of lives as narratives? On my account, no life is a narrative since no life is a representational artefact. Some dystopic future may introduce us to artificial or at least artefactual life made with the intention that it—the life itself—tell a story. Ray Bradbury's illustrated man, with his animated tattoos, has a body that tells stories; it might have been instead that his actions, preprogrammed in some way, told the stories. We are not yet at a point where such a life is available, and claims to the effect that lives are narratives are claims about ordinary human lives, past and present. But I am not sure that anyone seriously thinks that any life *is* a narrative, though they may think things which are easily confused with this. They may think that some act of narrative production is a condition for the flourishing, or perhaps even for the existence, of that life.[45] Galen Strawson has shown, I think, that this is not true, that one can live an integrated, coherent, and worthy life where the relations of earlier to later are not mediated by narrative (Strawson 2004). Recall our distinction between narrative and story, between the representation and the represented. If a life cannot (except in extraordinary circumstances) be a narrative, can it be the story told by a narrative? To think so is not so obviously mistaken as thinking that a life is a narrative.[46] Still, the idea does more harm than good. No one has the knowledge or power to make their whole life or even a significant temporal stretch of it correspond to a narrative they construct; at best, one's life and one's narrative of the life overlap, with lots of the life missing from the narrative and, no doubt, plenty of mistakes in the narrative about the life. But the Sherlock Holmes narrative is not an incomplete and partly mistaken account of the Sherlock Holmes story; the narrative determines what the story is, because the story consists of just those things which are true according to the narrative. Nor is it different for non-fictional stories. A biography of Churchill may get the facts wrong and leave out lots of important stuff, but the relation between that narrative and

---

[45] The debate on whether lives and other historical processes have a 'narrative structure', or something close to it, with supposed implications for realism about history, is not, I think, a debate about whether lives are narratives—not in my sense, anyway. See essays by Carr, Mink, White, and others in Roberts 2001.

[46] In a passage quoted by Strawson, Jerome Bruner goes from talking about 'the stories we tell about our lives' to claiming that the 'self is a perpetually rewritten story . . . in the end, we *become* the autobiographical narratives by which we "tell about" our lives' (see Strawson 2004: 435).

the Churchill story—the story told by that narrative about Churchill—is not similarly wrong and incomplete; the story, once again, just is whatever is so according to the narrative.[47] Narratives we tell about ourselves and our lives may be relatively faithful accounts; they may, in some circumstances and for some people, guide our actions and contribute to the worth of what we are and what we do—even Strawson may agree to that. But lives are not narratives, nor are they stories.

1.5. Implied Authors

I have insisted that narratives are understood by making inferences to the intentions of their makers. Narrative theory has a lively history of debating this issue, one often framed in terms of the 'implied author', an imagined or constructed agent, in the light of which the work is to be understood. Flagship examples include Tolstoy, who on close inspection turns out to be too morally unimpressive to illuminate *Anna Karenina*, so we are told, and in whose place we put an imagined figure of wide and deep moral sympathies. I am content to follow this pattern, more or less, but how does that fit with my insistence that narratives are intentional-communicative artefacts?[48] If they are, surely we ought to find out what intentions the maker of the artefact *really* had. Not so. Pragmatic inference is not a forensic investigation into a person's motives that involves sifting the evidence of diaries, letters, and the reminiscences of friends; it is a common-or-garden activity, over which we usually exercise little conscious control and of which we usually have little understanding, designed to produce an on-average good but not perfect match between speaker's intentions and hearer's uptake.[49] The regularity with which it is used together with its reasonable level of success in facilitating communication enables us to define a kind of meaning in terms of it, sometimes called *achieved meaning*.[50] Achieved meaning is what an attentive hearer, using pragmatic inference,

---

[47] See Louis Mink: 'Narrative history borrows from fictional narrative the convention by which a story generates its own imaginative space, within which it neither depends on nor can displace other stories' (Roberts 2001: 217). This feature of historical narrative is neither a convention nor borrowed from fiction.

[48] The question was raised by an anonymous reader. See also below, Chap. 4, sect. 2.

[49] In the higher reaches of criticism pragmatic inference can become exquisitely refined, but it is the refinement of that recognizably ordinary practice.   [50] On this, see esp. Levinson 2002.

can reasonably be expected to understand on the basis of what is heard. It is that meaning—reasonably expected communicative uptake—which the speaker succeeds in expressing: hence 'achieved' meaning. The idea of an implied author can now be explained, to a first approximation, in pragmatic terms. The implied author of the narrative is the (perhaps non-existent) figure whose intended meaning coincides with the narrative's achieved meaning.

This is a first approximation only. As we shall see, narratives come with points of view as well as with contents, and a full account of the ways in which an implied author is constructed needs to take point of view into account. Enough has been said here to indicate that the idea of the implied author is within the spirit of thinking of narratives as intentional-communicative artefacts.

1.6. Looking Ahead

The rest of this book will depend, in various ways, on the claim that narratives are intentional-communicative artefacts. It is a peculiarity of the recent study of narrative that writers have, on the whole, chosen to ignore the making of narrative, assuming that narrative is somehow best studied by treating its instances as internally structured objects which narrative theory aims to map but the origins of which we know nothing. Thus a great deal of time has been devoted to taxonomic projects which distinguish narrators at different levels, all considered to be 'internal to the narrative'. Authors themselves hardly get a look-in. There is something to be said for recognizing an internal narrator, and I will have more to say about this later. The point we need to start from is that any narrative we have is made possible by evolved human capacities for communication. And facts about this capacity—sometimes very unobvious ones, made visible for us by science—are crucial to understanding how narratives work.

2

The Content of Narrative

Narratives represent the people, things, events, states, and processes—real or imagined—that go to make up their stories. But I have said little about what distinguishes stories from the contents of other representational forms: theories, chronologies, lists, the interpretive ruminations we find in sermons. These other representational forms are able to tell us about people, things, events, states, and processes, without telling stories about them. What makes stories, and hence the narratives that represent them, distinctive?

2.1. Causes

An obvious suggestion is that narratives are distinctive in focusing on particulars, and on the particularity of their interactions over time. Interaction suggests causation, a notion which has been claimed to be central to narrative content.[1] And the unity of a narrative, some degree of which is required if we are to have a narrative at all, is partly a matter of causal unity. With a highly unified narrative, we find causal relations between events with a single subject, or at least rich patterns of causal interaction between events the subjects of which are a few central characters. Narratives, to summarize the proposal, are distinguished from other representations by what they represent: sustained temporal-causal relations between particulars, especially agents.[2] Other kinds of discourse focus on causes: scientific theories, for

---

[1] See e.g. Kermode 1981.

[2] See Carroll 2001a. Carroll focuses on the idea of *narrative connection*, which he explicates in causal terms, rather than on the idea of narrative. For, he says, we may call something a narrative even though it contains things which are not 'strictly narrative elements' (ibid. 21). Yet narrative connection and narrative are closely connected on Carroll's view: 'I suspect that when we call more large-scale

example. But theories stress generality, law–likeness, and abstraction, while narratives focus on the particular, the contingent, the concrete.[3]

The emphasis on particulars is surely right. Need the relations between particulars in a narrative's story be causal? Need all the entities of the story be temporally (and perhaps spatially) connected? Be wary, first of all, of sophistication in talking about causation in relation to narrative. Causation is a difficult notion, and there are widely differing views about what it is and about what is causally connected to what. At one extreme is the view that all causation is microphysical causation, with everything else simply supervening on the microphysical; apparent causal relations between macroscopic, mental, or social events then turn out to be mere illusions of causal connectedness. Taking such a view as this, and regarding the representation of causation as one of the essential tasks of narrative, would make nonsense of most of the narratives we actually have, which rarely speak of microphysical causation.

Here are two remedies. One is to tailor a notion of causation that allows us to say such things as that Emma's attempts at marriage-making cause a great deal of unhappiness, and that Iago's lies cause the death of Desdemona. The other is to allow a range of causal and non-causal relations between objects, persons, and events—we might call them relations of dependence—and to say that it is this larger class of relations, which includes the happiness of various people depending on Emma's activities, and the fate of Desdemona depending on Iago's lying, that narrative is concerned with. I have no strong preference for one of these solutions, but it is worth noting that there are conceptions of cause which are much more

discourses, such as histories or novels, narratives, we do so because they possess a large number of narrative connections or because the narrative connections they contain have special salience or a combination of both' (ibid.). Carroll justly emphasizes the role of questions in sustaining interest in narrative; narratives succeed he says, to the extent that they raise questions in the minds of audience members, who then stay with the narrative in order to have the question answered. This seems right as an observation about what makes narratives successful, but is not a condition on narrative itself; a narrative that fails to raise the right sorts of questions will fail to get an audience, but need be no less of a narrative for that (see e.g. Carroll 1990).

[3] Sometimes we make a distinction between narrative and drama (Scholes and Kellogg 1966: 4), but here I treat drama as simply a form that narrative can take: one with limits and possibilities distinct from those of the novel, the short story, film, and other narrative forms. Theatre is storytelling in a specific medium, without an internal (within the story) narrator of the kind we sometimes (not always) find in the novel (see below, Chap. 5, sect. 5). Drama generally concerns the thoughts and doings of particular people in their causal transactions with one another and the world. It has as good a claim to be called narrative as these other forms.

inclusive than the 'all causation is micro-causation' view. For example, the interventionist approach to causation claims that we have a causal relation between X and Y when an intervention which changes the value of X would change the value of Y.[4] This is likely to accommodate the cases of both Emma and Iago; intervening to change their behaviour in relevant ways would avoid the unhappiness, small and great, which they cause. But we should not struggle here to refine such notions so as to produce a general and philosophically defensible analysis of cause; the operation of narrative does not depend on any such notion, and we would do violence to many narratives by requiring them to observe the conditions of a precise philosophical theory of cause. In saying that the representation of causation is central to narrative, we are saying something about the centrality of represented relations which we would, in our philosophically unreflective moments, think of as causal, or perhaps merely as dependency relations, assuming we unreflectively distinguish these two classes. There can, it is true, be a narrative in which it is stipulated that there are no causal relations without intervening mechanisms, or that all causation involves conserved quantities.[5] In such a narrative we are required to take a specific and perhaps idiosyncratic attitude to causation, and what I have said just now would not apply in these situations.[6] Such cases are very unusual, and are no basis for generalization across narratives.

A challenge to the idea of causal connectedness—however that notion is understood—as essential to narrative, is offered by David Velleman. What is essential for narrative, he says, is an arc of development the audience finds emotionally satisfying in certain ways, however its events are represented as being connected. In a story that Aristotle relates, Mitys was murdered, and the murderer of Mitys went on to be killed by a falling statue of Mitys himself.[7] These events, the murder and the accidental death, constitute the material for a narrative, says Velleman, despite the lack of causal connection

---

[4] See e.g. Pearl 2000.

[5] For the idea that causation involves conserved quantities, see Dowe 2000. The possibility of causation, particularly psychological causation, without mechanism is argued in a series of papers by John Campbell, including Campbell 2007.

[6] In such cases questions arise as to the extent to which an author is entitled to stipulate the metaphysical or scientific facts about causation, and some such attempts may be deemed to fail on account of violating conditions which have been proposed in order to explain the resistance of readers to incoherent stipulations. (For an approach to one aspect of this topic of 'imaginative resistance', see below, Chap. 6, sect. 1.) I am assuming here that not all such stipulations would fall foul of whatever conditions on authorial say-so prove robust.   [7] Aristotle, *Poetics*, 1452a4–6.

between them; the emotional cadence provided by the juxtaposition of these events is enough. Or take E. M. Forster's idea that 'The king died and then the queen died' is not a narrative ('plot', in his terms), but 'The king died and then the queen died of grief', with its suggestion of causal connection, is. But 'Let the queen laugh at the king's death and later slip on a fatal banana peel: the audience will experience the resolution characteristic of a plot' (Velleman 2003: 7).

Let us distinguish two claims. One is that causal relations between events are not necessary for a narrative. The other is that bringing about the effect of an emotional resolution is necessary and sufficient for something to be a narrative. Velleman seems to be committed to the second as well as the first. He says that 'a description of events qualifies as a story in virtue of its power to initiate and resolve an emotional sequence in the audience'. Suppose someone found emotional resolution in the deduction, according to physical laws, of a certain pattern of particle interaction. No doubt this would be unusual but such a deduction, or the representation of it, would not come to be a narrative if, for some reason, all or most of us started finding such emotional satisfactions in particle physics. We could say that the emotional response in question is the one provoked by narrative, but that kind of response would have to be specified in some narrative-independent way if it is to help us understand what narrative is. I see no reason to think that there are emotional responses we have to narratives and to nothing else. It is worthwhile, then, to consider whether we can continue with the traditional project of trying to say at least something informative about the nature of narrative by way of specifying its representational features, taking into account the challenge to the idea that the representation of causality plays a particularly important role here.[8]

Before I take this up, I note one other claim that Velleman makes, intended to shed doubt on the explanatory potential of narrative:

the audience of narrative history is subject to a projective error. Having made subjective sense of historical events, by arriving at a stable attitude toward them, the audience is liable to feel that it has made objective sense of them, by understanding how they came about. Having sorted out its feelings toward events, the audience

---

[8] As the next chapter will show, I do not, in the end, claim that all that is distinctive of narrative is explicable in terms of its representational features.

mistakenly feels that it has sorted out the events themselves: it mistakes emotional closure for intellectual closure.   (Velleman 2003: 20)

If Velleman is right, the point generalizes beyond historical cases: we should say also that when we feel that the events of a fiction have been explained by the narrative, this is because we have made merely 'subjective' sense of them. Intellectual closure is an ambition of serious fiction as well as of non-fiction and, if Velleman is right, it is an illusion to suppose that it is ever achieved; it would also then be difficult to see how narratives could be a pathway to moral knowledge.[9] We do not have to go so far; we can say that narratives (fictional or not) have the potential to explain but that we also sometimes are led into error by our sense of emotional closure, thinking that we have a narrative explanation when we do not, or that we have a stronger explanation when what we have in fact is weaker.[10]

Back to the role of causality. I will take the story of Mitys, his murder, and his murderer's death as representative of a class of cases in which apparent lack of real connection between events goes with a strong sense of narrative; I will call it *The Murder of Mitys*. And I will distinguish this case from some others that may come to mind. Andre Bazin praised De Sica for his use, in *Bicycle Thieves* (1948), of sheer happenstance, as with the group of seminarians sheltering from the rain—an event which turns out to have no connection with the story. The lack of connection does not compromise the narrative, but this case is very different from that of *The Murder of Mitys*. By the time we see the seminarians, *Bicycle Thieves* has achieved considerable narrative momentum through its presentation of causally related characters and incidents; the seminarians come and go, and make no difference to the story—though their presence is a significant element in the film's realist style. The problem with *The Murder of Mitys* (imagining it to be suitably filled out) is that the two most salient events of the story seem to be causally unconnected; an intervention which prevented Mitys' death would have had no effect on the subsequent and fatal event, 'statue falls on man'. Then there is Huxley's *Eyeless in Gaza*, where the heartless affair of Anthony and Helen is interrupted by

---

[9] For a positive account of the role of narrative in moral deliberation, see Misak 2008.

[10] In the quoted passage, Velleman does at one point speak of the audience as being 'liable' to think that events have been explained by the narrative.

their having a dog dropped on them from an aeroplane—literally out of the blue. There is something anomalous about this episode, but there is too much conscious working against the grain of narrative expectation for this to be a good specimen for the kind of analysis that is wanted here. And, while the causal history of the dog is, or seems to be, unconnected to any of the salient events of the story to that point, the dropping has consequences further on. Some of the things I shall say later on might (or might not) help us to understand aspects of these episodes from *Bicycle Thieves* and *Eyeless in Gaza*, but these cases are not ones to start with.

Perhaps we are judging the story of Mitys to be a narrative, not on the basis of our emotional response to it, but because, at some level, we cannot rid ourselves of the presumption that there is a connection between the murder and the accidental death. It is difficult not to think of the story as one in which the murderer gets his just desserts. But justice is not served by coincidence; it requires a dependency relation between the crime and the subsequent disadvantage—death in this case—accruing to the criminal. Perhaps, remembering earlier remarks, we should say that this relation of dependency need not be thought of as causal. Perhaps, as I have said, there is a way of thinking about the world according to which there are non-causal dependencies between events, and the case of Mitys is of this kind. If so, let us by all means say that what matters to narrative is its representation of dependencies in general between events, many of which will be causal but some of which may not. I think we still have a problem: take the story of a man who successfully battles a life-threatening disease but who is killed in an unrelated car crash the day after his discharge from hospital. Might not this provide a compelling narrative? We might think of this as another case of hidden dependency; somehow, the story implies, the recovery from illness disturbed the balance of fortune owed the man, and the car crash served to re-establish it. I cannot quite believe that other readings are not possible. Couldn't the unrelatedness of the events be the point of the story?

What we have in such a case is, I agree, a narrative. We need, therefore, to accommodate the fact that there is here a notable absence of dependency at the point one would otherwise expect to find it, and that this does not destroy the claim that what we have is a narrative. But we need to accommodate it within a framework which allows for more than just a narrative/non-narrative distinction. Such a framework follows.

2.2. Narrativity

Lewis Namier's *Structure of Politics at the Accession of George III*, with its meticulous analysis of the allegiances of individual MPs, dealt a blow to the Tory-versus-Whig interpretation of eighteenth-century politics.[11] It is standardly contrasted with the richly narrative histories of Macaulay and the Trevelyans. But Namier's history is not devoid of narrative, since he illustrates his general theses with examples of particular behaviour and motive which are presented in narrative form. We need some fine distinctions when comparing these works. If we take seriously such general definitions of narrative as that of Genette—'a linguistic production undertaken to tell of one or several events'—we can say only that all are narratives, as is 'I walked to the shop'.[12] We should add that the events are to be represented as causally related (so there would have to be more than one). But causation is required for walking, and walking to the shops involves starting and stopping, which ought to count as two separate events, irreproachably causal in their relations. And causation is not absent from Namier's account; when he tells us that Lord Rockingham wrote to the Earl of Newcastle about closing the secret service accounts he tells us of particular physical and mental processes that are thoroughly causal.

Perhaps we are stuck with a conception of narrative that includes, but does not discriminate between, Macaulay's and Namier's very different histories, as well as minimal items like 'I walked to the shop'. Peter Lamarque (Lamarque 2004) thinks we are, that we are simply mistaken in thinking that narrative is an interesting category. We think this because there are, as a matter of fact, some interesting narratives: the novels of Jane Austen and Charles Dickens, the great epics, the great narrative poems. Lamarque is partly right; narrative as a category is not, I shall argue, very interesting. If that was all there was to it, the situation would be puzzling. It would be as if we were persuaded that the category *middle-sized thing* was interesting just because there are interesting middle-sized things. Call that an error of overgeneralization. This does not seem to be an error

---

[11] Namier 1929.
[12] Genette 1980: 30; see also Abbott 2002: p. xi. Genette's definition has the additional disadvantage that it applies only to narratives in language. Barbara Herrnstein-Smith's definition—'verbal acts consisting of someone telling someone else that something happened'—is equally problematic (Herrnstein-Smith 1981: 228).

we are naturally prone to. There ought to be some special reason why we are prone to overgeneralization in the case of narrative and not in other cases, like that of middle-sized things. As a matter of fact, I do not think that the error in the narrative case is one of overgeneralization. It is a less-obvious error, hiding behind an ambiguity in the question. Should we be interested in whether this or that is or is not a narrative, or should we be interested in whether this has a greater degree of 'narrativeness' than that? I believe that it is the second thing that we should be interested in. This is sometimes called *narrativity*.[13]

Anyone who, like me, thinks that the categorical concept of narrative is not interesting owes us an explanation of why so many people think otherwise. On Lamarque's view, we think that narrative is interesting because there are some interesting narratives. I offer a different explanation. It is that we are quite often uncertain as to whether the right approach to a given concept is to treat it as categorical or gradational. According to Susan Haack (Haack 1993), justification is gradational while knowledge is categorical. But this is disputed: Stephen Hetherington argues that knowledge itself is gradational (Hetherington 2001). I won't try to decide who is right, but the dispute suggests that deciding between categorical and gradational accounts is often difficult. Narrative, I submit, provides a further instance of this. People who say that narrative is interesting are, I say, confused: what they actually find interesting is the concept *thing high in narrativity*.

Support for the idea that we confuse narrative and narrativity comes from the fact that we tend to use 'narrative' in ways that depend on a sometimes contextually determined contrast with other things. Contrast Namier with Macaulay and it is natural to count only the latter's work as narrative; contrast Namier with my shopping list and it is the former that deserves the title. At a higher level of abstraction, contrast narrative

---

[13] For a recent survey, see Prince 1998. 'Narrativity' is a term used in different ways; other senses of 'narrativity' include that of Greimas (1977), who uses it to name a level of autonomous meaning that survives translation between languages and even between media (see also Bremond 1964). My use carries no implication that any such autonomous meaning exists. Galen Strawson uses 'narrativity' to refer to a certain view of life as understood in terms of narrative; see his excellent and provocative (2004), with which I have no quarrel here; see above, Chap. 1, sect. 4. Noel Carroll says that by distinguishing between narratives, annals, and chronicles we avoid the need for the concept of degree of narrativity (in something like my sense) (Carroll 2002: 34). Even if we reserve 'narrative', as Carroll suggests we should, for items with significant, salient narrative connections, there is plenty of room left for judgements of degree, and hence for narrativity.

with mathematical physics and it will seem natural to count parables and character studies as kinds of narratives.[14] On other occasions, we might *distinguish* narratives from parables and character studies, on account of the fact that the two latter kinds have generalizing tendencies that do not fit well with the particularizing, sequential aspirations of narrative. Narratives tell of causally related sequences of event tokens, distinguished by their involvement with particular objects and agents, while parables draw general conclusions from the particular, and character studies use the particular to illustrate general traits in a life.[15] What seems to be going on here is that context determines different threshold levels of narrativity, which we recognize by calling anything above the threshold a narrative. When the contrast is with something so *un*narrative-like as mathematical physics, the relevant threshold is very low, and so parables and character studies make it over the bar. Making parables and character studies the relevant contrast case signals a substantially raised level of the threshold.

In calling something a narrative, we may be doing any of three things. We may be contrasting it with things which, like general theories, are simply not narratives at all. We may be placing it on a scale of narrativity somewhere above a certain, contextually determined, threshold. We may be placing it in the class of what I will call *exemplary narratives*: a sustained account focusing on the histories of a few highly interrelated persons and their fortunes, replete with information about connections of dependency (which, for simplicity, I will assume to be causal dependencies), all this held in place by something I have not focused on so far: thematic unity. We find combinations like this exemplified in a great deal of literature, popular and canonical: in the novel, the short story, but also in drama and in film. Things of this kind would count as narratives in just about any context, no matter what contextually determined standard applies. In what follows I will give as examples of narratives things in this third class. Speaking generally, I will sometimes use 'narrativity' to remind us that we are discussing something that comes in degrees, but mostly 'narrative' will do equally well, and I will use it; talking, for example, about the relations between narrative and causation is easily understood as asking us to think

---

[14] On the contrast between narrative and character study, see below, Chap. 3.
[15] See Goodman 1981.

about how degree of narrative is affected by variation in the representation of causes. I turn now to that topic.

2.3. Weighing Factors

We may now think again about the relation between narrative and the representation of dependency, made problematic by the (apparent) lack of dependency in *The Murder of Mitys*. Consider again our class of exemplary narratives with their rich, particularized, and unified histories of cycles of thoughts, actions, and contingencies. What makes it the case that things combining these distinct features are seen as belonging to an interesting kind—the kind of thing that immediately comes to mind when we think of narrative, and in which human beings seem to show such a degree of interest? An obvious hypothesis is that exemplary narratives are excellent vehicles for the description of the motives and behaviour of individual people, or small numbers of people acting in consort or in competition or both, that things of this form are perhaps better suited than is any other representational device for conveying what particular people do or have done and why, and that this sort of information is of inexhaustible interest to us.[16] Why of inexhaustible interest? The answer, I suspect, has something to do with the circumstances in which our minds were evolving in the Early and Middle Stone Ages.

I reserve these speculations for an appendix to this chapter; what I say there will connect with issues dealt with much later concerning the notion of character and its role in narrative. Just now I will focus on the narrative practices of more recent ancestors. For its combination of the features I have said are important for narrativity—focus on highly interrelated persons, their actions, motives, and fortunes, richness in causal connectedness and

---

[16] It is no accident that Namier's work, with its low level of narrativity, left his history without much sense of 'adult human beings, taking a hand in their fates and fortunes, pulling at the story in the direction they want to carry it, and making decisions of their own'. For that, as Butterfield notes, 'we must have a political history that is set out in narrative form' (Butterfield 1957: 206). There is some reason to think that the narrative form tends to push us towards essentially human models of thought and action even when our inclination is to reach for quite different models. Experimental work by Barrett and Keil indicates that people who officially subscribe to the view that God is infinite in power and knowledge easily fall back on a much more limited, human-like conception of God's mind and action when presented with narratives which describe God's interventions in particular situations (Barret and Keil 1996; Barrett 1998).

connectedness by thematic unity—the following from J. H. Plumb provides as good a brief example as we shall find of something that brings narrative order and compression to a complex, even chaotic sequence of events:

No sooner had London been filled with speculation than it was learned that the Queen was dying. Would Bolingbroke have time to secure his party in power even if he obtained the white staff? Then it was learned that Bolingbroke was dining with Sutherland, Stanhope and the leading Whigs. The Privy Council met, and possibly with the connivance of Shrewsbury, the Dukes of Argyle and Somerset, both Whigs and loyal Hanoverians, attended. Bolingbroke was cornered; the dying Queen made Shrewsbury lord treasurer and the crisis was over. Time, if nothing else, had defeated the Jacobites and made George I's accession certain.   (Plumb 1956: 37).

In these few sentences, Plumb summarizes the complexities of the succession, emphasizing the shifting alliances and oppositions between leading figures against a background of personal and party interest. Plumb's attempt at generalization in the final sentence quoted finds a spurious inevitability in the process—but a tempting one given the degree of order his narrative has imposed on events.[17]

I have spoken of exemplary narratives as the natural vehicles of the sort of social information important in the environment of our evolutionary development—and now, for that matter. More on this in the appendix. But exemplary narratives will always have come in different grades or degrees, and there is no particular point of reduction in this degree, below which the form ceases altogether to serve this function. In practice, people's narratives fall short of the ideal in one way or another, with irrelevancies, failures of thematic unity, absence of crucial connections—faults for which further conversational exchange could provide some repair. So it is natural to suppose that our emerging conceptualization of this form allows a wide range of exemplars and has no clear boundary. That, I take it, is the concept of narrative we actually have. When picking exemplars of the category there is a tendency for us to focus on those items which are either very high in all the qualities listed, or which, while high in many, are notably and perhaps deliberately anomalous in their very low degree of one or other of them, where there is a good narrative-promoting reason for the anomaly. Such a

---

[17] Perhaps this illustrates an aspect of the pseudo-explanatory potential of narrative: a certain kind of prose generates an emotional cadence (Velleman) that makes the outcome seem more rationally, less contingently, related to its antecedents than it really is.

reason would be the difficulty of combining all these features, given the aim of the narrative. In a narrative committed to the systematic exploration of the theme of happenstance and its role in subverting justice or some other perceived good, it is necessary to violate the condition of causal connection, or at least to compromise it significantly, as happens in *The Murder of Mitys* and in the story of our recovered but unlucky patient. And we may well think of a version of a story like this as 'very much a narrative', or, in my terms, high in narrativity, even though failing to score as high as it might in terms of causal connection. Suppose there is a lot of causal information concerning the murder itself, and concerning the fall of the statue; we might then say that it does as well in causal terms as it can do, given its aim.

The cases of Mitys and of the recovered patient who dies in the car crash should not bother us much—as long as we do not see causal relatedness as the heart and soul of narrative. But causation is important in narrative; by and large we expect narratives to tell us a lot about causes, and to have their most salient events strongly embedded in causal contexts. Note that, even in a very thin version of the story of Mitys, there is information on causation at least implied. There is a unified, if rather shadowy subject, the murderer, who is central throughout and whose personal continuity is surely a causal matter; a statue gets to be *of* Mitys only in virtue of some causal connection between them. We would not have anything like the claim to narrative that we do have if the story went: 'Mitys was murdered; later a statue of Mitys fell on someone who had nothing at all to do with Mitys.' And even less narrative-like is this: 'Mitys was murdered; later a statue of someone fell on someone else; neither of them had anything at all to do with Mitys.' That narrativity varies to some extent with causal information is surely correct.

People have occasionally asked whether there could be a narrative of spatio-temporally disconnected events. In some such stories, the spatio-temporally separate streams of events converge or diverge, and hence have some sort of connection; so let us consider only wholly disconnected sequences of events. In some such stories, people move between different time series, thus introducing causal connections (assuming personal continuation requires causal continuity) between the different series; so let us consider only stories with no such transfers.[18] Should we say that in such a disconnected case we do not have one narrative, though we may have

---

[18] Stories of these kinds and their relations to narrative are discussed in LePoidevin 2007: chap. 9.

two or more narratives stuck together in a single discourse, much as we have with a book of short stories? If that is so, we have a discourse which dissects into separate narrative parts between which there are no common personal histories, no antecedents or consequences of events. Might there still be something present in such a case which is relevant to judgements of narrativity: thematic unity? The distinct parts of this discourse might have thematic unity in one sense, focusing on some aspect of conduct and its consequences: greed, jealousy, etc., as with portmanteau films such as *Les Sept Péchés capitaux* (1962).[19] We need to distinguish different kinds of thematic unity: general and particular. The thematic unity of the discourse just imagined is general, the point of the discourse being to illustrate a general theme from separate particular instances. This sort of unity is not enough to make a single narrative of what would otherwise be distinct narratives. The thematic unity that is relevant to narrativity is particular: unity is provided by a focus on some common thread in the activity of particular persons in particular connected circumstances, though narratives often do have, in addition, general thematic unity in that we are invited to generalize from the case in question.[20] A discourse concerning spatio-temporally-causally-personally unrelated events is not a (single) narrative, as long as it has only general thematic unity, though it may dissect into parts which are each as fully narrative as can be.

2.4. Causal History

I have avoided an approach to causation in narrative which requires us to be specific about what causation is. But there is a question to answer. Whatever sort of thing causation is, what kind of information about the causes of things do we expect from something high in narrativity? It would be absurd to think of even exemplary narratives as providing conditions sufficient for the occurrence of an event; outside of mathematical physics,

---

[19] Strictly, this is not an example of narrative streams occurring in separate space-times, but the stories do not exploit the possible connections that their occurrence within what is in fact a common space-time allow, or so I'll assume for the sake of the argument.

[20] In some portmanteau films—not *Les Sept Péchés capitaux*—there is some element of causal connection between the stories, but not enough to create a significantly unified narrative, as with *Dead of Night* (1945).

no one ever does that. One proposal is that we can expect narratives to provide INUS conditions in J. L. Mackie's sense: insufficient but necessary parts of conditions that are themselves unnecessary but sufficient.[21] This is still too strong; for one thing, INUS conditions require the assumption of determinacy. Something far weaker will do. David Lewis has argued that explanation is the provision of information (some information—never all) about causal history, where the causal history of an event is a relational structure: a set of events related by causal dependence (Lewis 1986). You can provide information of this sort in different ways: by singling out one event within that structure, by specifying several events that form all or part of a cross section of the causal history, by specifying a causal chain or a branching structure within the history. And you can provide information about causal history (and hence do some explaining) in less-specific ways. You might say only that the causal history involves events of a certain kind, has a certain kind of cross section, or involves a certain kind of causal chain. You might say merely that the pattern of events and their relations is in some way like another pattern of events (one we are more familiar with, perhaps). You might say that the pattern is one that tends to have a certain kind of effect, as with teleological explanation. Lewis even allows negative information to count; you can explain (better: do some explaining) by saying what was not involved in the causal history.

Since Lewis allows so much that falls short of specifying particular causes to count as information about causal history, this notion might be thought unhelpful when we are considering narrative. It is surely characteristic of narratives to focus on the specific and the particular. True, but the demand for specificity need not be the demand for information about what the specific causes of an event were. Causal information of a very weak kind may make a substantial contribution to a narrative, without seeming anomalous or calling into question our judgement that what we have is indeed a narrative. Consider this case of negative causal information:

1. Albert was strongly suspected of the murders, and indeed there was much evidence against him. In the end, it turned out that he was innocent, and his suspicious presence on all these occasions was just coincidence.

---

[21] See Carroll 2001a. Mackie's original paper ('Causes and Conditions', *American Philosophical Quarterly*, 2 (1965), 245–65) is reprinted, along with several critical commentaries, in Sosa and Tooley 1993. See esp. pp. 8–9.

The information this provides is highly specific, concerning Albert and the causal history of a particular murder, though it fails to specify a cause. What we expect from a narrative is highly specific information about causal history—and (1) provides it.[22]

2.5. Coincidence and Humean Cause

Here's another reason for doubt about the role of causation in narrative. Consider this:

2. The wind blew; the tree shook; the apple fell.

This sounds like a narrative, though a thin one. Part of the reason is the implication that these events are causally connected; to assume otherwise would be to accuse the speaker of violating the condition of relevance.[23] Suppose we now add:

3. By the way, none of these events actually caused the other.

Adding (3) to (2) means that we no longer have a narrative, since the implication in (2) of dependency between the events listed has been cancelled; perhaps we have a chronicle instead. But suppose that in place of (3) we had:

4. By the way, although all these events occurred in such a way as to give every impression of causation between them, the world described in this story is a Hume world: a world in which there is constant conjunction, just as in the actual world,

[22] See Auerbach's discussion (1953: chap. 4) of Gregory of Tours' *History of the Franks*, for a subtle exploration of the interplay between causality and specificity, and the relation of both to the presentation of a vivid and concrete narrative. Hayden White discusses a kind of writing he calls the *annal*, which, he says, falls short of being a narrative in various ways (White 1981). His example is from the eighth-century *Annals of Saint Gall*, a disconcertingly unconnected list of years with at most a brief comment against each (some years have no entries against them). The entry for the year 712 is 'flood everywhere'. This minimal account is certainly thick with causality; we already know what kind of event is in question here, roughly what its cause is, and can guess at some of its effects. But this is causality without much specificity. (Note the spuriously high degree of specificity in the entry for year 732: 'Charles fought against the Saracens at Poitiers on Saturday'.)

[23] At least, that would be so in most conversational contexts. One can imagine strange contexts in which the remark would count as relevant without the implication being assumed; suppose we knew that if a certain conjunction of unconnected events—the blowing of a wind, the shaking of a tree, the falling of an apple—happened to occur, then the gods would be kind to us.

but no substantive causal relation between events. In this world events seem to be causally related, just in the way they are in the actual world. In fact one could not tell by observation which of these two worlds you were in. But these events are not really causally connected.[24]

I am not inclined to say that the addition of (4) to what previously looked like a narrative means we no longer have one. Indeed, if we thought that what went before was high in narrativity, adding (4) does not seem to change much. Does this mean that cause is irrelevant to both narrative and narrativity? The problem here is that it is difficult to see (4) as annihilating cause, perhaps because we are inclined to take a Humean view of causes; if cause is Humean, then (4) is just contradictory, telling us that there is plenty of cause in the story but no cause. So I do not think we should treat (4) as seriously challenging the idea that cause is an important ingredient in a judgement of narrativity. And, if (4) really does abolish causes in the world of the story, it does not abolish the impression that it is a world with causes; moving points of light on a screen, if they move in ways that mimic billiard ball collisions, can seem causally connected even when we know they are not. At the very least, judgements about narrative seem to be linked to the representation of relations *like* causal relations.

2.6. Salient Possibilities

Providing causal information about an event may involve providing information about things made possible by causal antecedents of that event. We would be providing causal information about outcome P if we said that some factor in the causal history of P made it possible (or probable to some degree) that something contrary to P would happen. P may then have an interest for us in that its occurrence rules out what we took, up to that point, to be a certain possibility. Up to the moment where Jim leaps from the *Patna*, believing that it will sink and that the passengers will die, what we are told about happenings on board leaves it open as

---

[24] Carroll discusses a case where the discourse announces at the end that all these events have happened in a world with 'no causes, just coincidences'. He says that this is in fact no narrative. I take it that Carroll has in mind an addition more like my (3) than my (4). See Carroll 2001a: 35.

to whether he will stay. That he abandons the ship and its passengers seems to be determined by rather arbitrary factors. The possibility that Jim would stay is, to a certain point, a very salient possibility in the story, the question of whether he will stay is likely to occupy the reader at this point, and its having been a possibility to that point remains a salient fact thereafter.[25]

Gerald Prince suggests that it counts towards our confidence that a piece of discourse is high in narrativity if the discourse specifies not merely what did happen but what might have happened (Prince 1998). This is not an invitation to list all the logical possibilities; we expect this clause to be implemented by the provision of information about thematically relevant possibilities causally consistent with the information we have about events as they occur. Our sense of narrative may be enhanced by the discourse making salient that there are various outcomes which might happen at this point—that are consistent with how things are, or with how we know or believe they are.[26] Salient possibilities might be indicated explicitly. More often, the author will draw on common, importable, knowledge of causation. If we are told that the hero is clinging to a high ledge, context usually informs us of the relevant causal possibilities: he will fall, he will be rescued.

What determines, for a given narrative, whether something is a salient possibility? I answer the question in the next chapter.

Appendix: Cheap Talk and Costly Signals

I have suggested that our concept of narrative takes the form it does because things with just those features served, as they still do serve, as vehicles for the dissemination of certain kinds of information about agents. At a time in our relatively recent evolutionary history we became much larger brained, more intelligent creatures. This was a time when the groups in which we lived were becoming larger and more complex, probably with intense within-group competition for reproductive and other resources. In such an environment, and with the emergence of verbal language, being able to talk about, and hence to gain and communicate information about, other people's activities and their motives,

---

[25] In thinking about the connection between the salience of possibilities and questions, I am much indebted here to Carroll's account of 'erotetic narration' (Carroll 1990).

[26] The role of possibility in narrative is a consistent theme of narrative theory. See e.g. Iser 1989; Bruner 1990: chap. 2.

was hugely important.[27] The narrative form is exactly what enabled us to do all this—and still does.[28]

Can we be a little more precise about the selective forces at work here? The following is, I admit, no more than a plausible guess, but it is one which, as we shall see, sheds light on an issue that will confront us later on: the belief in character.

Humans are probably the only animals with language. But signals are common in the animal world. A signal may be a piece of behaviour, initiated by a specific situation, as when a vervet monkey gives a call which indicates to the group that a predator is near; it may be a more or less permanent visible trait, as with the peacock's tail which indicates—many believe—the health of the bird, and hence its desirability as a mate.

Vervet monkey calls are notable for their degree of differentiation: a different call for a different predator. With them, a relatively complex system of signalling has arisen which benefits all vervets, since all are vulnerable to predators.[29] Compared with the peacock's tail, these signals are cheap; the cost to a vervet that sees a predator of giving a call is small and the benefit to others large. Peacocks' tails are expensive in terms of the energy needed to grow and sustain them, and how difficult they make it for the peacock to get around.

Why has nature imposed such costs on the signalling of peacocks? One answer is that signals of fitness, if they were cheap, would be very unreliable, and hence ignored, and ignored signals, of use to no one, will not evolve. Signalling one's desirability as a mate is signalling between parties with conflicting interests. It is in the interest of all peacocks to signal their fitness as mates, whether they are fit or not, so signals of fitness available to all will be used by all. It is in the interest of peahens, for which the signals are intended, to distinguish the fit from the unfit, and signals of fitness used in the same way by all peacocks tell the peahens nothing.

---

[27] Robin Dunbar argues that language evolved as a mechanism for cementing social bonds, at the point where hominid group size became so large that grooming—the prior mechanism for managing social relations—became impossibly time consuming (Dunbar 1996). For a broad ranging reflection on the role of gossip in relation to social stability, see Gluckman 1963.

[28] For an evolutionary approach to narrative, see Sugiyama 2001. Sugiyama emphasizes the role of narrative in conveying foraging information, also noting that foraging and other kinds of technical and natural history information are generally interwoven with social themes. Typical themes of the foraging tales of the Ju/'hoansi people (a San society of the Kalahari) include many that are highly social: 'problems of marriage and sex, the food quest, sharing, family relationships, the division of labour, birth and death, murder, blood-vengeance, and the creation of the present world order' . . . as well as 'the origin of meat, animals . . . and the balance of power between men and women' (quoted from Biesele 1993: 17 and 23). Sugiyama also notes the tendency in hunter-gatherer societies for information to be conveyed indirectly, in the form of narratives of personal experience rather than 'in the form of lists or lectures', though lists occur significantly often within stories.

[29] See Cheney and Seyfarth 1990: chap. 4.

If, on the other hand, signalling fitness bears a cost that only the fit can pay, the signal will be reliable and may evolve.[30]

We expect signals to be costly when there is incentive for signals to be deceptive. That is how it is when there is conflict of interest, as there is between males who want to convince females of their fitness and females who want to distinguish the really fit from the pretenders. Where there is little conflict of interest concerning the subject of the signal—as with vervet avoidance of predators—there is no need for signals to be costly.[31]

The emergence of fully articulated language has given us an enormously flexible, and cheap, system of signals. With language, we are able to indicate the precise location of predators, their type, the number of them, the direction they are headed, their speed, what the signaller had for breakfast, what she would like for dinner, and just about anything else she wants to say, all for the price of the energy used in vocalization. With language, it costs a speaker no more to make a deceptive remark than it does to make a reliable one; there is no way to impose selective costs on utterances in a way which reflects their use in situations of conflicting interest. This is because language works by combining signals. Suppose we want to make it more expensive to say 'I want a goat' than to say 'I want a rabbit', given that we want people to claim the more valuable item only when they really need it, and hence only when they are willing to bear the higher cost of signalling. That means assigning a higher cost to 'goat' than to 'rabbit', making it undesirably more costly to signal 'I do not want a goat' or 'one of your goats has escaped' than to signal the same thing about rabbits.[32] Unsurprisingly, what we end up with is a complex system of signalling within language with more or less uniformly low costs for all signals.

Given that languages are cheap signalling systems, should we assume that the capacity to use language evolved in an environment where there was little conflict of interest between agents? That is unlikely: most theorists of mental evolution think that the massive growth in human cognitive power was fuelled by conflict of interest within and between human groups; an arms race developed in which increments of smartness, especially in regard to figuring out what others will do while hiding your own real intentions, were strongly selected.[33]

---

[30] The foundational work on costly signalling is Zahavi 1975. On costly signalling, reliability, and reputation as enduring literary themes, see Flesch 2007. Flesch argues that the pleasures of fiction are not those of identification with characters but the opportunities that fiction offers to monitor the behaviour of characters.

[31] Predator warnings can be costly in the sense that the one who calls may attract the notice of the predator. But such signals are not costly in the sense relevant here, for in this case there is a cost only if the signal is reliable. Also, I assume here, for the sake of the argument, that vervet signalling has as its proper functioning the alerting of group members to danger; this has been questioned.

[32] See Lachmann, Számadó, and Bergstrom 2001.   [33] See e.g. Trivers 1985.

With so much one can say at so little cost, with so little discouragement from being deceptive, and so much to be deceptive about, how did language ever evolve?

There is another factor that we must consider in accounting for the emergence of linguistic signalling systems. Signallers are not the only ones to pay costs; receivers may also pay costs in order to provide a high-quality assessment of the signal. This is noticed in many animal signalling systems. In some species, males attend at certain sites, or leks, for display. Female sage grouse prefer males with regular attendance on a lek over a period of days, attendance which it is costly for the females to monitor; they may also be in danger through being in proximity to males whose displays attract predators.[34] Linguistic signals also are intrinsically difficult to assess—so difficult in fact that for many of them no realistic assessment can be made because the facts are unavailable to be verified or the time and effort required to verify them is prohibitively expensive. With language, we seem obliged to take on trust signals we have every reason to think unreliable.

In seeking a solution to this problem, the first thing to be said is that cheap signals *can* evolve in situations of conflicting interest, if there is social enforcement of honesty.[35] Punishment for deception means that intrinsically cheap signals become expensive when they are known to be deceptive, and if the probability of being unmasked is high, the expected disutility of signalling deceptively may be significant. There are limits, of course, to the capacity of a single person to punish another for being unreliable, and in many cases no serious punishment is available to the aggrieved party. At this point language rescues itself: language enables aggrieved parties to share with others their beliefs about the speaker's untrustworthiness, the effect of which may be to damage the speaker's reputation and their capacity to draw on assistance, since people will no longer believe that the assistance will be reciprocated.[36]

Does the appeal to language as a spreader of reputation really help here? It is as possible, after all, for agents to signal misleading information about people's reliability as about anything else. But there is a way in which such information can be kept reasonably honest. Testimony concerning someone's unreliability need not consist in a simple, unelaborated assertion; it can be developed into a narrative

---

[34] Dawkins and Guilford 2003: 866.   [35] See again Lachmann, Számadó, and Bergstrom 2001.
[36] Robert Frank reports that 'when an experimental subject is told that his partner already has defected in a prisoner's dilemma, defection is the almost universal response' (Frank 2001: 73). People interested in the evolution of co-operation and morality have emphasized the role of reputation in determining an individual's fitness: performing acts of helping towards unrelated persons (or, in the case of related persons, acts the cost of which are not adequately compensated by genetic pay-off) may provide you with a reputation that enables you to benefit later on from some advantageous exchange with someone who prefers you to a partner with lower repute (Alexander 1987: 37 ff.; Trivers 1971). Recent evolutionary theorizing has emphasized the role of reputation in allowing reciprocal helping, not based on kinship alone, to develop. See Nowak and Sigmund 1998.

which describes the context along with details of the interaction, and a plausible account of motivation. The more detail the story contains, the more checkable its claim becomes, either through the test of inner coherence or through verification of the details, some of which the hearer may have direct or indirect experience of, or can cross-check with other, independent sources. The more detailed and more substantial a narrative is, the more difficult it becomes to tell a convincing lie by its means.[37]

My suggestion, therefore, is this: that the human capacity for linguistic communication co-evolved with a taste for significantly narrativized accounts of people's behaviour. The elaboration of language made ever more complex narratives possible, while the growing preference for narrative served to dampen the tendency to use language deceptively, by facilitating reliable information flow concerning deceptive behaviour. In the appendix to Chapter 5, I add to these considerations an argument for narrative as reliable because of its association with hard-to-fake expressions of emotion. At the end of this book (Chapter 11: appendix) I will connect these speculations with another puzzle: the high degree of reliance we place in the notion of character as something explanatory of behaviour.

I have spoken as if the evolution of a preference for narrative formulations of information has a biological explanation. And so, perhaps, it has; the idea is not, at any rate, an absurd one. But my account could be framed instead as a piece of (very early) cultural history. The preference for the narrative mode might not be carried through the generations by biological forces, genes perhaps; it might be sustained by cycles of cultural learning, whereby infants and children adopt a narrative mode in imitation of their care givers. If this pattern of cultural inheritance began early enough in our species, it might have been carried wherever the human diaspora went, preserved to this day in the storytelling habits of every culture. It might even have become the subject of the Baldwin effect—a (disputed) evolutionary mechanism whereby some highly adaptive behaviour which begins life as learned falls under biological control and

---

[37] Blakey Vermeule (2006) explores the tension in so much literature between the form's own exploitation of our taste for gossip and our always wanting to dissociate ourselves from gossip. Why are we so (officially) opposed to gossip? Vermeule cites explanations by Pascal Boyer (Boyer 2001: 141) according to which (1) we dislike being gossiped about and (2) we want to be seen as fastidious in our treatment of information about others. There are other possibilities, some of which might have played a role in the evolution of attitudes to gossip: while gossip is undeniably useful as a means to impart information about people's reliability and honesty, a manifestly high level of dependence on gossip advertises the limitations of one's own powers of judgement in matters of personality and character, and encourages attempts to manage gossip in such a way as to mislead one. The best mix of strategies would then be to be highly attentive to gossip but highly adept at disguising one's attentiveness. (On the role of ideas about character in the evolution of reliable signalling, see Chap. 11: appendix.) We can also see why gossip is so unsubtle, rarely delivering a nuanced verdict about someone's vices and virtues (see again Vermeule 2006: 110); the proper function of gossip was to deliver a memorable verdict on trustworthiness, as free as can be from the noise of ambivalence.

then simply emerges in development, thereby avoiding the costs of learning.[38] What matters is that we are able to see that the reason it has been sustained, by whatever forces, is that it contributes to the maintenance of (relatively) honest signalling.

[38] For an excellent account of the Baldwin effect, see Papineau 2005.

3

Two Ways of Looking at a Narrative

Chapter 1 took a distant view of narrative, one that brought into focus the processes that go into narrative-making; Chapter 2 moved in closer, offering an account of the story-content of narrative. These correspond to the *external* and *internal* perspectives.[1] Adopting the external perspective, we see a vehicle, something that represents a sequence of events in virtue of the activity of an agent we call the author. Adopting the internal perspective, we examine the world of the story as if it were actual; we speak and think directly of the characters and events of the story, though much of this speaking and thinking may be make-believe. The interaction of these two ways of seeing and thinking is crucial to understanding how narrative works. Our expectations about a narrative, our desire for explanation of what happens, and our sense of what is satisfactorily explained, are all a product of the interaction between these two factors. By getting us to adjust the resources we allocate to the two different perspectives, narratives manipulate our expectations, affect our sense of what is probable, and shape our willingness to grant plausibility to events within the story.

I start by arguing that the external perspective is essential to an understanding of narrative itself; this complements some of the results of Chapter 2. I then show how this addition gives us additional resources to account for difficult cases. I take a particularly problematic narrative, *Last Year in Marienbad* (Resnais, 1961), seeking an answer to the question,

---

[1] Here I am indebted to Peter Lamarque. See Lamarque 1996, esp. chaps 2 and 8. This distinction is closely related to one (or several) variously described as between discourse and story, *recit* and *histoire*, *syuzet* and *fabula* (see e.g. Chatman 1990). Peter Goldie (2003) distinguishes between internal and external perspectives, but for him an internal perspective represents or 'otherwise indicates' the point of view of one or more story participant; this is not required (though it is not ruled out) on my account.

what sort of narrative, if any, is this? Section 3 takes up a question raised at the end of Chapter 2, concerning what I called there 'salient possibility'; this will give us another reason to invoke the external perspective. I also offer an analysis of what it means for a narrative to be, as we say, 'improbable'. In Section 4 I examine a relation between narratives and their contents which I call 'representational correspondence'; adjusting the degree of representational correspondence, it turns out, is a way of managing some difficult relations between the internal and the external perspectives.

3.1. Limits to the Content Approach to Narrative

Specifying what sorts of things are represented in narrative—what we have called the story-content of narrative—is helpful if we are trying to understand what distinguishes narratives from other kinds of representations. Does it give us all we need? No. If degree of narrativity were determined solely by story content, there would be no difference in narrativity without difference in story content. Nelson Goodman imagines a case where this is not so. He asks us to consider the material in a narrative reordered so as to group the events not by temporal and causal relations but by their illustration of personality and character traits.[2] We start with *The Life of Nelson*—birth, early life at sea, command, great victories, death—and end up with *The Character of Nelson*—chapters on Nelson's bravery, his leadership, his intemperate courting of disaster. Need there be a difference between these two from the point of view of what is represented as occurring in the story? There will, perhaps, be differences between them concerning what is explicitly represented. But we saw in Chapter 1 that we cannot afford to identify story content with explicit content: narratives always have implicit content. We can grant that there are temporal and causal relations between events it would be easier to glean from the *Life* than from the *Character*. But ease of access does not make the difference between what is represented and what is not. Difficulty of access can be hard to distinguish from indeterminacy, where there just is no fact of the matter as to what the narrative represents on some issue. But

---

[2] See Goodman 1981. For more on character, see below, Chaps 10 and 11.

I see no difficulty in supposing that, in the case of the life and the character study, differences in ease of access do not make for differences in determinacy of representation: whatever is determinately represented in the one is determinately represented in the other, and whatever is to a degree indeterminate in the one is to that degree indeterminate in the other.

Goodman says that the transition from the life to the character study is a transition from a narrative to a non-narrative. It is hard to see why the life should not be a narrative to *any* degree; compared with my shopping list it counts as a pretty decent one. Better to think in terms of our degree of narrativity. *The Life of Nelson* can plausibly be thought to have a higher degree of narrativity than *The Character of Nelson* does. That is enough to generate a problem for any purely internalist account of narrative, for a purely internalist account says that there is no difference in *narrativity* without a difference in story content.

If there are differences in narrativity which are not accountable for in terms of differences of story content, what accounts for them? I say that it is *difference in expressed authorial attitude to story content*. There will be things about *The Life of Nelson* that indicate that temporal and causal relations were intended by the maker to be seen by the reader as especially significant: we are intended to read it *as* a life, and not as a character study. This will probably not be a matter of what the author explicitly says; an author need not announce that she is writing a life rather than a character study. Rather, the way in which the material in *Life* is organized will be expressive of certain kinds of interest and focus, while the organization in *Character* will indicate foci of other kinds. In particular, the material in *Life* is likely to be presented in such a way as to indicate that the author's primary focus is on causal-temporal relations between events across the lifetime of the subject, and in particular on how events at earlier times brought about events at later times. And the organization of material in *Character* will indicate a focus on certain relatively enduring traits, with the temporal dimension subservient to the illustration of these traits. Thus, progression through the text is unlikely to be progression from earlier to later, but rather from one trait to another, with no systematic correspondence to the direction of time.

We can now see what was wrong with our earlier account of narrative, that it should fall victim to Goodman's puzzle. That account derived from taking the internal perspective alone. It was right in focusing on representational features of narratives to do with unity, time, specificity, and causation. But it ignored expressive features of the work: features that function to indicate the ways in which authorial interest is directed towards unity, time, specificity, and causation. Narrativity is therefore a notion to be accounted for in terms of story features and expressive features.[3] Narrative can be understood only by combining the internal and external perspectives. The idea of expressive features of a narrative will be examined more thoroughly in Chapter 5.

3.2. Telling the Time in *Marienbad*

I said that a mark of narrative is richness in the representation of temporal relations. But there are occasions when a discourse is infuriatingly unspecific about crucial elements of timing, and yet uncompromised as a narrative. How can that be? Because it may be clear, when the discourse is considered as a whole, that time is a significant concern of the author, who wishes us to think of temporal relations between events as salient, even though we are not told as much as we would like about them.[4] Here, the very lack of temporal detail puts time high on the agenda and makes the discourse high in narrativity, just as lack of specificity about motive puts the subject of motive high on the agenda for an audience at *Hamlet*. In such a situation time has low status so far as story content goes (less is represented about time than we expect or want) but a high expressive status; the narrative is expressive of concerns about temporal relations. On the other hand, a discourse may indicate that time is not intended to be

---

[3] Notice that I have not provided a way to calculate something's degree of narrativity, or a way to judge the relative narrativity of two things. I am claiming only that degree of narrativity supervenes on story features and expressive features. And, for all I am claiming here, this may be taken to mean only that a person who assigns narrative N a certain degree of narrativity ought, in those circumstances, to assign the same degree of narrativity to anything indistinguishable from it in terms of story features and expressive features. Because such judgements are highly sensitive to context, it will not be the case that this generalizes across worlds: we cannot say that if Smith judges N to have a certain degree of narrativity he ought to do the same in all other circumstances, as long as those circumstances do not change N's story features and expressive features. And if such judgements fail to be objective—as in my opinion interpretive matters generally do—we cannot say that if Smith is justified, in given circumstances, in judging N to have a certain degree of narrativity, then Jones would be wrong in assigning a different degree of narrativity to N.

[4] For reasons that will be clear later, I am not distinguishing here between authors and narrators; see below, Chap. 4.

a significant ordering principle that we are to bring to the arrangement of the information with which we are presented, and the discourse scores low (at least in this regard) for narrativity. With the character study discussed above, we may have a situation where rich temporal relations are represented (explicitly or implicitly) but where little or no concern with time as an ordering principle is expressed.

There is an interesting example to consider in this context. *Last Year in Marienbad*, with its pervasive ambiguities and contradictions in the representation of space, time, and causality, as well as perception and memory, is often said to represent the breakdown of narrative. I am more inclined to say that the work exhibits the coming apart of the two aspects I have considered are determinants of narrativity: representation of story features and expression of authorial focus. For example, while the work expresses (partly through voiced commentary) an interest in time amounting almost to obsession, there is very little we can identify which represents temporal relations between events in the story. This is not, therefore, a work that is straightforwardly low in narrativity. Rather, it is a work that undermines our conventional assumption that, when we are judging degree of narrativity by reference to temporal information, we are to focus on story content. That general assumption cannot, I have argued, be correct, since lack of specificity about time in the story is compensatable by features expressive of a concern for time. The problem with *Marienbad* is the degree of trade-off it demands; we can think of it as high in narrativity if we are willing to shift the burden of temporality almost entirely from what is represented concerning the story to what is expressed concerning the intentions behind the story. There may be nothing in our concept of narrativity which determines whether this is a legitimate trade-off or not. In that case, *Marienbad* is not low in narrativity; it is simply indeterminate where it stands in this regard.

Marienbad underlines my earlier insistence that we concentrate on arte-factual representations and exclude from consideration non-intentional corpora which share certain representational features with genuine narra-tives. For these non-intentional corpora, analysis in terms of expression is unavailable, since expression, in the sense relevant here, is something rev-elatory of the states of the artefact-making agent. The thermometer of our earlier discussion produces a graph of temperature over several days, from which we can read off a great deal of highly specific causal information.

But the mechanical nature of the device, which is independent from intentional mediation, means that *nothing at all* is or could be expressed. A genuine narrative might be notably unexpressive, but its being so is a contingent and a salient fact about it, since it is of the nature of narrative to allow for an expressive aspect. The mechanical registration of temperature is, by its very nature, non-expressive.[5]

3.3. Possibility, Probability, Evidence

I ended Chapter 2 by asking what determines whether something is a salient possibility in a narrative. Recall: a salient possibility, at a given stage of a narrative, is one which we are, or should be, aware of as a non-negligible option for how things may turn out later in the narrative.

Can we know all the facts about what is a salient possibility by taking the internal perspective alone? We must not confuse this question with another: can we know all the facts about what is a salient possibility by considering only what is objectively probable to a given degree within the world of the story? The answer to the second question is no; taking the internal perspective allows us to look at a good deal more than just objective probability. People will often rate some outcome as a salient possibility in the actual world when it is in fact much less probable than some event they do not rate as salient—as when people worry about the dangers of flying and not about the more likely event of a car crash on the way to the airport. Narratives sometimes exploit these tendencies on our part; we are invited, implicitly, to bring to the world of the story our own suite of responses, including tendencies to focus on some objectively improbable outcomes and ignore others that are objectively more likely. But even an internal perspective which allows us to judge salient possibility without being bound to follow the dictates of objective probability is not equal to the task of identifying all that counts as a salient possibility. With narrative we are often guided by something else as well; our awareness—perhaps a

---

[5] Is not the graph at least the distant product of agency? After all, the thermometer was made with the intention that it would produce such graphs. True, but at most this establishes the presence of the highly unspecific intention: to represent the ambient temperature, whatever it is. We have here, at best, a product very low in narrativity because none of the specific representational details—things which matter a great deal in narrative—is intended. I am grateful to David Miller for discussion of this point.

not very conscious one—of the narrative-maker's own purposes. At that point the external perspective intrudes. Suppose that our story's hero has been shot and seriously wounded. The story, I will assume, is a naturalistic one that encourages us to import into its content the sorts of assumptions about causation we make concerning the real world. Serious bullet wounds are, we assume, life threatening, so the death of the hero ought to be a very salient possibility at this point in the story, by whatever internal standards we choose to apply. But if we are only one-third of the way through the story and the author would be faced with narrative difficulties as well as a rebellious readership if the hero died at this point, we may be confident that the hero is not going to die—though the author might wish us to be more uncertain.

This sort of inference, from the author's predicament to the likelihood of the hero's recovery, is not made on the basis of information from within the story. It is no part of the story that the hero is a creature of fiction unlikely to be got rid of by his creator. Does this mean that, in the case imagined, the importation of information about guns and their effects on bodies is blocked? No. We are not dealing with a science fiction fantasy about beings with peculiar invulnerabilities. While the importable causal information suggests one thing about the outcome, information about the author, his aims and his problems suggests something else, and we think that this is the dominant consideration. It might also happen that some event which, on importable-causal grounds, we would rate very unlikely to have any effect on the outcome, achieves the status of being a significant possibility simply because the narrative draws attention to it. In *Lonely are the Brave* (Miller, 1962) a rebellious cowboy (Kirk Douglas) is on the run from the law, and scenes of his pursuit are interspersed with shots of a lorry laden with plumbing supplies. The viewer understands that some sort of connection between these two strands of the narrative will be revealed, and does not take their juxtaposition to be a sign of narrative disunity. This cannot be based on anything represented in the story at the point where the viewer draws this conclusion. For what would that be? That cowboys and lorries are bound to meet up? It would be eccentric to think that the world of the story is one in which such a principle is true. Instead, the way shots are put together in the movie is understood to express an intention that some, probably causal, connection between the cowboy and the lorry will eventually be established. Nothing within the causal/evidential structure of the story itself, or in our own tendencies to judge the evidence, makes that probable until the last moments of the film. Yet the coming together of the cowboy and the lorry is a salient possibility from early on in the film; its salience depends on factors external to the world of the story.

Sometimes when we say that events in a narrative are improbable, we imply a negative evaluation of the work. We may feel that the coincidences in *Oliver Twist* are uncomfortably improbable. Judged by our normal, real-world-based ranking of probabilities for various outcomes, these coincidences are much more probable than the occurrences in any tale of the supernatural. Yet those of us who rate the probability of supernatural events at round about zero, may have no strong feeling of improbability associated with many ghost stories, and a strong feeling of improbability in connection with *Oliver Twist*, even though the probability that Oliver will turn out to be related to the woman whose house he is forced to rob is surely much greater than the probability that there are ghosts.[6] Sometimes writers on this issue talk of 'plausibility' or 'verisimilitude' rather than probability. These moves do not help, because they keep us within the sphere of belief, knowledge, and credence. The error is supposing that what we call improbability in fiction is an *epistemic* vice. I suggest instead that it is an *aesthetic* vice, accessible only from the external perspective. A most improbable event can take its place in a fiction without causing us unease, if the author's act of constructing the work—improbability and all—seems elegant, principled, uncramped; improbabilities in the epistemic sense can even be marks of a bravura performance. We call a fictional story improbable, meaning by this to express a negative judgement, when the action behind it seems to involve a clutching at narrative straws. Often, these judgements about performance are implicitly relativized to norms determined by the genre within which the author works. Ghosts and the like are *standard* for tales of the supernatural, and we do not fault the author merely for introducing them, just as we do not fault the bust-maker whose work is uni-coloured and provides for nothing below the shoulders.[7] Nor

---

[6] Compare Freud's explanation of why events that would seem 'uncanny' in real life often do not seem so when they are narrated as part of a story (Freud 1985). For more on this, see Currie and Juridieni 2003.

[7] For an illuminating discussion of standard and contra-standard properties in art, see Walton 1970. The example of bust-making is from the same source.

are improbabilities a mark of failure in works like Italo Calvino's *If on a Winter's Night a Traveller*, where coincidence is drawn on repeatedly. But, improbability can be grounds for complaint where it shows a failure to keep to a naturalistic framework to which the author seems otherwise committed and within which massive coincidence is contra-standard.[8]

Probability, in the sense relevant here, is a matter of evidential support. And evidence counts in narrative, even in fictional ones. Stories are under-motivated if they present no events which could count as evidence towards settling the questions they raise in our minds. But, evidence, like probability, is a topic that needs careful handling because of the dual perspective that engagement with narrative requires. Awareness of the two aspects of narrative—the internal and the external—has important effects on our treatment of events in a story. It makes us more willing than we would otherwise be to regard a given event as evidence for something, and evidence becomes a more than normally potent force for change of opinion. Suppose we are watching a film. The camera takes in the objects in the room, and pauses at one of them: a photograph, say. We think the photograph is a clue to something; a previously unsuspected relationship, perhaps. We shall not think this unless we also assume that the maker deliberately put it there with the intention that it should be taken as a clue to this relationship. Of course, it may be part of the story, in such cases, that the evidence is there by accident—think of the dead body photographed by accident in *Blow Up* (Antonioni, 1966). But we recognize that, at another level of organization, this is no accident at all. Not everything seen in a film is of significance, and not everything seen is there by design; but, if we think of something as evidentially significant for some aspects of the story, we must see it as present by design.[9] And, something signalled as evidence-by-design need not meet normal real-world standards of evidence, even in stories where those standards of evidence are the right ones from the internal

---

[8] This discussion represents an approximation. A more detailed analysis of naturalistic fiction would have to recognize the tension within the tradition of naturalistic fiction between conformity to real-world probabilities and the use of co-incidence, which is not completely contra-standard.

[9] Here there is a striking difference between the fictional and the non-fictional cases, for a documentary film may contain unsuspected evidence for some hypothesis relevant to its narrative. None the less, even in the non-fiction case, our treatment of the material as evidence is highly influenced by our assumptions about the ways in which the film-maker is structuring the material and the coherent intention with underlies it. Without some such basic assumption as this we could not make proper evidential sense of the material presented.

perspective. In M. R. James' story 'The Stalls of Barchester Cathedral', we learn early on that the aged archdeacon has died in a fall, at last to be replaced by Dr Hayes who has waited many years for the office. Readers immediately form the conviction that Dr Hayes was responsible for the death, though nothing that would standardly count as evidence for this conclusion has so far been presented; nor is there any rule of genre according to which clerical deaths in ghost stories are to be reckoned as due to ambitious colleagues. Still, the reader's conclusion is a reasonable one and, as it happens, justified in the light of what comes later in the story. By combining in one paragraph the news of the death and Dr Hayes' reaction to it, 'standing in silence before the window', James indicates a connection for which he gives us, as yet, no evidence other than his own intention that we should see things that way. Inferences like this make no rational sense when set against the evidence which is available within the plot itself; they are sensible only from a perspective which includes as evidence signs of maker's intention.

Taking the external perspective, we can see a range of relations between events that would not be visible from the internal perspective. Here I have focused on the ways in which epistemic relations of probability and evidence are enlarged/distorted by the external perspective. Other sorts of relations, not visible at all from the internal perspective, are sometimes made available from the external one; they are discussed under such headings as 'metaphor' and 'symbol'. I examine some of these in Chapter 9, and conclude that they do not always deserve the attention they get.

3.4. Representational Correspondence

Why, in *Double Indemnity* (Wilder, 1944), does the door to Walter Neff's (Fred MacMurray) apartment open outwards? One answer is that, for some reason, the building was eccentrically designed. An entirely different kind of answer says that Wilder needed to place it that way so that Phyllis Dietrichson (Barbara Stanwyck) could not be seen in the corridor by Barton Keyes (Edward G. Robinson), and he needed to bring this about for dramatic effect. Seeking an answer of the first kind—an answer given from the internal perspective—we are asking what Kendall

Walton calls a 'silly question'.[10] On the doctrine of silly questions, we ought not to seek an internal explanation when to do so would require us to elaborate improbable scenarios that distract us from the work's real qualities and purpose, and where there is some evident external explanation, like the one just offered. Sometimes the identification of a question as 'silly' indicates, not so much a good dramatic reason, but an authorial intervention designed merely to raise our awareness of the artifice involved in narrative composition. Ivy Compton-Burnett gets rid of one set of characters by having them fall down a ravine—an intrinsically improbable event in the Home Counties, as Hilary Spurling observed. Compton-Burnett could have achieved the same effect in various, less-improbable ways, and chose this one, presumably, as a means of defying naturalistic technique.[11] In such cases as these we are not to deny that the door opens outwards or that the characters fell down the ravine—we just should not expend energy on thinking about how, within the world of the story, this came about.[12]

Other cases are different; Walton gives the example of Othello, bluff man of war, who produces, spontaneously and apparently without effort, poetic statements of surpassing beauty.[13] The question, 'how is it that Othello is so poetically talented?' may be silly, but the reason this time is that, in the world of the story, Othello is *not* an outstanding poet; none of the characters in the play is, despite the fact that the words they utter actually constitute beautiful poetry. Similarly, it is generally silly to ask why, in opera, people dying of consumption or wounds sing with extraordinary power and control—if the request is for an internal explanation. For in the world of the story, they are not singing at all. In such cases, the question is silly because of limitations on *representational correspondence*. For a given representational work, only certain features of the representation serve to represent features of the things represented. In opera, the singing of a performer does not represent the singing of a character, characters in Shakespearean drama are not, or not always, represented as possessing extraordinary powers of poetic expression, despite the fact that they are

---

[10] Walton 1990: sect. 4.5.

[11] See also George Wilson's treatment of certain narrative effects in von Sternberg (Wilson 2003).

[12] Sometimes the shadow of the external perspective falls so hard on the narrative as to destroy its interest as a story. In Russell Rouse's 1952 film *The Thief*, which observes the restriction of containing no audible speech, the most salient reason why someone does not answer the telephone is that this would violate the film-makers' self-imposed restriction, thus reducing to a minimum the interest of the character's motivation.   [13] See Walton 1990: sect. 4.5.

represented as uttering just those combinations of words that the actors playing them do utter, where those combinations are, in fact, highly poetic. In such a case, we have a breakdown of representational correspondence for some higher-order property: there is representational correspondence between the words uttered by the actor and the words uttered by the character, but, while the words uttered by the actor constitute great poetry, they are not represented as constituting great poetry in the mouth of the character.[14]

In other cases, the costs of denying representational correspondence are too high to make this a worthwhile strategy. Take another of Walton's silly questions: why are all the diners in Leonardo's *The Last Supper* sitting on one side of the table? In painting, we normally assume that spatial relations between the representations of characters represent spatial relations between the characters themselves, according to some prevailing convention or principle of perspective. We would abandon representational correspondence for *The Last Supper* if we said that, while the geometry of the drawn figures has them in a certain configuration, we should not assume that the people there represented are represented as being in that configuration. To do so raises too many difficult and distracting questions about what the true spatial relations between the subjects are, especially given the importance in the picture of certain details of those relations, such as the relative positions of Jesus and Judas. To appreciate the picture we need, it seems, the conventional assumptions about spatial correspondence, but these assumptions bring with them the unwonted consequence of an implausible layout, and we are likely to feel uncomfortable when we notice this. We do not feel correspondingly uncomfortable about Othello's speeches.

One effect of the anomalous global layout of the characters in *The Last Supper* is that we tend to concentrate on the local spatial relations, many of which are not similarly anomalous; it is not anomalous that one person is sitting next to another, at a greater distance from a third, that one person is turning towards, or speaking to another, or gesturing in a certain way. In all these respects, *The Last Supper* is replete with relevant and coherent detail. In other cases, the external constraints on a representation—the

---

[14] See also Walton on the case of Emily Dickinson's verbosity in *The Belle of Amherst* and its collision with the representation of her as excessively shy (ibid. 175–6).

constraints, self-imposed or otherwise, on the maker—cannot be ignored by the shift from global to local features. Richardson's Pamela Andrews has always been suspected of a calculating attitude to the protection of her virtue, and readers, adopting an internal perspective, note her tendency to detail every compliment, gift, and improper advance that comes her way. Pamela is so voluble on these topics that it is difficult not to see in the narrative a picture of calculating selfishness, though other aspects of tone and structure in the book suggest quite the opposite intent. The problem arises because Richardson chose the epistolary form, which he more or less invented, and was thereby obliged to make Pamela herself the source of all our information on such matters, especially concerning intimate details about which another correspondent could not plausibly know, and whose reporting of them would anyway be less dramatic.[15] Knowing this provides a resolution of sorts: we can now see a coherent intent as to the nature of Pamela's character, and we explain the difficulties in the way of coherently embodying that intent in the text by reference to self-imposed constraints of genre. But the difficulty does not entirely go away. It remains hard for us, as it apparently was for a contemporary audience, to hear Pamela's narrative as a record of virtuous conduct. And the problem cannot be avoided by shifting from global features to local ones; it is exactly in the details of her recounting that Pamela's virtue comes into question. Is the problem resolvable in the way the *Othello* problem is: by denying representational correspondence to a higher order property? Adopting such a solution would mean accepting that the words on the page represent the words Pamela writes, but denying that the act of writing such words would constitute an act of immodesty. Two things speak against this strategy. First, the denial of representational correspondence for such things as the poetic talents of the characters was more or less a tacit theatrical convention in Shakespeare's time; Richardson would not, I think, have had the protection of any corresponding convention for the epistolary novel. Secondly, there are undeniable attractions in construing Pamela as not wholly good, whatever the author's intent. The assumption is one which meshes well with our real-world knowledge and from which we are able to make a large number of interesting inferences, elaborating a narrative of conflicting desire and self-deception.[16] No such interesting interpretive

---

[15] See Kinkead-Weekes 1962.   [16] See Sperber and Wilson 1995: chap. 3.

options open up for us by taking seriously the thought that Othello is a great but underappreciated poet.

In this I go somewhat against the prevailing direction of the argument of this book, for I have been basing a great deal on the idea that we need to understand narratives as intentional creations of people who want to communicate a story; reading *Pamela* as a record of calculating greed or even of more or less innocent self-deception runs counter to what we know of the author's intentions. True, we have available to us the implied author, and we might argue that there is a reasonable way to understand this hypothetical persona as intending a much more flawed picture of the book's heroine than Richardson himself intended. My own unscholarly reading of the novel makes me doubtful of this; anyhow, it must be counted a possibility that a very careful and informed reading would not open the door to a depiction of Pamela-as-less-then-fully-virtuous via appeal to the implied author. If that possibility turns out to be actual, even the mad-dog intentionalists I keep company with ought not to rule automatically against such a depiction. We make nonsense of narratives by assuming them *not* to be the products of intentional-communicative acts. But, once the project of understanding a narrative in this way is up and running, we ought not to be blind to possibilities the maker did not see—possibilities which may provide interest and instruction unavailable to us if we stick rigidly to the path of authorial intention. And the counter-authorial reading is not one arrived at by dropping basic intentionalist assumptions; the problem arises because, fictionally, Pamela speaks her own words and we are as able to apply our mind-reading skills to fictional utterances as well as to any other. Sensitive readers then naturally find it difficult to avoid hearing those words as expressive of calculation, or self-deception—or something else not wholly virtuous.

In the situation just described, the competent reader who takes such an interpretive detour will be aware that their reading is a deviation, and that there is a tension between the communicative meaning of the narrative and how they are choosing to understand the character of Pamela Andrews. With *Pamela*, the tensions between the way we are intended to see the story and the (perhaps) unintended combination of properties of the storytelling vehicle which make seeing it that way difficult have no satisfactory resolution that I know of. In the case of *Pamela*, these tensions, as I have described them, were not intended. In other cases the author creates and exploits these sorts of tensions, doing something that seems to collapse the internal and external perspectives into one colourfully incoherent story. In *Duck Amuck* (Jones, 1953), Daffy Duck finds himself initially without scenery and then shifted unpredictably from one uncharacteristic and humiliating costume/location to another by an uncooperative animator.[17] In *Rosencrantz and Guildenstern Are Dead* the causal deviancy of the play's world is indicated by having it begin with a series of coin-throws with an unlikely outcome: ninety-two consecutive heads. This is not merely an indication that strange causes are at work within the world of the play. The unlikely sequence signals the dependence of events on external factors: the decisions of the play's author about what will happen. What is unusual here, and difficult to make sense of, is that authorial determination of events has become part of the story's own content, with the characters vaguely and uneasily aware of their own fictional status. This device, familiar from Pirandello's *Six Characters in Search of an Author*, gets a reversal of sorts in Wes Craven's *New Nightmare* (1994), where it is fictionally the case that a character from previous movies breaks into the real world of moviemaking that created him.

In cases like this, the internal and external perspectives seem to collapse into one. This is not really so. However hard the narrative-maker tries, he or she can at most engineer a fictional collapse; the real things accessible from an external perspective on *Duck Amuck*, and *New Nightmare* remain aloof. *Duck Amuck* provides a fictional story about the interaction between Daffy Duck and a fictional maker—it turns out to be Bugs Bunny. Even if Chuck Jones had put himself in the story as an uncooperative animator he would be there only as a character in a fiction, with his own real activities that result in this enlarged fiction of animator vs character standing outside and beyond the representational limits of that fiction.

---

[17] Purported collapse, in my sense, occurs when external facts are represented as becoming part of the content of the narrative itself, and hence internal. I do not automatically count it as collapse when, as often happens, both domains are represented within the same vehicle. Thus, literary authors sometimes explicitly comment on their capacity to shape the fates of their characters. Schlockmeister William Castle appears on screen in *Mr Sardonicus* (1961) to ask the audience for a judgement on the villain, and Ingmar Bergman interviews his actors in *A Passion* (1969). Such activities do not automatically insert themselves into the world of the fiction itself, and do not in fact do so in *Mr Sardonicus* or in *A Passion*.

Cases like *Duck Amuck*, with their feigning of collapse, are not really exceptions to the rule that a duality of perspectives—internal and external—pervades the experience of narrative, from the most conventional and anonymous instances up to the most self-consciously paradoxical. For the rest of this book my concern will be with intermediate cases: cases where the author, without generating a clash of perspectives, acts so as to make the external perspective salient and rewarding of attention, through devices of narration which I shall explore.

4

Authors and Narrators

Being artefacts, narratives have makers; in the case of literary narratives, we call them authors. In some cases there are many makers, each with a different role, as in film, and we are not always able to find just one among them with sufficient authority to count as an author; rather, the act of authorship is conducted jointly. Narrative-making may proceed by accretion rather than by joint action, as with novels where one person writes a first chapter, passing it to the next in a chain of authors. Messier, less co-operative cases occur, as when one person steals the partly completed text of another and finishes it in their own way. Whether we find narrative unity in such gerrymandered cases depends on our getting from our reading or viewing the sense of there being an agent with a unified set of intentions of which the work is the outcome. We would then be appealing to the implied author: the imagined agent whose intentions coincide with those which ordinary pragmatic inference suggests were productive of that text.

4.1. A Distinction without a Difference?

It is tempting to think that we can separate two activities: narrative-making and narrative-telling. Makers are (roughly) authors, while tellers are narrators. Recent theorizing about narrative has been almost exclusively about narrators. But I do not wish merely to redistribute attention more equitably so that authors get a look in. I say that, for virtually all cases of narrative we are likely to come across, there is no distinction that should or can be made between authors and narrators, for there is no distinction to be made between narrative-making and narrative-telling. Recall the point that narratives are communicative artefacts: things made in such a way as to communicate, and not merely to represent, their stories. True, someone might write a story which someone else reads out, or writes down, or otherwise assists in making available to an audience; that is not the author/narrator distinction as it functions in discussions of narrative. I might communicate with you by letter; that requires a postman to deliver the letter. The postman does not thereby take on the role of narrator in our communicative exchange. Narrators, as they are discussed in critical and academic debates on narrative, are beings about whom it is sometimes appropriate to ask such questions as: 'how does he/she know about these things?', 'is he/she reliable?', 'what is the narrator's point of view'. Answering these questions may be important for someone who wants to understand the narrative. None of this applies to the agent who merely acts as a facilitator or postman. The postman will have knowledge, values, and an outlook, but none of that sheds light on the narrative he delivers, since, by hypothesis, the words and sentences we read do not at all depend on, and are not expressive of, these characteristics; we are entitled to think of them as dependent on or expressive of someone's intentions only if we think that person the maker of the work. The author of the letter, novel, or poem is its narrator in the proper sense: the person whose intentions have to be understood if we are to understand what is being communicated to us. The author is the narrator: the teller whose point of view does so much to illuminate the narrative itself. The postman, the amanuensis, and the talking-book reader are people for whose actions we are grateful, but they are not narrators.

What about those narrators *in* stories, like Dr Watson of the Sherlock Holmes stories? Surely we do not identify that narrator with the author. I agree. It is part of the Sherlock Holmes stories that the stories are told as known fact by Dr Watson, not that they are so told by Conan Doyle, so we should not think of Watson as Doyle under an assumed name. But Watson is not a real narrator, any more than he is a real doctor or Holmes a real detective. Watson, Holmes, and the other characters do not exist and the exploits they were involved in did not occur. Rather, it is part of the story (taking the stories as a single whole) that Holmes is a detective and Watson both a doctor and a narrator. Watson is, fictionally, a narrator. It is also part of the story that Watson is the author of the stories he tells; it is no part of these stories that he found them somewhere or that they were dictated to him by Holmes. This sort of narrator, where there is one, is, according to the story, the author; and where there are many such narrators, as with epistolary novels like *Dracula*, we have to count it as fictional that there are many authors, acting in this case serially rather than jointly. So in cases like that of Watson and the Holmes stories we have no grounds for distinguishing narrators and author, though we have grounds for distinguishing between someone being an author/narrator and it being part of the story that someone is an author/narrator. Bearing in mind an earlier distinction, we can say that Watson is the *internal* author/narrator and Doyle the *external* author/narrator. If Doyle had represented himself as an agent within the stories, as someone who knew Holmes and told of his adventures, and thus had told a fictional story partly about himself, he would thereby be an internal and an external author/narrator. As things actually turned out, he is simply the external author/narrator. More on external narrators later.

Taking the internal perspective, we treat Watson as the sole direct source of information, and by and large we treat him as reliable. Some internal narrators have a more problematic relation to their stories. Some are notably unreliable, as with the lies and self-delusion of Barry Lyndon, and (less clearly) the delusions of the governess in *The Turn of the Screw*.[1] In these kinds of cases it is part of the story, not that the narrator is telling us what he or she knows or thinks probable; the narrator is telling us a mixture of knowledge, lies, self-deception, delusion, and plain error. But these are still cases of internal narrators: people who stand in such a relation to its events as to make it appropriate to raise questions about their epistemic responsibility. In making their narrators unreliable, both James and Thackeray raise questions about the failure of these characters to respect norms of truth, relevance, and reliability in representing events the way they do, and these issues are resolved—to the extent that they are resolved at all—within the story itself. Questions like this do not arise concerning James and his construction of *The Turn of the Screw*, or Thackeray and *The Luck of Barry Lyndon*. James and Thackeray do not know about, or tell lies about, or become deluded about the characters and events of their stories: they imagine these characters and events, and they communicate with us so that we may imagine them also.[2]

---

[1] We need to distinguish an unreliable narrator from an unreliable work. Briony's narrative in *Atonement* is unreliable, but the novel is not, given that the final part makes clear the unreliability of what has gone before. A work is unreliable if its narrator is unreliable in a way that the work does not make manifest to us, but works without narrators can be unreliable also; see Currie 1995.

[2] Are not the real authors of fictional works epistemically responsible when they get certain kinds of facts wrong, such as frequently seemed to happen with Ian Fleming? Only when they intend to get it

A narrator might become even more detached from the reality she describes without ceasing to be an internal narrator. She may convey nothing but ravings bearing little relation to what is true in her story, if anything is, and still be internal to the world of the story. Raving is a case of failure to exercise epistemic responsibility, though it may be a non-culpable failure.[3] And, there will be cases which render it unclear whether we should call the narrator internal or external; a mixture of truth, self-deception, and mere fantasy may slide over into something so dominated by unconstrained imaginings as (arguably) to count as a case of authorship of fiction rather than internal narration. As so often, we should not expect sharp distinctions in this area. It is clear that the internal narrator, raving or not, is, according to the story, the author.

We sometimes find an internal narrator, as with Dr Watson, and sometimes we do not, as in *Middlemarch*—or so I claim. In stories of the latter kind, no internal narrator is explicitly introduced, and the writing does not seem to carry with it hints of such a person. Nor is there indirect evidence, such as a limitation on what is narrated, which would correspond to the point of view of a non-magical agent. In these stories, a good deal is said that no ordinary mortal, however reliable and insightful, would be likely to know, and that may be one indication that there is no internal narrator. But we do sometimes acknowledge internal narrators who, for reasons we are not encouraged to enquire into, know about things which ordinary persons could not know or which it would be very improbable that they should know; this is one aspect of the fact that certain lines of inquiry about what happens in a fictional story amount to asking 'silly questions'.[4] So, the signs that the narrator knows too much are not always clinching evidence that this narrator is external. There are no firm rules to guide us here. All I suggest is that we do not postulate internal narrators unless there is positive reason to do so, especially where such a narrator, if acknowledged,

---

right—otherwise their failings, if any, are aesthetic. Internal narrators cannot get off the hook by saying that they did not intend to get it right.

[3] Ravings are briefly discussed by David Lewis (Lewis 1983: 266 n.).

[4] On silly questions, see above, Chap. 3, sect. 4. The never-glimpsed character Addie Ross in Joseph L. Mankowitz's film *Letter to Three Wives* (1943) offers at certain points a voice-over commentary on conversations she could not possibly hear by any naturalistically respectable means; Addie Ross (voice-over by Celeste Holm) is not really the internal narrator of the film but she does undoubtedly belong to the world of the film's story, despite her apparently magical capacity to hear and to know, and the film's seeming inconsistency with magical causation.

would have to be regarded as omniscient and where omniscience is out of keeping with the other conventions the work adheres to. While there are plenty of internal narrators, the postulation of an internal narrator is neither a general necessity nor the default option; it is something that calls for evidence. I consider some contrary arguments in Section 5 below.

Taking the external perspective, we have no such decision to make, for here we always find a narrator—the (real) author. In the case of a non-fiction narrative this narrator's role is like that of an internal narrator; the role is an epistemically responsible one. The external author/narrator of non-fiction may be a sober and reliable historian, an unscrupulous propagandist or a deluded exponent of crackpot ideas; in all cases, failure to tell the truth, to include relevant facts, or to provide a properly balanced account raise questions about the extent of the author's/narrator's culpability. As we have seen, the situation of the external author/narrator of fiction is different. He or she offers the story as something to engage with imaginatively rather than by way of belief, and there is no expectation that what is said by the author/external narrator will be true.

4.2. Implied and Second Authors

So far, a pretty economical system. We no longer have to decide whether the agent in question is a narrator or an author—they are always both—but merely whether he or she is internal or external. We must now make it more complicated. It sometimes happens that we need to postulate an external narrator distinct from the real author, because the voice which presents the story to us cannot, for some reason, be identified with the voice of the author. Interesting cases have been made for saying that this or that narrative voice from outside the fiction is not really that of the author. Cases like this get labelled indifferently as *implied-author* cases, but they come in two distinct types, and to underline the difference I will apply that label only to the first of the two.

The first, by now very familiar, type occurs where we have some reason to think that the personality one would, on the basis of reading the novel, attribute to the author is distinct from the personality one would attribute to her on the basis of a wider acquaintance with the facts of her life: Tolstoy and Fielding have both been said to be different, less-attractive people than the personas their works project. In cases of this kind we naturally think of the author as either unaware of the difference, being perhaps not very knowing of their lesser selves, or at most as consciously 'upgrading' their personas for the purpose of public display.[5] A different kind of case, less discussed, occurs when the author deliberately creates a 'second author' with a point of view different in subtle or dramatic ways from their own, and tailored to the work's artistic project.[6] As with so many of the distinctions employed here, this one is going to cause uncertainty in its application and there will be cases that are simply indeterminate as between the two options. But the distinction is real, and our perception that the case is of one kind rather than the other is likely to affect our engagement with the work.

In a case of the first kind we may imagine the narrative having been made by someone with the persona that the work itself projects, rather than by anyone with the persona of the actual maker. We can do this in either of two ways: we can imagine an implied author distinct from the real one, or we can imagine, of the real author, that he or she has a persona different from the persona he or she actually has. I can see no particular reason to favour one or the other of these options a priori, though advocates of the implied author have generally written as if the preferred option was the first of these two, as the terminology of 'real author' and 'implied author' suggests.

In a case of the second kind—second-author cases—the author is speaking ironically or in some other pretend mode and in doing so manages to create a consistent impression of narrating from some stable, imagined perspective.[7] Consider how this arises first of all in ordinary conversation. I may tell you a story (assume it is a fictional one) and at the same time impersonate a mutual friend's way of telling. If all goes well I manage two things: to tell you a story and to entertain you with my impersonation of the other's style. My performance creates two fictions: one is the story I tell and the other is a story in which it is not me but the mutual friend who is speaking.[8] Similarly, the author of a fiction may make it fictional that

---

[5] The classical statement is Booth 1983, esp. chap. 6.

[6] The term 'second author' I owe to Dorit Cohn 1999. See below, text to n. 9.

[7] For detailed discussion of irony and its relation to pretence, see below, Chap. 8.

[8] An ironic performance does not always require me to imagine that someone other than you is speaking; you might take yourself as the target of your irony, or the performance may require me merely to imagine you having a persona like that of our mutual acquaintance. I focus above on cases which do require us to imagine a speaker distinct from the actual one, for these are the cases that

someone other than herself is the author of this fictional story. Dorit Cohn argues that this is how it is with Thomas Mann's *Death in Venice*, wherein Mann projects an (external) narratorial personality excessively hostile to Aschenbrenner's predicament.[9] In second-author cases such as this it is natural, though perhaps not obligatory, to think of the second author as a genuinely different person from the real author, rather than merely imagining an alternative persona for the one, real author. The choice between these alternatives will not affect anything I say further on.

So cases of both these kinds—implied and second-author cases—require us to imagine either a new author or a new authorial persona. This complicates our simple taxonomy of authors/narrators, but it does nothing to pull apart the concepts author and narrator. We also in such cases end up with an *embedded* narrative. With *Anna Karenina*, we readers construct a story according to which a generous and broad-minded person writes a story according to which a woman has an unhappy affair and kills herself; with *Death in Venice*, the author constructs a story according to which a narrow-minded and unforgiving person writes a story about a man who falls unhappily in love with a young boy and dies. In both cases one story is embedded in another.

Embedding turns out to be a slightly complicated concept; it is worth a moment's attention to its clarification. Embedding occurs when (i) there are stories, S1 and S2, and (ii) those things which are so according to S2 are, according to S1, so according to S2, but (iii) those things which are so according to S2 are not so according to S1. Thus, *The Murder of Gonzago* is embedded within *Hamlet*: things which are so according to *Gonzago*, such as that Gonzago is murdered, are such that it is so according to *Hamlet* that they are so according to *Gonzago*. But it is not the case, according to *Hamlet*, that Gonzago is murdered, for Gonzago is not a character in *Hamlet*.[10] *Gonzago* is the embedded story, and Hamlet the *embedding* story.

---

parallel the cases of interest here: cases where we are to imagine an external author/narrator distinct from the actual one.

[9] Cohn 1999. One controversial aspect of Cohn's reading is its dependence on extratextual sources such as Mann's own correspondence (see ibid. n. 15).

[10] One story can be embedded within another without there being any specification of the content of the inner story, just as there can be a person who is a character in a story without anything (else) being specified concerning that person; it is then part of the outer story that everything that is part of the inner story is part of the inner story, but there are no propositions listable as contents of the inner story.

In *Death in Venice*, a second-author case (so I will assume), it is Mann himself who is the author of the embedding fiction. In implied-author cases like *Anna Karenina*, the real author is not the author of the embedding fiction. Tolstoy did not write a story according to which a wise and sympathetic person wrote a story about a woman who had an unhappy love affair and committed suicide. It is we readers who place Tolstoy's fiction—the one exclusively about Anna Karenina—within a larger embedding fiction according to which the author of *Anna Karenina* was wise and sympathetic. For all their differences, cases of both kinds give rise to embedding.

Embedding is very common: it occurs whenever someone within the world of story S1 tells a story, S2, according to which various things are so, but where those things, or some of them, are not so according to S1. Thus, the testimony of people in error, liars and the deluded, whenever these things occur in stories, are cases of embedding. Does this make our category a uselessly bloated one? Not if we make some easily available distinctions within it. *Death in Venice* and *Anna Karenina* are cases of fiction embedded within fiction, as are *Hamlet* and Michael Frayn's *Noises Off*, with its embedded play *Nothing On*. A murder mystery wherein various characters tell misleading stories to the police is non-fiction embedded within fiction, for what is so according to the mystery story itself is that someone makes some lying assertions, not that they narrated a fiction. A history which recounts a diplomat's lying account of her country's motives is non-fiction embedded within non-fiction. With these sorts of divisions within it, embedding is not a useless concept.

Something like embedding has been discussed often enough by narrative theorists. Genette discusses levels of narration within such stories as *Manon Lescaut*, wherein the Marquis de Renoncourt tells of the telling by Des Grieux of his adventures with Manon in France and in Louisiana.[11] This is not, in my terms, a case of embedding because what is so according to the narrative of Des Grieux is also so according to the narrative of the Marquis: Des Grieux's telling extends the world of the Marquis's narrative by providing information (reliable, we are given to assume) about events spatio-temporally and indeed causally connected to the story-framing

---

[11] See Genette 1980: chap. 5.

meetings of the Marquis and the Chevalier: Here, condition (iii) of my definition of embedding is violated. If we replace that condition with

(iii*) those things which are so according to S2 are so according to S1

we get a condition satisfied by stories such as *Manon*: call these cases of *extended* narrative. The distinction between embedding and extension is important: rather obviously so in non-fiction, since it is vital to our understanding of a history as to whether quoted testimony is treated as reliable by the history itself. It is important in fiction if only because a number of narratives profit by managing to create uncertainty about which definition applies. In many mystery stories we are unclear for some time as to whether the inner character's narrative constitutes an extension of the outer narrative or is merely an embedding within it; with *The Usual Suspects* (Singer, 1994) we are likely to be entirely mislead about this until the end. With Henry James' *The Turn of the Screw*, *Rashomon* (Kurosawa, 1950), and other tales, we may be unable to decide, even at the end, which category applies to a given part of the narrative.

4.3. A Concession

I have been insisting that there is no reason to distinguish the role of the narrator and the role of the author. There are, or might be, a few occasions when we do need the distinction, and I have been exaggerating the strength of my case. Here is the sort of thing I have in mind.

Scheherazade tells the stories of the *One Thousand and One Nights*. According to the story she has 'collected together a thousand books of histories, relating to preceding generations and kings, and works of the poets' and these are the material for her storytelling. I assume she tells the stories in her own words and perhaps with other embellishments and general tweaking of the tales. So far no problem. She has authorial responsibility for the stories she tells, though her stories depend, perhaps closely, on other acts of narration, as Shakespeare's did. But change the story a bit, and have her memorize the stories of others, merely repeating them to Shahryar. Then she is no longer the author of the narrative she tells. Ought we not to count her as a narrator in some reasonably full-blooded sense? She is not a mere deliverer of mail in this context, since much of our interest is in her motivation for telling these stories and—given the consequences of a wrong choice—her choice of stories.[12]

I agree that this would be a case where we want to count Scheherazade as a non-authorial narrator in some sense which is of significance to understanding and appreciating the narrative. But let us hold on to an important point: the case is exceptional—indeed, I had to turn a real example into an imagined one in order to find the exception. Almost all the time we need not distinguish the roles of author and narrator.

Even without the (largely) spurious distinction between author and narrator, we have a tricky taxonomy of narratives. In the simplest cases we have just an author/narrator, who tells a story, and in the story itself there is no narrator. Then we have authors/narrators who create internally authored/narrated stories, authors/narrators who create surrogate authors/narrators of whom it is part of the story that they create a further fiction, in which it may or may not be the case that there is an internal author/narrator. Then there are authors/narrators who do all that, plus making their stories multilayered, so that characters in one story are authors/narrators of stories-within-the-story, as Scheherazade externally authors/narrates the stories in *One Thousand and One Nights*. There is not much point in trying to map these bewildering possibilities exhaustively; we need only remember that the resources are there when we want them for particular cases. In general, we should go for the simplest description of the work that makes good sense of its narrative structure.

4.4. A Note on Non-fiction

In developing this taxonomy I have spoken mostly about fictional cases. Do we need a different set of categories for the non-fictional case? Surprisingly, no. One plausible but misleading thought here is that, with non-fiction, we do not need an internal/external distinction, because the world of the story is just the real world within which the real author operates. This is not so. The 'world of the story' is just a convenient shorthand for 'whatever is so according to the narrative'. In this sense, there is a

---

[12] Or, she is like a postwoman, who receives a series of letters you write, reads them, and decides which ones to deliver.

distinction between the real world and the world of the story for history and journalism just as for fiction. With non-fiction we aim for or expect a degree of correspondence between the world of the story and the real world which we do not find in the fictional case; the regulative aim of non-fiction is that what is so according to the narrative be true. But this regulative aim is frequently not met in full, and we need the distinction as much in the non-fictional case as in the fictional case; without it we do not have the resources to describe a history as unreliable. In that case it makes sense to ask, for non-fiction, whether there is an internal narrator. In some cases there is and in others there is not. A biographer may make his or her own activities part of the story, as Boswell does in *Life of Johnson*, and Michael Ignatieff does in his biography of Isaiah Berlin.[13] In such a case, the real author/narrator is also an internal author/narrator. In other, more self-effacing narratives, there will be an external author/narrator but no internal counterpart, as with Claire Tomalin's *Samuel Pepys: The Unequalled Self*.[14] Further, an unscrupulous biographer might invent a wholly misleading story about how the biography was written by a character he or she tries to foist on the reading public, describing this person's difficult relations with the subject, when in fact no such character exists. In that case we would have (deplorable) non-fiction with distinct internal and external author/narrators, the latter being non-existent.[15]

Historical writers sometimes project personae as marked as those of authors of fiction, and there may be reasons why it would be helpful to the creation of the right narrative mood for the author to project a narrative voice distinct from her own natural voice. This sounds like the invocation of my 'second author' category. But we should be careful not to multiply such cases beyond necessity. I won't count it as a case of 'needing to invoke

---

[13] Ignatieff 1998.   [14] Tomalin 2002.

[15] Different forms of non-fiction are marked by the author/narrator's different epistemically responsible relations to the events he or she describes: the autobiographer tells partly on the basis of personal memory, while the historian or biographer tells, by and large, on the basis of testimony. Isaiah Berlin's biographer, Michael Ignatieff, tells partly on the basis of his personal recollection of interviews with Berlin, as his narrative makes clear; there are elements, therefore, within the work which count, by my lights, as autobiographical. Suppose that Leonard Shelby, the main protagonist in Christopher Nolan's film *Memento* (2000), were real. He comes to the end of his adventures and decides to write the story of his life after losing his memory, relying on all the notes, photographs, tattoos, and other records he accumulated during those adventures. It seems to me helpful to classify this as biography, since what he writes is wholly from a third-person perspective. Once again there will be cases it is impossible to classify unambiguously.

a fictional author' when there is reason to think that the author's way of narrating history is somewhat different from her unguarded barroom conversation; that would mean invoking the fictional author in just about every case. People present themselves in different ways in different contexts; yet, it is one and the same person doing it. Only if we have a clear case of someone consciously creating a personae specific to the historical project in hand and seriously discontinuous with their standard mode of academic discourse should we wheel on the idea of a second author. How we identify such cases I do not know; my interest here is simply in allowing for their possibility.

4.5. Should there be a Presumption in Favour of the Internal Narrator?

Some narratives, I have said, have no internal author/narrator. This turns out to be quite a controversial claim, and there are a number of objections to it that we must consider. (Since this claim is generally formulated in terms of narrators and not of authors, I will formulate it that way myself, but I am not going back on the idea that narrators *are* authors.) The dispute is not about whether there sometimes or often are internal narrators; it is granted on all hands that the work itself often makes it clear, or at least strongly suggests, that there is such a narrator. The argument is about whether we should postulate an internal narrator even when there is no positive evidence for the existence of one. It is an argument about the existence of what George Wilson calls *effaced* narrators (Wilson 2007). A believer in effaced narrators need not hold that every narrative has an internal narrator; at a minimum, the claim is that we should assume that there is an internal narrator unless there are strong positive reasons against this hypothesis. In that case there will be cases where we will postulate an internal narrator despite the fact that there is no evidence for the presence of such a narrator, and that is exactly what is involved in postulating an effaced narrator. However, in order to be comprehensive I must consider here also some arguments which, if they were sound, would require us to believe in the existence, for every narrative, of an internal narrator. Also, since I am reviewing a number of arguments I can keep within a reasonable compass only by considering them as they apply to the case of text-based narratives. Arguments have been put for the existence of internal narrators in film; this is generally acknowledged to be a more difficult proposition to establish than the one for text.[16] Since I will reject all the arguments as they apply to text, the case for effaced narrators in film is left in at least a very weak position.

The first is an argument to the effect that effacement is not always a reason for failing to see the hand of an internal narrator—or something like one. I mentioned *Dracula*, with its series of distinct narratives, each with an explicit narrator, stitched together into a whole. Who did the stitching? Do we not have to assume the existence here of someone who at least did an editorial job? But there is no internal evidence for the existence of this figure.

Why, exactly, do we have to assume that there is an editor for *Dracula*? Because we otherwise have no explanation for how it came to be that all these distinct narratives are presented to us as a single story. But recall our discussion of silly questions. We do not look for an (internal) explanation for why the disciples are all on one side of the table, preferring an external perspective according to which this was an aesthetic decision on Leonardo's part. Similarly, we are not obliged to seek an internal explanation for the fact that the distinct narratives of *Dracula* are presented as a unity. If we had to find an internal explanation, postulating a hidden author/narrator would be a good option; but we do not have to.

It might be replied that, by making the narrators of the distinct parts of the story very salient, the work foregrounds issues of ownership and knowledge in ways which do encourage us to ask the question who put all this together?—a question which cannot automatically be regarded as silly. If that is so, then there is a ready answer, for the argument depends on the premiss that the existence of an internal editor is indicated within the work

---

[16] For an articulate and detailed account of the idea of the (internal) filmic narrator and what it might do for us as consumers and interpreters of cinematic narratives, see Levinson 1996. Much of Levinson's argument is given over to the role of the narrator as presumed source of film music, a topic I shall not be able to take up here. I will, however, comment briefly on one issue, though a not very prominent one, in Levinson's exposition, because it seems to contradict my assertion that narrators are narrative-makers. Levinson quotes with approval a remark of Chatman's: 'Cinematic narrators are transmitting agents of narratives, not their creators' (Levinson 1996: 150). But a later note (p. 154) suggests that Levinson's view is somewhat different, namely that narrators (in my sense internal narrators) provide access to events understood as constituted independently of their activities. Once we distinguish narrative and story, we can agree that the narrator creates the narrative without, necessarily, being the agent responsible for the events of the story itself.

itself, though perhaps not very directly. We have, in this case, a positive (positive to *some* degree) reason to postulate an internal editor, and so we have no model for the postulation of *effaced* internal narrators.

The next argument would, if sound, establish the necessity for postulating an internal narrator in a very wide class of cases. It is nearly universal that spoken or written stories are represented by means of a past tense. By saying such things as 'he went into the room' or 'he had gone into the room' the narrator indicates a relation of temporal priority between the act described and the act of narration.[17] And, we expect the narrator to use the past tense even if the (fictional) story is set in what is, from the perspective of the author's act of composition, the future. How are we to understand this relation if not by postulating an agent who provides testimony of what is past? In the case of the novel set in the future, this agent cannot be the author of the fiction; it seems that we have to postulate an internal narrator, narrating after the events of the story, even though there may be no other indication of such a narrator and even where there is reason to deny such a narrator's existence, as with an end of the world story or other tale that cannot be told. And, if this reasoning is sound, it is surely sensible to abandon resistance to the effaced narrator thesis altogether and admit that narratives constructed by means of the past tense imply the presence of an internal narrator quite generally, and not merely in the case where the events are set in the future.

One response has it that, while we cannot think of the real author as standing in the future of the events of the story, we are free to construct an implied author who is. This strikes me as creating more difficulty than it avoids. It is generally agreed that the situation of the real author highly constrains us in choosing an implied author—we should not see *Anna Karenina* as the product of someone with a twenty-first-century sensibility. And if a novel is set 10,000 years from now, what idea shall we form of an implied author required to live at that time?

A better solution is simply to deny that the use of the past tense requires us to understand the act of narration to be in the future of the story's events. This is just one more example of failure of representational

---

[17] With the second example differing from the first in that the second, but not the first, indicates that the going into the room was prior to some other, now past, event of the story which is narratively privileged and may be thought of as the 'present' of the story.

correspondence.[18] In assertoric discourse, one function of past tense constructions is that they represent the pastness of what is represented relative to the act of assertion. Any ordinary non-fictional narrative report is therefore bound to use the past tense.[19] And, we would expect fictional discourse to use it as well, because we do not wish to have explicit markers of a narrative's fictional status any more than we (generally) want actors to come on stage reassuring the audience that no murder is really happening or that no lion is really present. So there is a good reason for using the past tense in fictional narration, a reason which does not depend on assuming that its use has the same representational function that it would have in non-fictional discourse.

The next two arguments are quite general ones to the effect that, of its very nature, we have to assume an internal narrator for a fictional text-based narrative. The first argument depends on the widely accepted premiss that the author of a fictional work is pretending to make assertions. This claim must, I think, go with the idea that the audience of the fiction is to imagine the indicative sentences of the work to be asserted—otherwise the pretence would seem to be a private one with no consequences for the reception of the work. But is it not in that case at least very plausible that the audience is to imagine that someone asserts these sentences, and hence that this person is in a position to know that they are true? At the very least the asserter must belong to the world of the story, for how else could such assertions be credible? And, all this amounts to the requirement that the audience imagine that there is an internal narrator. But, if this is something that the work requires the audience to imagine, we have the best reason we could have for saying that it is true in the story that there is an internal narrator.

In fact, this is *not* something which, in general, the work requires us to imagine. As Wilson himself insists, we are free to imagine that an internal narrator—one within the world of the work and epistemically limited in the way that ordinary people are—knows things which no ordinary person can know, without having to imagine some way in which he or she can know this. Similarly, we may imagine the propositions of the work to be assertions, without imagining anything about how they got to be asserted. While this is, I think sufficient answer to the objection, another answer

---

[18] See above, Chap. 3.   [19] By 'ordinary' here I mean 'not based on precognition'.

is available: that authors of fictional narratives need not be pretending to make assertions. Sometimes they do, as when they narrate ironically.[20] In other cases they are merely making *fictive* utterances, characterized by the intention that the audience will imagine the contents of our utterances, along with their conversational and other implicatures. So there are two reasons to deny that readers are obliged to imagine that the sentences of the fiction are assertively uttered, though it is agreed that they do imagine this in some cases.[21]

The next argument is similar to the previous one in that it appeals to (putative) facts about the ways in which an audience will receive and process the sentences of the text. Suppose that, attending to a narrative, we read or hear 'Smith noticed a tree. The tree was shedding its leaves. It had slender branches.' The reader will assume that there is one tree in question: seen by Smith, shedding its leaves, possessing slender branches. And we assume this, not because this is deducible from the meanings of the words and their order, but because we assume that the speaker has in mind a certain tree, which he or she is referring to throughout the passage; this tree is the common referent of 'a tree', 'the tree', and 'it'. We must, therefore, be assuming that we are being told about a particular tree by someone who has that tree in mind. But, being the usual sort of fiction, there is no such tree, no Smith, and no speaker. None the less we imagine that there are these things, including the speaker, who counts as an internal narrator. Once again, it is admitted by all parties that readers do sometimes understand there to be an internal narrator who has in mind the things of which he speaks. The question is whether there needs to be one, and the present argument is meant to show that there does.

It won't do in this case to run the earlier argument to the effect that we do not have to imagine all the consequences of what we do imagine. For in this case the idea is that we *use* the idea of an imagined speaker who has someone or something in mind in order to track the referents of 'a tree', 'the tree', and 'it'. That we are doing this may not be very salient to us, but lots of what we imagine about fictional things is not very salient. What matters is that this imagining is part of imaginative project we are engaged in when we read the story.

---

[20] See below, Chap. 8.   [21] On fictive utterance, see Currie 1990: sect. 1.4.

There is a parallel argument concerning conditionals. Someone might say, 'if someone notices a tree and the tree is shedding its leaves, then . . .'. It is evident that I understand that the antecedent of the statement involves there being one and the same tree which is noticed and shedding its leaves, but it cannot be necessary, in order for me to understand this, that I believe that the speaker has a particular tree in mind; given that this is a conditional, they probably do not. But perhaps it is essential for me to imagine, of the antecedent, that it is asserted, and, from within this little imaginative project, to process the antecedent as if it were an asserted sentence, in which case I would be imagining that the speaker has a particular tree in mind.

Now, in the case of the conditional, we may suppose that this imaginative project is at some stage dispensed with, and one ends up with a view (a belief) about what the actual communicative content of the utterance is. Now, the case of the fictive utterance is importantly different from that of the conditional. The fictive utterance, as a whole, is unasserted, whereas the processing of the conditional involves the processing of an unasserted part of something that is asserted. This difference need not prevent us from treating the imaginative project that goes into understanding the fictive utterance in a similar way—that is, as something to be discharged once its work is done. That the whole sentence, and the surrounding context of discourse, is a fictive one and hence something that requires us to imagine certain things should not prevent us from distinguishing sharply between two imaginative projects, one of which is basic and the other merely instrumental. The basic project is to imagine in accordance with what is true in the fiction, and the sentences of the fictional narrative are a guide to what is true in the fiction. The merely instrumental project is to deploy imagining in such a way as to understand what is being said by means of the sentences of the narrative. These are distinct projects and one would need a special reason for saying that we ought to collapse the imaginings they involve into one grand imaginative project. I cannot see what this special reason would be, unless it is that we ought to be imaginatively engaging with the narrative by way of the assumption that it contains an internal narrator. From the point of view of the argument we are considering, that would be viciously circular.

Simply put, the point is that, in order to engage imaginatively with a narrative, we may have, as a preliminary, to imagine various things which do not then come to be assumed to be part of the content of the narrative. In particular, in order to understand the narrative, we have to process its sentences as if they were asserted; but this does not mean that it is part of the content of the narrative that it is asserted. And there are other manifestations of this general phenomenon which indicate that I am not appealing to an *ad hoc* principle here. Kendall Walton gives the example of a photograph so taken that the person is visible only from the neck down. It may be that, in order to experience the proper effect of the picture, we have to imagine the man in the picture to lack a head. It is not part of the depictive content of the photograph that the man lacks a head.[22]

The final argument is due to George Wilson. He points out that within a given narrative, fictional or non-fictional, we often have to discriminate between utterances in different modes. Apart from indicative sentences, there are things which have at least the appearance of being questions. A narrator might say or write, 'Katie loves Hubble', following up with, 'Many people thought so, but was it really true?'

Therefore, at a minimum, we are going to have to draw some distinctions between the kinds of illocutionary force that fictionally attach to the propositional contents expressed in the narration . . . all these fictional assertions, suppositions, questionings, and whatever are intertwined in the unfolding discourse. It seems to me that it is most natural to imagine all this as the interconnected fictional *activity* of reporting and commenting upon the evolving narrative—the activity of an at least minimal narrating agency. Moreover, it seems to me that we are usually intended to imagine the narration along these lines.[23]

The issue of suppositions and questions, as they occur in narratives, does raise interesting issues. While it is easy to treat discourse in indicative mode as straightforward invitations from the author to imagine various things, thereby bypassing the need to imagine an internal narrator who asserts them, with questions it is less clear how this bypass operation is to be conducted. If there is a sentence in erotetic mode, but for which no corresponding sentence is attributable to any of the characters, are

---

[22] See Walton (forthcoming). The argument for the assumption of a narrator based on facts about language processing appears in Currie 1990: sect. 4.7, so I am arguing here against my own earlier self.
[23] Wilson 2007: 83, emphasis in the original. Wilson is commenting on views of Andrew Kania (2005) and Noël Carroll (2006).

we then obliged to think of this as a question put to us by an internal narrator? A question such as the one imagined by Wilson—'Was it really true?'—makes sense only, one may argue, on the presupposition that many people did indeed think that Katie loved Hubble. Since it is agreed on all hands, I hope, that nobody actually thought this, since Katie and Hubble do not exist, what we must have here is a question within the scope of what one imagines concerning the world of the story: that many people did indeed think that Katie loved Hubble. That is part of the pretence offered us by the fiction, and so it would seem that we have to understand the question itself as issuing from within the pretence created by the work. That requires us to imagine there being someone in a position to put the question, and that, surely, can only be the internal narrator.

There are two things worth saying about this. The first is that there are, in at least some cases, ways to understand the occurrence of questions in a narrative other than as questions arising from the musings of an internal narrator. When a narrative-maker wants us simply to imagine something—that Katie loved Hubble—he may simply write 'Katie loved Hubble' and have done with it. But narrative-makers sometimes want to control us in more subtle ways. The appearance in the relevant text of 'Was it really true?' might therefore be taken, not as a query issuing from within the story as to whether Katie really loves Hubble but as an indication from outside the story to readers to adjust their imaginative stance *vis-à-vis* the relationship between Katie and Hubble. What is it for us to adjust our imaginative stance? Just as we believe things with various degrees of credence, so we imagine things with various degrees of what I shall call, somewhat inadequately, imaginative conviction. Watching the movie, I may have a dawning suspicion as to the guilty party, which then climbs steadily to certainty by the end of the film. None of this is really belief—I do not believe a murder has been committed. So imagination must come in degrees that parallel these degrees of credence for belief. And the degree can go down as well as up; to the point where I come across the question 'Was it really true?' I might give a relatively high degree of imaginative conviction to the proposition that Katie loves Hubble, and the appearance of the question may have, and be intended to have, the effect of reducing this degree. Similarly, we might think that some commentary in indicative mode and ostensibly spoken from within the world of the story actually amounts to thinly disguised commentary from without. When

Angela Thirkell writes: 'Short of having Miss Holly to interpret for us, we cannot say what Miss Sparling thought of Mrs Perry'[24] it does seem as if the narrator is aligning herself with those within the world of the fiction who, deprived of enlightenment from Miss Holly, can only guess at Miss Sparling's views. Even in such a situation as this, we are not forced to the view that the narrator is internal. It may be that the best interpretation of the remark is that the narrator is pretending, just for the moment and with a certain rhetorical effect in view, to belong to the world of the fiction. This does not make it the case that the narrator *does* belong to the world of the fiction, no more than my thinking up a part for myself in *Hamlet* and leaping on stage to play it makes me part of Shakespeare's play. A fictional person at one level of pretence may pretend to belong to some other fiction without automatically coming to belong to it. It strikes me as better, in this case and in many others, to assume that what we are given to imagine is that the narrator pretends to belong to the world of Thirkell's story—not that she does belong to it. Why better? Because this assumption best underwrites the intent visible in this and similar passages, which is to provide, by means of an ironically tinged intervention, a playful reminder that there is something absurd about the pretence that these people—Miss Sparling and the rest—are real and that we are taking a serious interest in their fates.

I do not say that we could, or should, explain away all such apparently intra-worldly commentary in this way. My second point is that the right way to interpret a question such as Wilson's 'Was it really true?' is likely to vary between cases; within some narrative contexts I agree that the appearance of such a question would indicate that there lurks a so far invisible internal narrator. This is of some significance because Wilson offers the considerations I have quoted from him as part of an argument for the existence of *effaced* narrators. But the presence of an internal narrator may be signalled in various ways, and one of them is that we find some question in the discourse which, very plausibly, is attributable to such a narrator. In that case the narrator will be, exactly, not effaced; there will be some positive reason, though perhaps not a very strong one, for thinking that there is a narrator there. This leaves untouched the issue of whether we ought always or sometimes to accept the existence of effaced narrators.

[24] Angela Thirkell, *The Headmistress* (London: Hamish Hamilton, 1944), chap. 4.

Perhaps the only thing that separates Wilson's position and my own is a view about where the burden of proof lies. Wilson, I think, takes the view that we ought to regard the assumption of an internal narrator as the default position, whereas I am inclined to think that we always need some positive reason to think this. It is hard, as Wilson says, to know how to settle this issue. But we seem to agree on this: that it is not any sort of analytical necessity that narratives have narrators.

5

Expression and Imitation[1]

By 1830, Walter Scott had outsold Jane Austen, book for book, by a ratio of ten to one; by 1900, there had been 290 dramatizations of *Ivanhoe*.[2] His attention to scene, vivid historical placement, intense rendering of dialect, exactness as to dawnings of recognition and inner resolutions—then understood as a kind of psychological realism—created a framework of romantic attention his audiences were pleased to adopt, at least for the purpose of reading. He declined steeply in the twentieth century as public sensibility drifted away from the *Waverley* template.

In speaking of framework I mean to add something to our ways of describing the effects of narrative communication; a framework is a preferred set of cognitive, evaluative, and emotional responses to the story. The framework of a good narrative helps us engage appropriately with the story, enabling us 'to notice and respond to the network of associations that make up the mood or emotional tone of a work'.[3] But narratives do not generally come with a set of explicit instructions as to how and when we are to respond; I will argue that framework is communicated to us, not as something represented, but as something *expressed* in the process of representing the story. And framework, once communicated, will influence the response of the audience to the story, its characters, and events. They may adopt, in whole or in part, that framework, perhaps with the enthusiasm of Scott's audience. By contrast, some narrative-makers deliberately frame events in ways that do not come naturally, and good narratives often

---

[1] In this chapter and in Chap. 7, I am much indebted to Robinson 1985.

[2] See St Clair 2004. John Bayley says that 'Like Balzac, although much more inadvertently, [Scott] had made novel writing into a form of capitalism, and novel readers into rentiers' (Bayley 1995).

[3] Moran 1994: 86. See also Moran 1989 on the distinction between the content and the framing effect of metaphor (esp. p. 100).

challenge us to experience their events in unfamiliar ways.[4] We may see that as morally enlarging, either because it reveals merit in a point of view to which we were previously insensitive, or because it helps us understand, from the inside, the attractions of a distorted way of seeing things. But we do not always welcome, or approve, these attempts to frame our experience of the work; we sometimes experience *resistance* to framing. The chapter following examines this kind of resistance.

If an authorially validated framework is adopted, the audience will have an experience of sharing that depends on psychologically important mechanisms of joint attention and imitation. In this chapter, I focus on framing, the experience of sharing it can generate, and the mechanisms that govern it, looking well beyond the bounds of narrative to get a sense of how powerful and general these forces are.

5.1. The Framing Effect of Point of View

Framework or something like it is a widespread phenomenon of communication. Daniel Kahneman and Amos Tversky asked people to imagine that we are preparing for the outbreak of a disease, expected to kill 600 people if nothing is done (Kahneman and Tversky 1981). Two alternative programmes to combat the disease are proposed, with consequences as follows:

If Program A is adopted, 200 people will be saved.

If Program B is adopted, there is $\frac{1}{3}$ probability that 600 people will be saved, and $\frac{2}{3}$ probability that no people will be saved.

Of those asked to choose between the programmes, 72 per cent preferred A to B. Kahneman and Tversky then presented two further alternatives:

If Program C is adopted, 400 people will die.

If Program D is adopted, there is $\frac{1}{3}$ probability that nobody will die, and $\frac{2}{3}$ probability that 600 people will die.

---

[4] See Booth 1988 for a perceptive account of our relations with 'our best narrative friends'.

This time 22 per cent preferred C to D. But the two 'further alternatives' are the same as the previous pair, with their consequences differently described. Kahneman and Tversky explain the response by appeal to what they call a *framing effect*: framing the problem in terms of gains (the first way) elicits a different response from framing it in terms of losses. The first way elicited an attitude hostile to risk, with the prospect of certainly saving 200 lives being more attractive than a one-in-three chance of saving 600 lives; the second elicited an attitude hospitable to risk, with the certain death of 400 people being less acceptable than the two-in-three chance that 600 will die.

If we think of these scenarios as presented in narrative form, they seem naturally to differ in narrative point of view. One way points of view may differ is in respect of belief. But this is not the difference between Kahneman and Tversky's alternative framings of the disaster scenario. The differences between these points of view are to do with a tendency to focus on lives potentially saved as opposed to lives potentially lost; nothing in the two accounts suggests they are the product of distinct opinions on matters of fact. What is it, then, to have a point of view? The term has its origin in relation to sight, and theorists of narrative have treated visual perspective as somehow central to the idea of a narrator's point of view.[5] But neither restriction to nor central dependence on the visual case is required or helpful in understanding what it is for a narrator to have a point of view. Narrators have points of view in just the

---

[5] Genette speaks of 'vision' or 'point of view' (Genette 1980: 162), though later he seeks a term with less 'specifically visual connotations' (ibid. 189); Meike Bal says that 'whenever events are presented, they are always presented from within a certain vision' (Bal 1997: 142). Some writers even insist that narrators, while not within the story-world, still perceive the events they report (Phelan 2001). The emphasis on the visual is not confined to any particular school; Ian Watt, discussing the opening of Henry James' *The Ambassadors*, speaks of 'the characters' awareness of events: the narrator's seeing of them' (Watt 1960). Other writers have been tempted by a spatial interpretation of consciousness which allows them to say that narrating from a point of view has the effect of placing us inside the consciousness of the subject whose point of view orients the narration. Of Christopher Newman in *The American*, Henry James says that 'at the window of his wide, quite sufficiently wide, consciousness we are seated' (Preface to *The American*); according to Ian Watt, 'we and the narrator are inside Strether's mind' (Watt 1960: 266); Seymour Chatman, describing the 'mediating function of a character's consciousness' says that 'The story is narrated *as if* the narrator sat somewhere inside or just this side of a character's consciousness and strained all events through that character's sense of them' (Chatman 1990: 144, emphasis in the original); Norman Friedman says that the reader ostensibly listens to no one; the story comes directly through the minds of the characters as it leaves its mark there (Friedman 1955: 1176). Sartre characterizes the view as one according to which consciousness is 'a place peopled with small imitations' (Sartre 2004: 5).

sense that any finite agent has one: point of view arises from an agent's limitations of access to and capacity to act on the world. Finite agents have locations in space and time, with consequently limited access to other such locations, and must, in order to act, possess mental states which are *egocentric*: they are states which specify how things are in relation to oneself. I may know the precise spatial coordinates of an object as given in some objective way, but I cannot reach for the object unless I have some way of representing its position relative to my own current position.[6] The relevant egocentric states may be states which involve the concept of the self, as when I believe that the tiger is about to attack *me*, though they need not be; they may be states such as the belief that the cup is nearby, or the perception that the knife is out of reach.[7] Limitation in conceptual resources is itself an aspect of point of view, as with Henry James' Maisie, whose immaturity restricts her grasp of what is going on around her. Our limited capacity for action, and hence our vulnerability, also give rise to senses of threat and opportunity, with their attendant emotions, while our preferences and interests make unavailable to us what are, from other perspectives, adequate characterizations of things. What is valuable from my perspective might, quite legitimately, be valueless from yours.[8] Seeing it as valuable, only a restricted range of responses to it are possible for me.

I said that in acting some of the states on which I depend must be egocentric. A system wholly composed of non-egocentric states will never enable me to act. Arguably, without egocentric states, one could not be said to have psychological states in the ordinary sense at all; one could not, for example, have beliefs. For an agent with no egocentric states cannot act, and while a being that cannot act may have states which, in some sense, register conditions in the world, these are not the states we think of as perceptions, beliefs, desires, etc.[9] So we can think of the totality of an agent's psychological states as contributing to their point of view, while a proper subclass of those states—the egocentric ones—make possible the having of a point of view in the first place.

Thus defined, point of view is extremely inclusive; is it too inclusive to be useful in discussing narration? I believe not. A narrator or character's point

---

[6] For an exposition and development of this view, see Chen 2008. Chen's account restricts the notion of point of view to spatio-temporal point of view.   [7] See Campbell 1994: sect. 2.2.
[8] See Moore 1997, esp. chap. 1.   [9] See again Chen 2008.

of view is never given in full; what is focused on is always some relevant aspect of that point of view, usually some aspect which distinguishes that agent from other significant characters. The great generality of the notion of point of view is recognized in our acceptance that any of a vast range of characteristics *may* count as relevant to the specification of point of view, though most, on any given occasion, will not. Anything from a trivial and easily remedied failure to notice something through to a deep-seated mental disposition such as a tendency to pessimism or misogyny may be relevant to the specification of point of view. Proust's narrator at various points is physically placed so as to be unable to see something, and this highly contingent aspect of point of view leaves us in doubt as to what is going on; Humbert Humbert's sexual pathology—presumably not easily remedied—is the key to understanding the unreliability of his narration.

Difference of point of view is a concept that slices very thin. Two people may see or hear or tell or do the same things without their points of view being the same. If their points of view are distinct, then there must be at least one thing which one of them could see or hear or tell or do which the other could not.[10] To understand a narrator's point of view fully is to understand what resources for knowing, sensing, telling, and doing that point of view makes available. And two people may know and tell the same thing, but, given their different points of view, it may be surprising in the case of the one that she knows it and not surprising in the case of the other. Given A's point of view, it took insight to know that P, and courage to tell it, while B's point of view made P obvious and unproblematic. B cannot make it difficult for himself to know something that is in fact obvious to him, cannot make it an act of courage to tell that which for him has no consequences. The richness encompassed by point of view as I understand it is required if we are to do justice to our ordinary practices of describing differences of narrative points of view.

A narrator may tell us what he sees or has seen, but beyond this the narrator's point of view is not usually announced or described in the narrative itself: it is made evident by things the narrator does which are

---

[10] Strictly, we need to build in conditions here. One character can do something the other cannot do if the one can, say, lift the cup without moving to another seat, while the other can lift it, but only by moving.

expressive of interests, moods, emotions, evaluations, and the rest. As Mitchell Green puts it, 'In expressing ourselves we manifest some part of our point of view.'[11] A narrative expressive of a point of view is the sort of thing which would naturally be the product of that point of view, as an angry gesture is one expressive of an angry state of mind.[12]

Many kinds of behaviour may be expressive of a person's point of view: verbal and nonverbal action, involuntary behaviour, such as the depressed person's posture, as well as behaviour which is intended as expressive and which may, in addition, be, as Green puts it, overt: in such a case I make it clear that my behaviour is intended as expressive. Sincere assertions are examples of overt expression—of one's belief. By and large, we are most inclined to think of behaviour as genuinely expressive of a point of view when it seems *not* to have been intended as so expressive. Outside the realm of assertion, perceiving behaviour to be intended to express something about the agent's point of view tends to set off warning bells: the agent may be trying to manipulate us, and so the expressive behaviour may be an unreliable guide to their point of view.[13] Or that same behaviour will seem expressive of point of view in unintended ways; behaviour recognized as intended to convince us that the agent is honest may then be expressive of wholly other characteristics.

Highly contingent and transient aspects of point of view—recall Marcel's blocked view—say little about the character or dispositions of the person who possesses them, whatever their consequences for the narrative. Then there are differences in point of view which are more stable; parts, we may think, of a person's character.[14] Iago manipulates Othello's perceptual point of view, ensuring that he sees and hears certain things, and he does so confident of how Othello is disposed to respond: how he will be emotionally engaged by certain ideas, will pursue certain questions, ignoring things that for others would seem salient. Most of us reason in a certain way, give special weight to certain kinds of factors, attend to certain facts

---

[11] Green 2007: 1.   [12] See Vermazen 1986 for a careful development of this idea.

[13] Perhaps this is because expressive behaviours other than those involving linguistic assertion are not governed by conventions of truthfulness and trust (Lewis 1975). We do occasionally distrust people's expressions of belief, but by and large we treat them as reliable, even though we see them as being deliberate expressions. This connects, in ways I will not have opportunity to explore, with ideas about reliable signalling which I drew on in the appendix to Chap. 2.

[14] For doubts about the idea of highly stable, character-defining personal characteristics, see below, Chap. 11.

or possibilities more than to others; we have general beliefs and preferences which are resistant to revision and which affect our practical and theoretical reasoning; we have emotional sensitivities which highlight some options and obscure others. Because of its relatively sustained character and because it involves a variety of responses to a rich pattern of events, narration often manages to be expressive of something like a whole persona.

I have emphasized the points of view of narrators more often than those of (non-narrating) characters, and will continue to do so for a while. Two things need to be noted. The first is that characters who are not narrators have points of view, and much of the interest of narrative is generated by them. In a later chapter I will have something to say about this, emphasizing ways in which a narrator presenting events from his or her point of view can in some way *orient* the narration to a character's point of view. Secondly, we need to recall that there is often more than one figure who counts as the narrator of a given narrative: there are external narrators of various kinds and internal narrators, possibly several and possibly at different levels within the story. Watson telling us of Holmes and his triumphs, the historian explaining the origins of a conflict, the novelist communicating a ghost story: these are all cases where we can ask where the narrator's interest lies, what they value, what moves them. In a fictional story we may find distinct and sometimes competing points of view, the internal narrator being given to us as having one set of responses while the external narrator—the real author perhaps—manifests a partly conflicting set. In such a case the internal narrator may be given to us as morally or emotionally unreliable. My interest here is primarily with the highest level, most authoritative point of view manifested by the narrative; this is the point of view on which the framing effect of the story, considered as a whole, depends, though other, subaltern perspectives need to be understood if we are to get a rounded sense of the work.[15]

An external narrator's point of view will generally need to be described in ways different from that of an internal narrator, and the nature of these differences will sometimes be a matter of philosophical dispute. The external narrator of a fiction is someone for whom the events of the story are fictional, so we should not say, speaking very strictly, that

---

[15] As Jerrold Levinson points out, 'our image of the implied author of a novel is necessarily based, in large part, on our image of the narrator and how the narrator is managed or positioned by the author' (Levinson 1996: 152).

such a narrator believes, for example, that Jane Fairfax is unhappy at a certain point in the narrative, wishes that she were not and hopes that events will turn out in her favour. But we, the audience, are in exactly the same position—aware of the fictional status of the story—without that preventing us from having attitudes towards Jane and her predicament which we would naturally describe in just this way. We do not need to decide here the exact nature of these attitudes which are confined, it seems, within the scope of an imaginative project. For whatever is the right account as it applies to us, the audience, that account should do as the best, most fastidious description of the attitudes we find expressed by the external author/narrator.[16]

A final preliminary. Story and framework are distinct things, and they correspond to the answers we give to two distinct questions: 'what happens according to the story?' and 'in what ways are we invited to respond to those happenings'. But we generally cannot identify the one without identifying the other. The dependence of our knowledge of framework on our knowledge of story is obvious; we cannot see what the act of representing story events expresses unless we also know what it succeeds in representing, for what are expressed are attitudes and other responses to what is represented. And less obviously, dependence runs the other way: the framework itself partly determines how we are to take things that are said about the story's events. Is the preferred response to the narrator a sceptical one? Knowing the answer may depend on a sense of the mood or tone of the piece. If we take the narrator to be unreliable, we will have radically to rethink our assumptions about what happens in the story.

5.2. Conversation, Framing, and Joint Attention

While framing has a special interest for us in cases of great narrative art, the motives and mechanisms that govern its workings are visible in a much broader class of phenomena. Sharing information is not always the only or even the primary reason for communication, even among adults; we

---

[16] Thus, I disagree with Levinson when he says that the narrative-maker is 'not in the right cognitive position . . . will not actually have attitudes or views towards the fictional personages or occurrences involved in the story, knowing they are merely fictional' (ibid.).

have seen that much signalling evolved in situations of conflict which put a premium on misinforming your audience. And signalling can benefit the signaller in ways that do not depend on its informational content. Creating the right mood in someone whose actions may benefit or harm you can be important, and the history of human signalling is probably as much to do with this process of 'tuning' people's affective states as with information content, reliable or not. The ubiquity in human communities of music, with its movement-inducing rhythms and capacity to bring about a state of emotional harmony between participants, suggests that articulated but 'non-referential' sound production pre-dated language. It may even have been the evolutionary precursor of language; in some other species of primates, sound seems to be used in ways which are highly expressive emotionally, without having anything like a linguistic articulation.[17] We have language *and* music, but it is not at all surprising that language is capable to some extent of fulfilling the mood-inducing function that music carries out so efficiently. Even silent communication can play this role; here is an example I adapt from Dan Sperber and Deirdre Wilson.[18]

Arriving for a holiday at Lake Como, Janet throws open the balcony doors and, in a way that is visible to John, and is clearly intended to be visible, sniffs appreciatively at the air. What does Jane mean by doing this? That the air is fresh? The freshness of the air is already evident to John. Janet is arranging things so that she and John attend to the freshness of the air in a way that is mutually manifest to both of them. Janet is doing more: she is adjusting John's cognitive and affective take on the world: trying to get John to see the world in somewhat the way she is currently seeing it. There is a small, highly salient portion of the world visible to both of them, and Janet wants John to attend to that portion of it in the way that she is attending to it: appreciatively, gratefully, with excitement at the possibilities for the holiday that has just begun. She wants John to notice certain things; to engage imaginatively with certain possibilities which these things present; to see these things and possibilities as valuable in certain ways. She wants John to frame the visible world in a certain way. It would be vastly impractical—perhaps impossible—for Janet to try to *say* all this, to make explicit the way she wants John to frame the bit of world

---

[17] See Mithen 2005. For scepticism about the idea that music was adaptive because of its role in social bonding, see Patel 2007: 371.   [18] See Sperber and Wilson 1995.

they are looking at. It would also be pointless: the minimal gesture does the job very well.

John already shares the dispositions, preferences, and knowledge that make Janet's response to the view a natural one. To see the scene in the way that Janet does is more or less automatic for him: a kind of mental contagion I will explore in more detail later. Adopting a framework proffered by a narrative or by a conversational remark sometimes requires us to respond in ways that call for effort and mental flexibility, stretching ourselves conceptually and emotionally to participate in a way of seeing things which we do not spontaneously or easily enter into. If John were merely dropping Janet off at her destination, not expecting, or wanting, to share the holiday, his tasks might be harder and call on the conscious exercise of imagination. If John thoroughly dislikes fresh air, lake views, and Italian cooking the project will challenge his imaginative powers a good deal. Whatever the difficulties, they cannot be overcome by having John simply imagine certain propositions: that fresh air and lake views are invigorating; that Italian cooking is delicious. Imagining these propositions, which he will find easy enough, will not help him to enter into Janet's way of seeing things, which is what her appreciative sniff invites him to do. What he needs to do is to enter imaginatively into a framework that includes valuing these things, even though he may not really value them himself—or not so much as, or in the same way that Janet does.

Janet has arranged things so that she and John are jointly attending to something—the scene beyond the window. Frameworks are often found in situations of joint attention. Like Janet and John, most mature humans enjoy acts of joint attention, as with shared spectatorship. One reason this is attractive is that jointly attending to certain scenes has a tendency to bring about emotional harmony between the parties, and, since it is common knowledge between us that we are jointly attending, it may also be common knowledge that we are reacting in similar or complementary ways. Religious celebrations, with their combination of a common focus of attention and expressive auditory and rhythmical behaviour produce powerful experiences of harmony through framing. Where there is joint attending but where harmony cannot be established, as with spectators supporting different teams, tension is likely to result.

Children engage in acts of joint attention by the age of about eighteen months: they draw a caregiver's attention to some object or event, not because they want the caregiver to do anything—fetch a toy, say—but in order simply to bring it about that the child and the caregiver attend together to the object or event.[19] Joint attending is enjoyed by children for its own sake, and seems to be an important milestone in the development of normal affective relations with others. My second example of framework in conversation is a real one, reported by Robyn Fivush, between mother and child; here, joint attention serves to aid the construction of a narrative.

M: What happened to your finger?
C: I pinched it.
M: You pinched it. Oh boy, I bet that made you feel really sad.
C: Yeah . . . it hurts.
M: Yeah, it did hurt. A pinched finger is no fun . . . But, who came and made you feel better?
C: Daddy![20]

In this conversation, a brief, factually based narrative of past events is constructed; it tells us that the child was hurt, and felt sad as a consequence, but the intervention of daddy made things better. Note the extent to which the mother guides the construction of the narrative which this conversation embodies, prompting a reminiscence of how the child felt about the past event, and correcting the child's tendency to speak of the hurt in the present tense by explicitly contrasting the past pain with the later intervention by daddy, who 'made you feel better', thus bringing the narrative to a satisfactory closure. The mother guides the construction and ordering of represented events, taking care to place events in their correct chronological order, while at the same time providing a framework within which to engage with the narrative: recalling the hurt but discouraging a strong resurgence of negative emotion by emphasizing the positive turn of events after that. As Hoerl and McCormack put it, such guided narrative constructions enable mother and child to arrive at a 'shared personal and emotional evaluation of the past'.[21] I suggest that this sense of a shared personal and emotional evaluation survives and indeed flourishes in our most

[19] For an important collection of essays on joint attention, see Eilan, et al. (2005).
[20] Fivush 1994, quoted in Hoerl and McCormack 2005.
[21] Ibid. Hoerl and McCormack acknowledge a debt to the work of Catherine Nelson.

mature engagements with narratives, where the sharing has come to be between audience and the authorial personality manifested in the narrative itself.

5.3. Joint Attending and Guided Attending

We need to pause here because we cannot easily assimilate all or even most cases of attending to narrative to cases of joint attention. As that notion is commonly understood, joint attention involves a condition of mutual openness between the parties—an essential component in the situation of the mother and child described above. It is not easy to specify exactly what is involved in this, but no condition of openness can really be satisfied for the ordinary case of narrative communication when one of the two parties—in this case the author—knows nothing of the other, and may not even know whether there is such another party.[22] We might seek to avoid this problem by claiming that engagement with a narrative involves the pretence of genuine joint attending with another, just as it involves a pretence which gives rise to that fictional being 'the authorial personality' who, it is generally recognized, is not at all the same being as the flesh and blood author. While some encounters with narrative may be of this kind, many, I think, are not. Instead, I prefer to think of the typical situation of one engaged by a narrative as psychologically grounded in those capacities which make us apt to be seekers of joint attention, without itself constituting a case of joint attention in the strict sense. The experience of genuine situations of jointly attending to narrative is a formative and salient event in a person's development towards mature narrative engagement, and an influence on the later experience of engaging with the 'pre-packaged' narratives of literature, film, and the theatre. The enjoyment we get from the experience of attending with a narrative's authorial personality (however that notion is formally to be characterized) is of very much the same kind as the pleasure of genuinely joint attending,

---

[22] On the openness of joint attention, see Peacocke 2005. Peacocke opposes the idea that openness need be explicated in terms of common knowledge, proposing instead that we understand openness in terms of a condition of mutual perceptual availability; such a condition would not generally be satisfied in the narrative case.

and derives, I believe, from the same set of mental dispositions that underlie that other pleasure.[23]

So let us think of joint attention as a refined form of a more general phenomenon wherein one experiences the influence of another's attention to some object on one's own attention to it; call this *guided attention*. The refinement consists in the fact that, with joint attention, all parties are symmetrically placed with respect to the openness of the experience. We find examples of many kinds within this broad class of guided attendings. In the observance of tradition, for example, we attend to something in the service of sharing a response with those who may be long dead, and it is the thought of their (possibly idealized) response to the situation that modulates our own response to it.

The cases of guided attending I have discussed all have a distinctively emotional component.[24] They involve, and may be designed to involve, valued experiences of shared emotion, directed at a scene or object. I emphasize the role of emotion here because adopting a framework for a narrative means being *tuned* to the narrative's content; being apt to respond to it in selective and focused ways that show some stability over the length of one's engagement with its characters and events. Emotions bind together the elements of the narrative, placing some in the foreground, and making connections between what we know now and what is yet to be revealed.[25]

---

[23] There are other ways in which we jointly attend to narratives, as when you and I watch a film together, and this sort of joint attending can have significant effects on one's understanding and experience of the work. But, while this kind of joint attending deserves more attention than it has received, I am not going to explore it here.

[24] For the emotional significance of joint attention, see Hobson 2005, who argues that the experience of having an emotional reaction to an object corrected by an adult with whom the child is jointly attending is a source of the child's sense of objectivity (thanks to Tom Cochrane for discussion and reference). Note that I draw the domain of the emotions very widely. It is much larger than the domain we would get if we were to count emotions conservatively, including only those large-scale, recurrent, culturally salient affective states which themselves have distinctive narrative shape and a name we recognize as putting them on the list of emotions. In addition to love, fear, jealousy, disgust, and the other cases we easily recognize as emotions, there are small-scale nameless urgings that direct our attention to certain stimuli and prime us for action in *ad hoc* ways. When I speak hereafter about emotions I mean to include the small-scale as well as the large, the unnamed as well as the named. There are purposes for which this would not be a useful principle of grouping, but I think it meets the needs of the present case. In my very generous sense of 'emotion', at least a good deal of framework adoption consists in being apt to engage emotionally with the events and characters of the narrative.

[25] On the capacity of emotions to generate 'patterns of salience and tendencies of interpretation', see Jones 1996. See also Carroll 2001b.

And mood—as opposed to more specific emotional states—is an important ingredient in situations of guided attention to narrative, making certain emotional and evaluative responses to specific events more likely than others. Noël Carroll asks how it is that works of art create a mood in their audiences, suggesting that this often happens through a kind of overflow; we experience a specific emotion as a result of reading about the actions or sufferings of a character, and such emotions often leave one with an associated and relatively sustained mood (Carroll 2003). Perhaps this is part of the explanation, but works of various kinds are capable of creating mood more directly that this. Carroll mentions the famously mood-setting introduction to Dickens' *Bleak House*; here I consider the case of *Little Dorrit*, with its opening description of Marseilles. Very quickly, and well before we learn the fate or doings of any character, a certain mood is set by the descriptive choices Dickens makes; he speaks of the 'staring' white walls and streets, 'tracts of arid road', and dust 'scorched brown'. The intense heat, the water within the harbour, the blistered boats are what is represented, but their mode of representation expresses a certain, not easily described, mood of sombre oppression, though summer heat bearing down on a city lends itself equally to anything from a sense of anxious expectation to comic indolence. We have a sense of the narrator's mood, as expressed through his act of representation, and we quickly catch that mood ourselves; we need no specific, emotion-generating event in the story to create the mood.

Looking back at the mother–child narrative reported in Section 2, it is easy to see how the mother's changing tone of voice helps make emotional adjustments to the child's way of seeing things, leading, at the end of the exchange, to their jointly attending to the past in a harmonious way. When mother says 'A pinched finger is no fun . . . But who came and made you feel better?' we can hear the changing tone of voice that first encourages a regretful recollection of the pain followed by an upward curve of affect leading in to the child's delighted 'Daddy!' The dialogue exploits, without either party being aware of it, the child's strong tendency to imitate the mood expressed in the caregiver's utterance.

This example suggests that framing in narrative works in part by a kind of imitation that is unlike the conscious mimesis of the actor, and more a kind of mental contagion, something we as individuals know little about and have limtied powers to control.[26] This mechanism is worth looking at in some detail.

5.4. Imitation

First, a little on what we know, or think we know about the human tendency to imitate. We are, it turns out, astonishingly imitative creatures, and imitation probably plays an important role in the acquisition of skills and hence in the spreading of cultural practices, as well as in achieving harmony and solidarity between group members.[27] Very little of this is deliberately or consciously done, or noticed when done by others. We unconsciously adopt the tone of voice of someone we are listening to—and their mood as well.[28] We like people better if they imitate us (though we do not realize that this is why we like them), and we imitate people more if we like them.[29] The best way for a waiter to increase his or her tips is simply to make sure to repeat the order back to the customer word for word.[30] Certain pathologies remove the inhibition to imitation, leaving people in the grip of a drive to imitate in inappropriate circumstances.[31] Strength in imitation seems to go with high levels of empathy and with social understanding, and children with autism (a disorder marked by rigid, unimaginative thought) tend to be poor imitators.[32] As well as being good imitators, normally developing children are very sensitive to imitation of themselves: infants at fourteen months clearly distinguish between someone imitating them, and someone imitating someone else; they will 'test' the imitator by performing unexpected movements, gleefully keeping the game up for twenty minutes or more.[33]

There is nothing new in the idea that imitation is a subtle and powerful agent for generating and controlling feeling and action. Adam Smith gave it a large place in his theory of sympathy, and at the beginning of the twentieth century the social thinker Gabriel Tarde thought it 'the fundamental social fact'.[34] It has recently been suggested that the

---

[26] On the role of what he calls 'automatic processes' in causing us to adopt imagined points of view, see Harold 2005.　　　　　　　　　　　　　　　　　　　[27] See e.g. Tomasello 2000.

[28] See Neumann and Strack 2000.　　　[29] Chartrand and Bargh 1999; Balcetis and Dale 2005.

[30] van Baaren, et al. 2003.　　　[31] See Hurley 2004.　　　[32] See Hobson and Lee 1999.

[33] Meltzoff 1990.

[34] Smith 1979; Tarde 1903. For a summary of current evidence for this idea, see Dijksterhuis 2005.

evolution of imitative capacities explains the at first glacial rate of change in hominid technology—virtually static for a million years at a time—and its dramatic speeding up over the last quarter of a million years; as imitative tendencies increase it becomes more likely that the innovations of one person will be picked up and copied by others.[35] There is also impressive evidence, unknown to or ignored by opponents of censorship, that unconscious imitation plays a significant role in the production of violent and antisocial acts.[36]

5.5. Imitating the Unreal

You might worry about imitation as I worried earlier about joint attention: imitation cannot be the driving force behind framework adoption in the case of narrative, since the author is generally not present to be imitated, and may indeed be long dead. And imitation may account for changes in behaviour, but can hardly account for the sorts of subtle cognitive and affective changes that will be involved in adoption of a framework; whatever readers do, they do not copy the behaviour writers engage in when writing their novels.

The first thing to say is that there is such a thing as delayed imitation. We all know that we can imitate our friends after they have left the party, and infants at nine months will imitate up to a week after they have seen an initial behaviour performed.[37] More importantly, we shouldn't think of imitation as a matter simply of conforming our behaviour to that of another. Tarde was very clear that imitation is not fundamentally a matter of behaviour, but of adjusting one's state of mind to harmonize it with that of another, though he did not illuminate matters much by calling this the 'action at a distance' of one mind on another. This view of imitation as mental harmonization is spectacularly confirmed by recent work which focuses on ways people tend to imitate the mental processes—even, apparently, the

---

[35] See Sterelny 2003: chap. 8. Paul Harris and Stephen Want (2005) suggest that the emergence of complex tool construction, which they associate with the Upper Palaeolithic circa 50,000 years before the present, is due to the emergence of a new kind of imitative capacity, more sensitive to the success of innovation. They present evidence that such a sensitivity emerges in contemporary children around the age of three years.   [36] See e.g. Hurley 2004b. See also below, Chap. 11, sect. 1.

[37] Meltzoff 1985; Meltzoff 1988.

capacities for rational thought—of others. As Ap Dijksterhuis, a leader in this kind of work, says: 'we not only imitate the observable behaviour of others . . . we adopt multiple, sometimes rather complex aspects of others' psychological functioning' (Dijksterhuis 2005). These studies offer another startling insight: imitation may be triggered, not by the presence of a target agent-to-be-imitated, but merely by the thought of such an agent.

The experiments in question show how easy it is to cause people to imitate the cognitive and affective style of a stereotypical group member when they are asked to imagine one. Subjects asked to imagine, for just a few moments, a 'typical professor' turned out to do better on Trivial Pursuit questions than did subjects who had not been asked to engage in any imaginative task; subjects who had been asked instead to imagine soccer hooligans did even worse.[38]

It is unlikely that the participants in these experiments actually became more intelligent while imagining a professor or more brutish when imagining a soccer hooligan. Dijksterhuis and van Knippenberg suggest the following explanation. Intelligence is likely to be linked in the minds of participants with such traits as concentration, the use of varied strategies, confidence in one's abilities, and careful and rational thoughts. These are likely, therefore, to be prominent elements within a mental model built up through the act of imagining a professor, since professors are generally thought of as intelligent. The effect of the task, then, is to cause participants mentally to represent, in salient ways, certain connected mental traits and then to deploy their own capacities in imitation of these traits, just as we use our capacity to run when we imitate the running of an athlete. In the process, subjects come to exercise (for them) untypical levels of epistemic effort by way of an attempt to imitate the levels exemplified by the model, much as the vivid example of an athletic triumph might make you run that little bit harder during your daily exercise. The mind is, without your conscious awareness, adjusting its level of activity in various areas as a result of your contemplation of an imaginary mind in which those levels are habitually high. You are unconsciously imitating the characteristics of a mind you imaginatively construct, much as you unconsciously imitate the bodily movements and posture of those around you.

---

[38] Dijksterhuis and Knippenberg 1998, which drew on suggestive earlier work by Bargh, et al.

These experiments involve imagination, in so far as subjects are asked to imagine a professor or a soccer hooligan; should we say that subjects in these experiments came to imagine *themselves* to be professors or soccer hooligans? As far as I know, they did not report imagining this, but I grant that we sometimes imagine things we are not aware of imagining. Even so, I doubt that there was any *de se* imagining going on in these cases, for very similar behavioural results may be obtained even when it is pretty clear that subjects are not imagining anything at all. In an experiment due to Bargh and colleagues, a version of which I draw on for other purposes in Chapter 11, subjects who had been primed with words connected with the elderly were then apt to walk more slowly than were subjects not so primed; similarly, by being exposed to aggression- or rudeness- or politeness-related words subjects were apt to become more aggressive or rude or polite.[39] The relevant words were so mixed with other words that subjects would not know that a subset of the words were keyed to the theme of the elderly or politeness; it is unlikely that subjects were pretending to be or imagining themselves being elderly people or rude people. Rather, subjects were engaged in unconscious imitative behaviour triggered and controlled at levels below that where it would be appropriate to say that they were imagining anything about themselves or pretending to do anything.[40] In the case of 'imagining a professor', what is probably happening is that imagining something provokes imitative behaviour via a similar formation of mental representations, as Dijksterhuis and van Knippenberg suggest.

[39] See Carver, et al. 1983; Bargh, Chen, and Burrows 1996.

[40] I am indebted here to work by Gendler, who notes that 'It seems implausible (to say the least) that Bargh's elderly-primed subjects *believed* that they had suddenly turned into a bunch of geezers who needed to dawdle lest they overtax themselves. It is slightly less absurd to suggest that Bargh's elderly-primed subjects *imagined* themselves as old—or imagined someone else who is old—and, having so imagined, began to act in some ways as if the imagined content should govern their own actual behavior. But even this is a rather far-fetched explanation. (Among other things, in well-designed scrambled sentence tasks, subjects remain unconscious of the fact that a particular notion is being primed.)' (Gendler 2008b: 659). Gendler argues that a good deal of behaviour is explained, not in terms of belief, but in terms of the activation of 'behavioural repertoires', which she says are 'innate or habitual propensity[ies] to respond to an apparent stimulus in a particular way' (Gendler calls these *aliefs*). The unconscious forming of complex representations which then serve as models for equally unconscious imitation would seem to be closely related to this idea, since we might think of them as among the processes underlying these propensities. But it would not then be true to say that the propensities were always either innate or habitual; the behaviours exhibited by subjects in the word-priming experiments depend on the contingencies of the stimuli and might be quite distinct from any behaviour the subject would otherwise be likely to display. See also Gendler 2008a.

In general, then, imitation of the kind which is relevant to understanding the framing effects of narrative occurs in a wide variety of contexts, some under conscious control, some not. Some imitation is guided by imagination, as when my attempt at imitating you is helped by imagining myself in your situation, and some is merely provoked by imagination, as in the 'imagine a professor' case. Some imitation has nothing to do with imagining at all, as in Bargh's word-priming experiment. For our purposes, imitation provoked by and perhaps sometimes guided by imagination is of considerable significance, since an important effect of narrative is to prompt us to imagine various things. This is not the only way that framing in narrative promotes imitation; anything which serves to activate patterns of representation that coalesce around the idea of an agent will tend to have the same effect.

One thing to note is how easy it seems to be for imagination to provoke imitation. In the experiments of Dijksterhuis and van Knippenberg, no vivid and particularized examples were provided; participants were not, for example, shown film of highly accomplished professors looking thoughtful or expounding complex thoughts, nor were they given details of the biographies of particularly successful academics. They were merely asked to imagine 'a professor' for a few moments; a very vague request with no 'props' to make the imagination keen. It is all the more remarkable, then, that their experiments produced the effect they did. Sustained imaginative engagement with a vividly expressed and highly individuated mental economy through a long and detailed narrative can therefore be expected to have even stronger and more finely-tuned imitative consequences, with correspondingly powerful results in terms of framing.

I have emphasized how little 'cognitive stock' it sometimes takes to bring about a framing effect. But the framing effects of narrative, while they involve primitive mechanisms of guided attention and imitation, will, to various degrees, also involve such higher-level mental states as beliefs and imagination. In the experiments of Dijksterhuis and van Knippenberg, the mechanisms by which the effects are achieved must be sensitive to high-level inputs and be, to that extent, different from the primitive operations that bring about, say, imitative smiling in infants; subjects have to have beliefs about soccer hooligans and professors. This was brought out vividly in a version of the Trivial Pursuit experiment conducted on psychology students who were asked to imagine 'a neuropsychological patient' and were then asked to perform a test—the Tower of Hanoi test—at which these patients do badly.[41] The students' performance was adversely affected because they, unlike the rest of us, happened to know that such patients do not perform well on this test. This knowledge, providing them with a mental representation of someone with impaired epistemic capacities, then led them, without conscious awareness, to reduce their own epistemic efforts roughly in line with those of the represented exemplar. In these experiments and, I believe, in the case of narrative understanding, we are observing the combined effect of high-level conceptual abilities and low-level, automatic responses. In the experiments, the subject's knowledge of professors, soccer hooligans, and neuropsychological patients are creating detailed mental models which then are responded to imitatively, but without personal control or sometimes even conscious awareness. With narratives, the reader brings to bear vast quantities of real-world knowledge in constructing a picture of the author's mind on the basis of what she reads. But her imitative response to that mind may see her pulled in the direction of a point of view she has not chosen and which she may have some difficulty in resisting.

Much earlier in this chapter, I noted that non-narrating characters as well as narrators have points of view. Since then my focus has been on ways in which our responses to a narrative are shaped by the interests, values, and responses of the narrating personality we see revealed in the work. Much the same argument could be run concerning our responses to the characters of the narrative, whose psychological profiles may be very different from that of the authorial personality. And the evidence of our tendency to shape our thinking to correspond to that of an imagined soccer hooligan suggests that we are as apt to imitate unattractive characters as attractive ones. We are so prone to imitate and so little aware of what we are doing that I expect that empirical studies, if they could be undertaken with a suitable fineness of discrimination, would reveal a vast amount of imitative activity as a part of narrative engagement, very little of which is conscious but any part of which has the capacity to contribute to our conscious sense of how interesting, effective, and valuable the narrative is. Developing a theory of the kinds of effects on our engagement with the narrative that all those different possibilities for imitation have is something

[41] Turner, et al. 2005.

to be worked up to slowly; I do not propose to attempt it here. My focus is almost exclusively on imitation as a mechanism for narrative framing. I end the chapter with a summary of the emerging picture.

5.6. The Standard Model

We now have the materials to describe what I shall call the *standard mode of engagement* with narrative. Narratives, because they serve as expressive of the points of view of their narrators, create in our minds the image of a persona with that point of view, thereby prompting us to imitate salient aspects of it—notably, evaluative attitudes and emotional responses. In taking on those responses, we thereby come to adopt, wholly or in part, the framework canonical for that work. This has two significant effects. First of all, adoption of that framework will, in favourable cases, help us orient ourselves in rewarding ways to the represented events of the narrative; we will respond to the story's events in ways the narrative was designed to encourage and which are likely to comport with the aesthetic, psychological, and moral aims of the author. Secondly, we have the sense of sharing with the author a way of experiencing and responding to those events, leading to a sense of guided attending on our part. We need not think of this canonical framework as always intended; often narrative-makers express themselves unconsciously through their acts of narrative making, though seasoned exponents of narrative art may consciously manipulate the expressive aspects of their work. Consciously or unconsciously, they fashion personas which their narratives express and which may not correspond to their own real personalities. This is not a talent confined to literary geniuses; producers of formulaic romances are presumably adept at expressing the personality their readers are most at home with. Nor should we think of frameworks as always highly constraining. Some narratives express attitudes and feelings that embrace or at least acknowledge a range of specific responses and with which one can feel in tune while having an ambiguous, puzzled, or even paradoxical response, admiring and deploring the very same traits and actions. Other narratives do seem to impose more rigidity: Dickens and Trollope as contrasted with Austen and Henry James.

I have called this the standard mode of engagement; it is not the only one. As we shall see directly, readers sometimes resist frameworks, wholly or to a degree. There are readings of narrative 'against the grain', but, as this description suggests, they require effort. In other cases, the framework that goes with the work seems to be intended to be resisted, though it is not always easy to distinguish these from cases of two other kinds: those where the framework is one we simply see no merit in, finding it difficult to see how this could genuinely be someone's framework; and cases where the apparent framework is undermined by subtle irony expressive of some other, less-obvious point of view. There are also emotional and other effects that narratives have which do not come by way of the expression-imitation nexus I have described. The ghost stories of M. R. James are chilling, but the fear we experience is not had by way of imitation of any fear expressed by the work's authorial persona; that persona seems ironically detached from the horrifying spectral creatures he describes.[42] This sense of detachment affects our own responses in various ways, but it does not generally lead to a feeling of detachment.[43] The standard model deserves its name because it works easily and naturally in so many cases, and relies very little on conscious efforts to communicate on the part of the author, or on conscious efforts to comprehend on the part of the audience.

Appendix: Expression and the Reliability of Signalling

In the appendix to Chapter 2, I outlined a hypothesis according to which the human capacity for articulated language co-evolved with a taste for narrative, with the latter contributing to the solution of a problem about reliable signalling posed by the former. The idea was that significantly narrativized accounts of motive and action have advantages for those needing to get reliable testimony about the behaviour (including the linguistic behaviour) of those they may want to co-operate with; narrative requires a sustained, coherent account that makes contact with evidential sources at various points and which is consequently hard to make credible unless it is true or significantly verisimilar. We can see now that there are other ways in which an agent's narrative may be judged as reliable.

---

[42] M. R. James' technique is the opposite of that employed so often by Poe, who takes care to have his narrators express their own, often extreme, emotional reactions to the events they recount.

[43] One hypothesis is that the detachment of James' authorial persona serves to increase anxiety in the reader because it denies us exactly the comforts of a joint-attention-like experience.

If someone claims that it has been raining I may look for evidence which directly supports the claim: wet pavements, used umbrellas. Alternatively, or in addition, I may seek evidence which supports the claim that the teller believes that it has been raining, for in normal circumstances a high probability that your informant does not believe what she is telling you translates into a high probability that what they are telling you is false. And doubts about the teller's veracity are not much reduced by the teller's claiming to be truthful; a teller who expresses a belief she does not have is being uncooperative, and we cannot test cooperativeness by appeal to a mechanism that depends on it. So we look for other signs. First of all, we think that the most credible testimony of unreliability will come from those most directly affected by it, rather than from those who merely heard about it second hand. And we do not expect a narrative of unreliability given by an affected party to be a dispassionate recounting of incidents and motives; we expect it to go with significant expressions of emotional response to the behaviour, at least in the case where the behaviour reported is grounds for future non-cooperation. And expressions of emotion are hard to fake, especially where they need to be sustained over the course of a narration, where they can be expected to vary appropriately across the course of the narration as distinct events are reported, and where they must have multi-modal coherence, with tone of voice matching facial expression, gesture, and posture. So the expressive aspects of narration can be expected to have added to the selectively advantageous reliability of narrative as a form of testimony. In that case narrative as a vehicle for the expression of point of view is not an artefact of the literary or artistic employment of the form; it is part of what made us such enthusiastic consumers of narrative in the first place.

6

Resistance

In V. S. Pritchard's novel *Mr Beluncle*, the central character is made to some degree sympathetic despite a constant emphasis on his small-minded religious zealotry, selfishness, self-delusion, bullying, weakness of will, and other faults. Pritchard puts the brakes on our natural tendency to enjoy roundly condemning Beluncle's character, behaviour, and way of life, and by so restraining us he helps us understand the forces behind such an existence.

Cases like this involve awkward framing, here in the service of goals we may feel are worthwhile. But discomfort can arise from the sense that a narrative's framing effect is to encourage us to respond in morally or aesthetically questionable ways, with no resulting enlargement in prospect. Oscar Wilde said that one must have a heart of stone to read of the death of Little Nell without laughing. But laughing is not easy; most of us are drawn to the reaction Dickens so obviously wants, however cheap we think the pathos of his narrative.[1] That Dickens succeeds in having us respond in ways that contradict the pull of better taste or judgement is an indication of how important for understanding the attractions of narrative this idea of framing is.

6.1. Kinds of Resistance

There are many ways in which the narrative's point of view, and the framing effects which this point of view seeks to generate, may cause us problems. In the case of Little Nell we may resent a too-easy drawing on our emotional responses. With Evelyn Waugh, we may be disconcerted

---
[1] 'Cheap pathos' is Henry James' phrase, but from a review of Dickens' *Our Mutual Friend*.

by the ease with which we are made to respond with laughter to tragic events. A crudely racist poem or violence-celebrating movie may render us unable or unwilling to conform to its framing effect. Even an author whose point of view we generally admire may sometimes ask more of us than we can comfortably give, as with *Mansfield Park*, for a reader unwilling to grant so central a role to the virtue of constancy.[2] In cases of these kinds we have, to varying degrees, difficulty in bringing to bear a range of affective and evaluative responses which are encouraged by expressive aspects of the work's point of view. We are like people asked to enjoy an exercise routine for which our muscles and joints are unprepared—perhaps even constitutionally unsuited—and which may seem anything from interestingly challenging, through irritatingly pointless, to calculatedly cruel.[3]

Some of these effects have been discussed under the heading *the problem of imaginative resistance*.[4] Why, we ask, do we have difficulty imagining racism and sadism to be good, when this is what the narrative seems to ask of us, and when we are able with ease to imagine that donkeys talk or that a time traveller becomes his own grandfather? If we can imagine time travel scenarios while acknowledging their stark impossibility, why are there barriers to imagining a similar inversion of the moral order? If belief were at issue there would be no problem; we are resistant, most of us, both to believing racism to be morally right and to believing in talking donkeys. Why the asymmetry in the case of imagining? There are aspects to the problem of imaginative resistance, especially as that problem has recently been elaborated and divided, which it will be best for us to

---

[2] See MacIntyre 1981: chap. 16.

[3] In Currie 2002 I argued that we should recognize a category of states I called 'desire-like imaginings'. I suggested that imaginative resistance is not resistance to imagining that such and such but rather to having certain kinds of desire-like imaginings. While I still think that we need the idea of desire-like imagining, it is not necessary, for present purposes, to insist that they are the source of imaginative resistance. Instead, I can go downstream (causally speaking) to a less controversial set of entities: emotions evoked by fictions. People who disagree with me about whether there are desire-like imaginings might yet agree with me that we do have the difficulties outlined above in responding emotionally to narrative events in the ways the narrative's framework suggests we should. We need not argue about whether these emotions—were we to have them—would be generated partly by our having states of desire-like imagining.

[4] The problem was noted in Hume 1985 and the issue was revived in Kendall Walton 1994 and Richard Moran 1994. For a detailed clarification of the issues and a proposed solution, see Gendler 2000, to which I will refer again later. Weatherson 2004 is a further contribution to the topic, and distinguishes several distinct versions of the problem, all with somewhat different solutions. My focus here is on what he calls the imaginative puzzle.

ignore. But in one or two cases those who have addressed the problem of imaginative resistance offer explanations of effects which I also want to consider. For example, Tamar Szabo Gendler notes that we do not find it merely difficult or unrewarding to adjust our imaginings to fit what seems to be asked of us: we sometimes think that it would be wrong to try. Gendler argues that this happens when we sense a desire on the author's part to 'export' part of the story: to suggest that what is true of the fictional world—that racism is good, for example—is in this respect true of the actual world. More specifically, 'cases that evoke genuine imaginative resistance will be cases where the reader feels that she is being asked to export a way of looking at the actual world which she does not wish to add to her conceptual repertoire'.[5] Why should the threat of export, which involves the attempt to get people to believe something that is part of the story, provoke imaginative resistance? Why do not readers—even sensitive ones—cheerfully refuse the invitation to endorse the *truth* of the story's content—that racism is good—while at the same time indulging the apparently harmless pleasure of responding *imaginatively* to the story content in the way they are encouraged to do?[6] If we think of 'ways of looking at the actual world' as including a suite of emotional responses to situations, it is easier to see why we resist.

Note that how we feel about fictional things and events is how we *really* feel about them; fictions put us into distinctive and highly salient emotional states such as warm-hearted approval, anger, and loathing.[7] This can be objectionable for two reasons. First, we may worry that, in coming to feel that way about imaginary situations, we may put ourselves in danger of coming to feel that way about real situations. In view of the evidence for the effects of fictionalized violence on aggressive behaviour and attitudes, I think we are right to worry, since the evidence suggests that fictionalized situations that encourage violent feelings and responses from the audience may then promote violent behaviour in response to real ones. However,

---

[5] Gendler 2000: 77. See also Gendler 2006b, where she distinguishes between the problem of imaginative barriers and the problem of imaginative impropriety (p. 154).

[6] See Weatherson 2004: 12 for much the same point.

[7] Kendall Walton argues that our responses to fictions are best described as 'quasi-emotional' rather than as genuine emotions (Walton 1978). For the contrary opinion, see Currie and Ravenscroft 2002: chap. 9 and Sainsbury 2009: chap. 1. But this issue hardly surfaces in our ordinary, unreflective thoughts about fictional cases; prior to philosophical reflection, we all describe our responses to fictions as emotional.

since the evidence for this has required careful empirical study to extract, it is not clear how much this explains about our natural tendency to avoid generating affect through imaginative involvement with scenarios which seem to us immoral.[8] And, there is something else we can point to which, I suspect, does attach in deep-seated ways to our natural inclinations. We do not like to find ourselves close, in mind or behaviour, to those whose outlook or personality we deplore. In particular, we do not want to feel (that is, really feel) certain ways about imaginary situations, for that would bring us closer to those who effortlessly and naturally feel that way about them, because that is their natural stance towards such situations, real or imagined. We would be manifesting a response which we see in another as the expression of something deplorable, inauthentic, or otherwise concerning. On this account, resistance to engaging as Dickens wants us to with the death of Little Nell is a matter of not wanting to share with others—and in particular with the authorial personality—an expression of sentimental and indulgent feelings. The same reasoning explains why we are resistant to imitating behaviour (for example, an insulting or threatening gesture) we find deplorable even when the imitation would not have the consequences that make us deplore the behaviour imitated. Resistance to wearing a Hitler-style moustache may be partly an aesthetic choice, but it also exemplifies resistance to sharing. Seen this way, imaginative resistance exemplifies a more general phenomenon: resistance to sharing salient, but often evaluatively neutral, properties with people who we wish to dissociate ourselves from on broadly evaluative grounds.

One thought that occurs naturally in this context but which it has been difficult to formulate in a satisfactory way is that the resistance we encounter is due in some way to the impossibility or incoherence of what we are being asked to imagine. It is important to distinguish impossibility and incoherence here because some impossible propositions do not seem to be incoherent. We can see this if we distinguish between the question: what is so according to the story? and the question: what can I imagine?

---

[8] See Hurley 2004b. In all this I am taking as read the point that, along with such tendencies to resistance, there are countervailing pressures caused by anything from fascination with evil through to weakness of will. These are emphasized by Michael Tanner in his comments on Walton's original paper on this subject (Tanner 1994). The existence of these tendencies does nothing to make doubtful the phenomenon of resistance, though in particular cases their operation may obscure it.

Certain things which are impossible may be both so according to a story and imaginable. I am willing to accept it as part of a story about a great mathematician that the mathematician proves the consistency of arithmetic by finite means, and I think we are able to imagine this. None the less it is impossible in the strictest sense. On the other hand, Graham Priest has a story in which two paraconsistentist logicians discover a box which is empty and contains a statue. I am willing to accept this as part of the story, but I do not know how to imagine it.[9] Can we characterize the class of incoherently impossible ideas which resist the grasp of imagination? Weatherson argues that one kind of resistance-provoking incoherence arises when we are asked to imagine certain things being true at a lower level, where those things would constitute the reason for the holding of some higher-level truth, but also to imagine the failure of the higher-level truth to hold. Thus we are resistant to imagining that grass is red if we are also required to imagine that grass looks green to normal observers in normal circumstances, and we are resistant to imagining that all female babies should be killed when there is nothing, apparently, which is both so according to the story and able to provide lower-level reasons for thinking this.[10] There may be other kinds of incoherence which provoke resistance, and they may need to be treated separately; I won't try to deal with them. For neither impossibility nor incoherence is central to the kind of resistance—resistance to framing—which interests me here. I do not think there is anything impossible and certainly nothing incoherent about a story according to which non-white people are mentally and morally inferior; the story might be filled out in ways that make these judgements coherent, or it may be clear from the context that we are free to fill out the details in any way we choose. Still, many of us will experience some kind of resistance to such a story. And in the cases of Mr Beluncle and Little Nell, the mandated kind of imaginative engagement may be challenging,

---

[9] Priest 1997. Weatherson makes this point (2004: 8). The difficulty in imagining what is claimed to be true in this story is, I think, one reason why, as Daniel Nolan points out, an 'unreliable narrator' interpretation of the story is tempting (Nolan 2007); on this reading there is no empty box containing a statue, but there is a narrator (Priest) who falsely believes there is.

[10] Weatherson 2004. Against this, one may ask why we are able to imagine Othello saying all the poetic stuff that Shakespeare puts into his mouth, without imagining him to be a great poet, when, surely, anyone who did produce this stuff spontaneously would be a great poet (see above, Chap. 3, sect. 4).

or regarded as not worthwhile, or demeaning, but impossibility does not seem to be at issue.

In cases like Mr Beluncle or European superiority, it is helpful to remember that imagining this or that tends to bring with it certain emotional consequences for the imaginer. In cases where the context tends to suppress emotional consequences, we speak, not of imagining, but of supposing or assuming, as when I ask you to suppose that aggression is a virtue, as part of an exercise designed to improve your capacity to reason about moral propositions. In contexts where the supposition generates affect—as when I tell you a vividly unpleasant story from the point of view of someone motivated by the belief that aggression is a virtue—we have moved into the realm of what we more naturally call imagining, and in this context resistance may well be encountered, partly because of the uncomfortable sense of emotional sharing it generates.

Discussions of the puzzle of imaginative resistance have focused on fictional cases—naturally enough, given that the difference between the fictional and the non-fictional cases is that in the fictional case alone the events of the narrative are presented to us as things to be imagined rather than to be believed. Thus, fictional cases conveniently avoid the problems generated by confusing resistance to believing with resistance to imagining. In the non-fictional case, the unproblematic phenomenon of doxastic resistance is very evident; we do not always believe what a non-fictional work claims, and belief, if we arrive at it, may be preceded by significant doubt. But there may be imaginative resistance also in non-fictional cases, when it comes to the presentation of the point of view of one or other protagonist; we are not always willing or able to enter imaginatively into the viewpoint of Genghis Khan or Jack the Ripper in the way that a historical work encourages us to do. Not because we cannot imagine the propositions which form the contents of these agents' motivation, but because we are being asked to imagine them in a context where these imaginings will generate emotional responses we find unwelcome.

6.2. Abilities

Should we say that resistance, as I describe it, arises from our unwillingness to adopt a framework, or from our inability to do so? There is no general answer to this question. Whether we call any particular case in this region one of inability or of disinclination depends on our assessment of the counterfactual robustness of the conditions that lead to the resistance, together with a choice of a standard of robustness which is highly context-dependent. Given your beliefs about what is morally right, your desires concerning what to do in the face of moral wrongness, together with rather basic facts about the ways you respond emotionally and viscerally to things which strike you as starkly wrong, it is reasonable to say that you simply *cannot* engage imaginatively with literature celebratory of sadism in the ways its canonical frameworks suggests you should—though you also think that it would be wrong to do so if you could, and are unwilling to test the boundaries of your imaginative capacity by trying. If you had different beliefs, desires, and emotional responses it might be a different story, but the requisite changes would have to be dramatic. It is the relative robustness of the states and dispositions which prevent you from engaging with this narrative which makes 'cannot' seem the right description in this case. In other cases the change required would be less dramatic, as with *Mr Beluncle*. Here one might say that someone who fails to take up the challenge of that work's framework is someone who *will not* adopt it rather than someone who *cannot*. If we say that Albert cannot engage imaginatively with *Mr Beluncle* or with a narrative of sadism, that is true in something like the sense in which he cannot speak either Finnish or Martian. It is true that he cannot currently understand a word of either, but his not speaking Martian is much more counterfactually robust than is his not speaking Finnish.[11]

6.3. The Evolution of Resistance

Perhaps we now have a new puzzle: why do the emotions work like this? Why is it that we are able to imagine just about anything—including the goodness of racism and violence, as long as this brings no affect in its train? Why are we so emotionally inflexible that we cannot adjust the emotional consequences of our imaginings in the way that we can adjust those imaginings themselves?

[11] See Lewis 1976.

My guess is that cost and benefit give us the key to this puzzle. Flexibility of response to circumstance comes at a cost, so there must be benefits that justify those costs.[12] Suppose that the capacity to imagine evolved in our lineage for planning purposes. In order to plan effectively I need to imagine how things might go under various counterfactual assumptions; I need to imagine this or that being the case, or doing this or that. And what I need to know about these scenarios is how they will affect me—and that means, in almost all cases, how they will affect me, constituted as I am with my own basic values, tastes, and other emotion-generating dispositions. Not much need here for flexibility in emotional response.

Planning may not have been the only reason why imaginative capacities were selected in our lineage: capacity to read the minds of our fellows was probably an important factor in determining the fitness of our Pleistocene ancestors. Here again there need not have been much pressure to gain flexibility in emotional response for purposes of mind-reading. Social groups were small by our standards, and the people one came into contact with were mostly those with very similar experiences and aspirations who faced similar problems; there were not then the differences of access to wealth and culture that so greatly exaggerate the differences between people. If our minds had evolved in an environment as mentally diverse as the *Star Wars* bar things might have been different.

A problem with this appeal to evolutionary processes is that it looks as if we have vastly *more* flexibility in imagining this-or-that than we need either for planning or for mind-reading. We take in our stride the wildly false scenarios of science fiction, though they would have had no relevance to either planning or mind-reading in the Pleistocene. The solution here is to see that, for this kind of imagining, maximum flexibility is the lowest-cost option. According to simulation theory, the capacity to imagine operates by using the same inferential system that operates for belief; that is cheaper than building two parallel systems. Such a dual-purpose system has then to be insensitive to the doxastic status of the input; the system will run the same way whether the proposition is believed or not. It will run on anything that is a potential belief. So at the very least, anything we could possibly believe becomes something we could imagine. Now, there

---

[12] On mental complexity as response to circumstance, see Godfrey-Smith 1996.

are things we can imagine but cannot believe: that I am now dead, that the world has ended, that I believe P but P is false, for example. The last of these examples is significant, since acknowledging the possibility that your own beliefs might be false is very useful; a useful system of imagining should therefore exceed the compass of belief. And so, very probably, it would. A rule for inputs which said 'allow just those things which might be believed' would require a gateway capable of distinguishing believable from unbelievable propositions—no easy thing to create and maintain. Once the creature concerned acquires an articulated language, the simplest rule for imaginative inputs is *allow anything that makes sense*. So imagining this or that is under quite different evolutionary constraints from those that apply to the adoption of frameworks for imagining. Flexibility for framework adoption comes only at considerable cost, and the benefits of great flexibility with respect to frameworks were few in the relevant environment.

6.4. Confusing Framework and Content

Working out the events of a story is often subject to indeterminacies of interpretation: there may be nothing to choose between the assumption that something happened according to the story, and that it did not. There can be similar indeterminacy with respect to what is expressed, and so there may be irresolvable disagreements about framework. There may also be indeterminacies about what is story and what is framework. We are in that region where things 'present themselves sometimes as statements but at other times as programmes of action or announcements of a stance'.[13] With so much unclarity it is not surprising that narrative-makers confuse us, and perhaps themselves, by offering what looks like narrative content, or elements of story, but which, properly understood, amount to disguised exercises in framing. In this chapter, I will consider two prominent works, one filmic and one literary, which have profited by this confusion. They illustrate the ways in which a narrative may confuse us—and may be contrived to confuse us—about what is content and what is framework, promising a more balanced and harmonious relationship between these two

---

[13] Heal 2003: 27. Heal's formulation suits my purpose but was intended for another.

things than they in fact deliver. The cases also illustrate the fact that the kind of resistance I am examining often occurs in response to non-evaluative claims we find in a fictional work.

Kurosawa's *Rashomon* (1950) is a film in which the same events are described by different characters, whose accounts are translated into images by means of flashbacks: we see what happens, according to each account. These accounts are different in crucial ways, particularly to do with the assignment of responsibility for the events. *Rashomon* is commonly said to illustrate the relativity of truth, and I think there is grounds for saying that this is how it is meant to be taken.[14] But I hope I am not alone in experiencing resistance to this intention; this sort of philosophy is too banal to add anything interesting to the story, and indeed it detracts from it. So I prefer not to adopt the framework here suggested by the narrative itself: a framework which requires me to see a certain kind of significance in the events of the story. I choose not to see those events as significant in that way.

At various points in Proust's *À la recherche du temps perdu*, Marcel experiences episodes of memory, most notably the incident of the madeleine. Along with descriptions of these events, Proust gives us, through the voice of Marcel, a very lengthy philosophical account of the nature of time, which is supposed to be illustrated by and in some way explain these experiences. This philosophy of time has many aspects; part of it seems to involve the idea that each person has an essence that stands outside time and which experiences the fusion of temporal moments from this external perspective.[15] This idea strikes me as very implausible, as making dubious sense, and certainly not as supported by the narrative's account of the experiences Marcel undergoes. The story looks better without that idea and once again I feel entitled to put it to one side.

These look like cases of resistance to metaphysical ideas.[16] Could my concern in these metaphysical cases be, at bottom, a moral one? Perhaps these claims about truth and about time are ones I associate with self-indulgent philosophizing, and indulging oneself philosophically may be a

---

[14] But note the well-worked-out non-relativistic reading in Richie 1972.

[15] For discussion, see Currie 2004: chap. 5. For a more detailed and scholarly analysis with similar conclusions, see Dancy 1995.

[16] Weatherson 2004 notes the possibility of imaginative resistance to metaphysics; but his '*Wiggins World*' case is an example of failure to make something part of the fiction's content.

bad thing to do; if the metaphysics in question was one I firmly rejected but for which I could see respectable arguments, I might not be so resistant.[17] But this cannot be the whole explanation. Ghost stories traffic in all sorts of entities and events I regard as epistemically unrespectable, yet, given the right kind of story, I am happy to imagine them existing and happening. Appeal to the idea of indulgent metaphysical thinking will not take us far in explaining my reactions to these works. For similar reasons, the difficulty with the indulgent metaphysics cannot be that I worry that by imagining these things I will end up believing them. The same consideration would create a barrier between me and the ghost story, and no such barrier exists.

My objection to the metaphysical ideas of *Rashomon* and of Proust is not so much to their epistemic weakness or metaphysical indulgence, but to their lack of impact on the content of these narratives. Successful ghost-story writers manage to embed their ghost metaphysics firmly in story-content. I do not mean by that that the stories always forbid a naturalistic reading; in some of them the supernatural might conceivably be explained away. But the supernatural is always a live explanatory option, and bears on particular events, their causes, and their effects. And, while a few authors have raised the genre to a high art, success in this is not so very rare; ghosts are the sorts of things that are apt to fit nicely into story-content, and one does not have to be a literary genius to make a ghost story work tolerably well. Ideas of the supernatural have, of course, advantages of vividness and emotional pull. But even some general and abstract metaphysical ideas occasionally make a significant impact on story content; David Lewis claims that there are time travel stories within which a consistently developed non-standard metaphysics of time governs the development of plot.[18] By contrast, the psychological and objective events of *Rashomon* and of Proust's novel seem unaffected by the metaphysical ideas in question; if it were not for Marcel's endless theorizing, sober readers would never infer Proustian notions of time from the plot. *Rashomon* and Proust's novel announce (in different ways) their metaphysical themes, without going to the trouble of showing how the metaphysics is integrated into the story—something, I

[17] I could be badly wrong about all this: about the works concerned, and about the merits of the philosophical ideas I have mentioned. That does not matter. The point is that, feeling this way makes me resist the imaginative invitations of the work. No doubt you can illustrate the phenomenon from your own experience.

[18] See Lewis 1976. On the relations between science fiction and narratives of the supernatural, see below, Chap. 9.

suggest, that would be just about impossible. Their resort is therefore to metaphysics as framework: they suggest to us ways of seeing the material as more profound than it would otherwise seem; they suggest to us certain attitudes and emotions we might have in response to this deeper message.[19] We are encouraged to see episodes of memory as portentous in vague ways, to adopt a rather knowing and superior attitude towards testimony, with hand-wringing about scepticism thrown in. This is metaphysics as anxiety—but without meeting the cost of making plausible or even visible anything to be anxious about. Oscar Wilde said that a sentimentalist is one who wants to enjoy an emotion without paying the cost of it. There is a sort of metaphysical parallel to sentimentality in such works as *Rashomon* and in Proust's novel as well: they invite us to admire certain exciting prospects, but they take care to show only a far distant and very blurred view, thus avoiding the hard work of making coherent sense of the idea they want us to be excited by. Their performance is like that of an artist who, lacking fine drawing skills, suggests we look at their work from a distance at which fine drawing will not be evident.

This does not mean the end for these narratives. Proust's novel cycle is full of literary and psychological value which survives the rejection of his metaphysics of time; Kurasawa's film has its virtues. Indeed, I have suggested that these works are experienced as more engaging, interesting, and valuable without the framework designed to push emotional buttons when time, memory, and truth are mentioned. This suggests an asymmetry in narrative between story-content and framework; frameworks seem to be to some extent optional, detachable things, or things which we as readers and viewers are in some—perhaps limited—position of authority over. We do not have comparable authority in story-content. Suppose I find certain speeches of Miss Bates in *Emma* to be too crudely characterized. So I fashion a new character for her, and make corresponding changes to the text. Surely I have ceased to engage with the original story, taking it instead as the basis for the construction of a new work of my own. That does not seem to be so obviously what I am doing in the cases of *Rashomon* and of Proust. With story-content, the author simply stipulates what is to be the case; while we are under no obligation to engage imaginatively with any

---

[19] Barnett Newman's much-derided titles suggest a framework that the work often does not live up to.

work at all, once we do choose to engage with it, we accept the author's say-so.[20] Not accepting that say-so is then a sign of disengagement. With framework, it seems as if something is presented on which there might be a certain amount of freedom for the audience.

Why should this be? Perhaps the answer is this. While story-content can be characterized in objective, observer-independent terms, framework is essentially a matter of response. In presenting a framework, the author suggests a way of responding to content. In matters of response, we do not easily accept the absolute authority of another. It is reasonable to think that the author is well-placed to make suggestions about how to respond to the story, but not reasonable to think him or her in a position absolutely to dictate terms.[21]

My worries about *Rashomon* and the Proust cycle are these. There is, first of all, a failed expectation that the proffered metaphysics will be built into narrative content; what we actually get is little more than a suggestion about how to see and respond to the events of the story by projecting onto them a general, vague emotional colouring. Yet even this exercise provides few if any opportunities for making interesting connections between events of the story and depends for its emotional force on our being persuaded that there is more depth in the metaphysical thoughts than in fact there is.

6.5. Conclusion

Resistance to framework is something we sometimes do well to overcome; on other occasions resisting seems the right thing to do. We may resist because we do not have or cannot summon the emotional resources to respond in the suggested way, or because by so responding we would feel uncomfortably close to a personality whose natural emotional responses we find alienating. Our rigidity in this regard—our lack of capacity and/or motivation to alter our emotional responses—is probably accountable for

---

[20] Except, perhaps, in those cases where the author specifies a set of circumstances, but then goes on to claim something I have called *incoherently inconsistent* with these circumstances. Consider again an earlier example: we would baulk at the author who, having told us that in the world of the story grass looks green to normally sighted people in normal circumstances, goes on to insist that, in that world, grass is red. On this, see Weatherson 2004. See also above, this chap., sect. 1.

[21] Again, I have found Weatherson 2004 useful here, though I am not sure he would agree with the point made. See also Yablo 2002.

in evolutionary terms; such flexibility was expensive to engineer, and not worth the cost. Some worries we may have about the metaphysical background to a narrative are best accounted for as the vague sense that the metaphysical ideas in question do not mesh well with story content; they are meant instead to help implement a framework within which the story's events seem more consequential than they are.

7

Character-focused Narration

Narrators have their points of view, and we have seen how powerful can be the framing effects of those points of view. But our interest in narrative is also with the points of view of characters. The mere representation of what a character does and says may be expressive of that character's point of view, but there is in addition something the narrator may do, through the act of narration, which is expressive of the character's point of view; the narration may be in some way aligned to the perspective of a character, without it being placed directly in the hands of that character. I will call that *character-focused narration*; it is a technique notable in the later work of Henry James. My treatment of this idea will be different from that often presented in the literature on narrative theory, which is influenced by the work of Genette. I will explain and reject Genette's account in Sections 1 and 2.

My proposal draws on the ideas of the previous two chapters, and a passage from Jowett's version of the *Republic* neatly summarizes the leading idea: '[W]hen the poet speaks in the person of another . . . the narrative of the poet may be said to proceed by way of imitation.'[1] As before, imitation is understood to include the fleeting, sometimes unconscious, sometimes internalized mirroring that goes on in response to a person before us or in our thoughts, as well as more self-conscious and sustained activity.

---

[1] Plato, *Republic*, trans. Benjamin Jowett, Book III. 'Imitation' is now thought an unsatisfactory translation of *mimesis*. See Halliwell 2002. A treatment of imitative narration similar to my own is developed in Gunn 2004. Gunn's treatment is especially valuable for its analysis of ways in which a narrator may subtly modulate between imitative and non-imitative narration within the space of a sentence.

7.1. Genette's Distinction

One of Genette's innovations in narrative theory is his distinction between
'the question *"who is the character whose point of view orients the narrative
perspective?"* and the very different question *"Who is the narrator?"'* (Genette
1980: 168). Other narrative theorists have, Genette tells us, failed to
distinguish these questions; they have made distinctions between points
of view, but these distinctions do not correspond to real differences. The
theorist Stanzel distinguished narration by one of the story's characters, as
with Ishmael in *Moby Dick*, and narration 'in the third person' but 'according
to the point of view of a character', as with Strether in *The Ambassadors*.[2]
But this, says Genette, is no difference in point of view, because Ishmael and
Strether occupy the same 'focal position' in the two narratives (1980: 187).

I shall reject Genette's claim that there may be differences concerning
the identity of the narrator without there being differences in the point
of view of narration. But there are incidental features of the examples he
gives which it would be best not to exploit against him. We might say
that, since Ishmael and Strether are different characters (in different stories)
with different points of view, there must be a difference in point of view
between the two narratives. Genette could have avoided this difficulty
by offering a different comparison. Instead of comparing *Moby Dick* with
The Ambassadors, he might have compared the actual *Ambassadors* with a
hypothetical *Ambassadors**, the difference between them being this: that
while the narrator of *Ambassadors* is a non-character narrator narrating
according to the point of view of Strether, the narrator of the *Ambassadors**
is Strether; otherwise the two are as similar as can be.[3] And, Genette's claim
would be that these two narratives differ with respect to the question 'Who
speaks', because they have distinct narrators—indeed, narrators of distinct
kinds—but do not differ with respect to the question 'Whose point of view
orients the narrative perspective?', since for both the answer is 'Strether's'.

---

[2] Genette cites Stanzel 1971.
[3] There are probably different ways that two narratives fitting these descriptions could be 'otherwise
as similar as can be', and so there are different candidate narratives, all with an equal right to be
considered *Ambassadors**. So nothing I have said picks out a unique hypothetical variant of *Ambassadors*.
Rather, I have picked out a class of such variants, and should be charitably understood as claiming that
any member of that class would suit Genette's purposes as a contrast to *Ambassadors*.

In that case there is no difference between these narratives with respect to point of view; so Genette might claim.

We might also object that *The Ambassadors* does not consistently narrate according to the point of view of Strether, there being many occasions where, for example, the Narrator refers to things that Strether does not (yet) know.[4] We may take the claim of point of view equivalence between the two works to be restricted to those parts of *The Ambassadors* where the narrator does adhere to Strether's point of view. I will argue that the equivalence claim, even thus restricted, is false.

Though Genette insists that there is no difference in point of view of narration between *Moby Dick* and *The Ambassadors*, he does not tell us what criterion he is using to assess whether, in some comparison between narratives, there is or is not a difference of narrative point of view. He could claim the following as a reasonable criterion: there is such a difference just in case the two narrators are narrating from different points of view. Unfortunately, this criterion will not deliver the distinctions Genette wants to make. For Genette does not claim, of *Moby Dick* and *Ambassadors* (and, presumably would not claim, of *Ambassadors* and *Ambassadors**) that they are narrated from the same point of view; while he says, uncontroversially, that Moby Dick is narrated from Ishmael's point of view, and would say, again uncontroversially, that *Ambassadors** is narrated from Strether's point of view, he does *not* say that *Ambassadors* is narrated from Strether's point of view. He says that the narration is 'according to', or 'oriented by' the point of view of Strether. There is a difference between *having* a point of view and *restricting oneself to* a point of view; Genette's careful terminology seems to recognize this, though he does not also recognize that the distinction is fatal for his theory. We have seen that to have a point of view is to have certain capacities or resources for knowing about, telling of, and generally responding to the world. The resources of someone with a certain point of view, P, and another, who, in telling a story, merely restricts herself to the communication of information available from P, are quite different. The second holds herself to a rule to tell in a way that corresponds to the way she would tell if she possessed P. The first, whose point of view is P, does not hold herself to any such rule; her behaviour is constrained by P itself, and not

---

[4] See Tilford 1958.

by any decision to act in accordance with P. Thus, the narration of *Ambassadors*, even under the assumption that it is consistently restricted to what Strether knows, is different, in ways that are relevant to point of view, from that of *Ambassadors**, and also from that of *Moby Dick*—and in this latter case not merely because the two have numerically distinct narrators. The capacities of the two narrators are different, regardless of whether one of them chooses to obey a self-denying ordinance in exercising those capacities.[5]

Stanzel was not wrong, therefore, to see the difference between narration by a character and narration 'according to' or 'oriented by' a character's point of view as a difference with respect to point of view. Neither were Brooks and Warren wrong, as Genette very puzzlingly claims, when they treated the difference between character narration and narration by an omniscient author as a difference with respect to point of view—even assuming the omniscient author to be narrating 'according to' the point of view of the character.[6]

While Genette stops short of saying that the narrator may narrate from the point of view of a character, he shows a hankering for this simple idea—its influence is surely visible in his thought that there is no difference in point of view of narration as between *Moby Dick* and *The Ambassadors*. In fact, there has, since Henry James, been a slide towards the simple idea. Of *The Ambassadors*, James himself wrote that 'Strether's sense of these things, and Strether's only, should avail me for showing them.'[7] Speaking more generally, he said that 'there is no economy of treatment without an adopted, a related point of view'.[8] The theorists Beach and Lubbock quickly distilled from the later Jamesian canon, and from the armoury of commentary which James put around it, the rule that action is to be shown, not told. Their emphases are slightly different: Beach contrasts the intrusive 'impudence' of an omniscient narrator moving from psyche to psyche with the 'close-woven psychological tissue' of James, arguing that James' commitment to illusion required 'consistency in the point of view', which he achieved most completely in *The Ambassadors*;[9] Lubbock focuses on the decision not to make Strether the narrator; to have done so would

---

[5] Arthur Danto (1984) makes a parallel point when he notes, apropos an exhibition at MoMA, the disparity between the 'primitivism' of Picasso and the point of view of the African mask-makers who influenced him.

[6] Genette cites Brooks and Warren 1943: 589.　　[7] Preface to *The Ambassadors*.

[8] Preface to *The Wings of the Dove*.　　[9] See Beach 1918: chap. 5.

have weakened the desired sense of an immediate connection between the reader and Strether's state of mind. While Lubbock is sensitive to the variation of effect in James, his summary, unanalysed judgement is always that the story is told from Strether's point of view.[10] The implication, a little clearer in Lubbock than in Beach, is that the story is narrated, not by Strether, but from Strether's point of view.

I will have more to say about *The Ambassadors*; it is a good illustration of the fact that external narrators often modulate their narrations in complex and subtle ways, orienting to a certain point of view for a brief space—often less than a full sentence—weaving in and out of speech modes in ways which, perhaps surprisingly, we follow with relative ease. We seem to be highly attuned, as practitioners and as audience, to this process whereby one person lets another's point of view guide their own behaviour. This narrative modulation is just one form of a broad class of behaviours which includes parodic and ironic performances as well as acts of imitative learning. Imitation will, unsurprisingly, be our guiding idea here.

In summary, then, we need to recognize two distinct notions concerning point of view. One is the idea of narrating from a point of view; what needs to be said about this is that everyone always narrates from his or her own point of view. The second is the idea of narrating according to a point of view. I am allowing—indeed I will insist—that one can narrate according to a point of view other than one's own, or, in Genette's other terms, one can orient one's narrative to the point of view of another; this is what is happening in (parts of) *The Ambassadors* and in other works. What we do not yet have is a clear explanation of what this amounts to, something I will develop in the next two sections. But, whatever it does amount to, it does not justify Genette's claim that there can be differences between works concerning the identities of their narrators, yet no difference concerning the points of view from which they are narrated.

7.2. The Knowledge Criterion

Genette might be quite wrong in his judgements about what constitutes a difference of point of view, yet right to separate the questions: whose

---

[10] See Lubbock 1921, esp. pp. 161 ('the point of view is primarily Strether's'), 165 ('Strether's point of view still reigns'), and 167 ('our point of view is his').

point of view 'orients' the narrative? and who narrates? There is an obvious difference between deciding who the narrator is, and deciding which, if any, character's point of view serves to orient that narration. What, then, can be said by way of explanation of the notion of narration oriented to a point of view? Genette offers a theory, but it is unsatisfactory. For him, the difference is to be spelled out in terms of difference of quantity of information:

1. A character's point of view orients the narrative if the narrator says only what that character knows.   (Genette 1980: 189)

In such a case, the character concerned is the *focal* character, and we have an *internally focalized* narrative, an idea I will return to in Section 4. Call (1) the *knowledge criterion*. As Genette realizes, a narrative need not consistently maintain its restriction to the point of view of a given character; it may shift away from internal focalization altogether (as *The Ambassadors* frequently does), or it may move from one focal character to another. The knowledge criterion will not help us much in trying to identify these shifts. The most it can tell us is that, if a narrator relates something a given character does not know, then that character is no longer the focal character (if they ever were). But the fact that the narrator tells us something that a character does know gives us only very weak grounds for concluding that this character *is* the focal character, if there is one. A traditionally omniscient narrator may tell us something that one or more of the characters knows, without the narration suddenly becoming oriented to that character's point of view; and if two or more characters know what is being told, how are we to decide which is the focal character, if either is? Genette may reply that such ambiguities will tend to wash out during a sustained piece of internally focalized narration, because sustained narration which conforms consistently to the knowledge of a given character will tend to make the perspective of that character very salient, enabling us to identify the orienting point of view. Even if this is true, an important point is being missed: as we shall see, authors are capable of extremely subtle modulations of point of view, shifting the orientation of their narrations within a brief space of time—sometimes within a given sentence—between points of view.[11] The knowledge criterion will not help us track these micro-modulations.

---

[11] Genette acknowledges this: 'Any single formula of focalization does not, therefore always bear on an entire work, but rather on a definite narrative section, which can be very short' (Genette 1980: 191).

The use of a character's point of view to 'orient' the narrative is not something we can account for in terms of conformity of narrated information to what is known by that character. And that is to be expected. We saw in Chapter 5 that having a point of view is more, much more, than merely knowing some things and not others. Two people might know much the same thing and yet have widely differing points of view. We need to allows that a narration may be oriented to a certain point of view in many ways, each corresponding to the many manifestations of point of view. Subjects are distinctive epistemically, and so knowledge is an important aspect of point of view. So also are such things as location, perceptual orientation, habits and capacities of mind, modes of emotional response.

It is not hard to see where the material for a better account of orientation to a point of view will come from. I have already sketched a theory of the way in which narrators' actions are expressive of their points of view; we need only now adjust this account to fit the present case.

7.3. Expression

Narrators sometimes describe the points of view of their characters. In Dorothy L. Sayers' *The Unpleasantness at the Bellona Club* (1928) Inspector Parker is questioning a suspect:

> 'How the hell should I remember?'
> Parker disliked a swearing woman, but he tried hard not to let this prejudice him.

This tells us something about Inspector Parker's point of view, but without resulting in anything which could reasonably be said to constitute narrating *according to* that point of view, for in this passage Sayers' narrator retains her normal, rather impersonal style. In describing this aspect of Parker's point of view, Sayers does not do anything that is expressive of that point of view.

The expression of point of view is something I have already discussed at length. But something more is needed here. Our interest is not in the case where a narrator does something expressive of his or her own point of view. We need a mechanism by means of which one person can do something expressive of *another's* point of view. The mechanism is imitation; just as readers may imitate the responses and evaluations of narrators, so narrators may imitate those of their characters. That is what is involved in orientation to a character's point of view. What is *not* involved is the narrator taking on, coming to occupy, that point of view.

How does one imitate a point of view? We have seen a tendency to announce the subjectivity of point of view, tempting us to say that what is being imitated is goings on within a private sphere of consciousness, the inner mental life of the agent whose point of view this is.[12] But there is no adequate, purely phenomenological approach to point of view which brackets the world and focuses on the subjectivity of the point of view itself. We do better—as I have been insisting—to think of point of view as a way of responding to the world. And the narrator who tells us about things and events in the world of the story, may tell us in ways which imitate the responses to that world which are characteristic of the point of view in question.

Remember that we are not to confine our attention to direct behavioural imitation, which occurs when I imitate some specific behaviour of yours—the way you just now uttered that sentence, the way you dropped that plate yesterday. To understand orientation to a point of view we need a general sense of imitation which includes, for example, my uttering a sentence you have never uttered, but saying it in a way which brings to mind your characteristic mode of utterance. By imitating some aspect of a person's way of behaving—their 'style', as we say—I may manage to do something which is expressive of their point of view. What I am imitating is behaviour which, were they really to engage in it, would be expressive of their own point of view. The narrator who narrates according to a point of view is like the person who, though they are not sad, expresses sadness through the adoption of a certain posture, facial expression, and tone of voice. Such a person can be said to imitate a sad person, and by imitating the behaviour they express the sadness that causes the behaviour. And imitation as I want to understand it may contain elements of caricature, as when I exaggerate aspects of your verbal style or mode of dress or gait while managing to present them as recognizably your own; exaggeration may be the means by which my imitation becomes salient. We shall see

[12] See above, Chap. 5, sect. 1.

that narration which is oriented to a character's point of view may also involve exaggeration.

Some will argue that we express only that which belongs to us; we cannot, literally, express sadness when we are not sad, for expression is a causal notion: to be expressive of a state or tendency the behaviour has to be caused by that state or tendency.[13] We need not decide this issue. If you think that expression is causal, you may still allow that in imitating another, I can do something very like expressing that person's state: I can make it fictional, in a vivid and affecting way, that I express that state. My behaviour will have the appearance of expressing that state, just as the actor's movements may have the appearance of striking a blow. What I say here about expression through imitation can be rephrased, for those who want it rephrased, in terms of fictionally expressing, or making it fictional that one expresses, a state or tendency. And even those who want the distinction will agree that the mechanisms by which we recognize and respond to real expression are the same as those by which we recognize and respond to the activity of making it fictional of oneself that one expresses something.

Go back now to Genette's primary example of character-focused narration. The narrator of *The Ambassadors* does not narrate from Strether's point of view, but he does, sometimes, narrate according to that point of view, by doing things which count as expressive of Strether's characteristic way of responding to the world—his point of view. How does he do that? First of all by imitation: by imitating modes of speech which, as we come to see, are characteristically Stretherian modes. In a literary narrative the narrator has only language, and whatever is imitated must be imitated by using language. In thus imitating these modes of speech he expresses aspects of Strether's ways of thinking about, responding to, or dealing with the world. In speaking this way, the narrator is behaving in ways which are expressive of characteristics which lie behind Strether's speech, as we may express a person's hesitant or angry frame of mind by speaking in his or her characteristically hesitant or angry way. Ian Watt, describing the opening of *The Ambassadors*, notes that

There are 6 'noes' or 'nots' in the first 4 sentences; four implied negatives— 'postpone'; 'without disappointment'; 'at the worst'; 'there was little fear': and two

---

[13] See Vermazen 1986 for discussion.

qualifications that modify positiveness of affirmation—'not wholly', and 'to that extent'. This abundance of negatives . . . enacts Strether's tendency to hesitation and qualification.   (Watt 1960: 259)

And, when 'the consoling reflection that "they [Strether and Weymarsh] would dine together at the worst"' is followed by 'there was little fear that in the sequel they shouldn't see enough of each other' we find James imitating a style of speech (Strether's own) that demands that 'open statement be veiled in the obscurity of formal negation'.[14]

In narrating in this way, what, precisely, is the narrator imitating? I have said that this kind of imitation need not be the direct reproduction of a character's words or thoughts (as we shall see, imitation is often more effective when it is not direct reproduction). The narrator may not be speaking quite as Strether has spoken. But if the *style* of speech is right, it may communicate the frame of mind, or the disposition to approach the world, which we suppose Strether to have. Indeed, it would impose a strain on our sense of the work's psychological realism were we to suppose that the narrator's imitative acts mandate us to imagine some exactly corresponding thought or utterance on the character's part. We need not assume that the idea that the delay in meeting Waymarsh is 'not insupportable' is a thought explicitly had by Strether; the narrator's formulation may do no more than reflect a tendency on Strether's part to think such thoughts, or be an analogue of an affective response that remains, with Strether, unconceptualized.[15]

There is also an element of caricature in James' adoption of Strether's style—more qualified and indirect, probably, than Strether really tends to be, but none the less indicative of the personality we are about to meet. This signals an irony in James' exposition: a pretence on his part that qualification and indirection to this degree is an appropriate vehicle of communication when in fact, as a sensitive and diligent reader may come to see, the aspects of Strether's point of view of which these tropes are

---

[14] Ibid. 265. In the same spirit we may point to the 'massed block[s] of portentous qualifications' (ibid. 263) that James provides.

[15] Orientation to point of view is harder to achieve in film, at least where it goes beyond the use of point of view shots. Notable attempts include the use of glossy, cold colours and uncomfortable camera angles to express something about Sylvia Plath's state of mind in *Sylvia* (Jeffs 2003). The result, as an expression of Plath's mood, is hard to distinguish from the mood conveyed by the narration itself. See also the discussion of 'indirect or reflected subjectivity' in Wilson 1986: chap. 5.

expressive are the source of some of his problems.[16] But character-focused narration can have an ironic effect without resorting to caricature. This example is from James—M. R. James this time. Mr Dennistoun is at work in the Church:

It was nearly five o'clock; the short day was drawing in, and the church began to fill with shadows, while the curious noises—the muffled footfalls and distant talking voices that had been perceptible all day—seemed, no doubt because of the fading light and the consequently quickened sense of hearing, to become more frequent and insistent.[17]

The reader will not suppose that the narrator's remarks on the noises and their relation to fading light represent the facts of the story; there is too much reason to think the true explanation more sinister. But the explanation in terms of fading light and quickening sense is one that would appeal to Mr Dennistoun, a typically Jamesian academic, nervously completing his examination of the Church. James' narrator imitates, just for a moment, the perspective of Mr Dennistoun, and gives the appearance of being someone who thinks (and how obviously wrong he is to think it) that the apparent increase in these disturbing noises might be thus innocently caused. The narrator could have said, flatfootedly, that Mr Dennistoun told himself that the cause was not sinister, but he would not have so vividly conveyed the pressures on Mr Dennistoun's thinking, or encouraged us to imagine ourselves in Mr Dennistoun's position, comforted by this unrealistic thought. I will say more on the empathy-generating effects of character-focused narration in Section 6.

Earlier I noted that behaviour is considered most expressive when it is not intentional. But when we are dealing with a narrator whose verbal

---

[16] In another author, less given to indirection himself, the irony would be more obvious. Watt's analysis makes it clear how James' 'enactment' of aspects of the point of view of Strether is emeshed with his own point of view. Watt shows, for example, how, in the same first paragraph, 'elegant variation and the grammatical subordination of physical events' express 'the general Jamesian tendency to present characters and actions on a plane of abstract categorization' (Watt 1960: 259). Indeed, the points of view are not always distinguishable. Watt notes that 'in the later novels . . . we do not quite know whether the awareness implied in a given passage is the narrator's or that of his character. [B]ecause the narrator's consciousness and Strether's are both present, we often don't know whose mental operations and evaluative judgements are involved in particular cases' (ibid. 261). The narrator's own point of view is dominant in the second paragraph. On irony as a form of pretence, see below, Chap. 8.

[17] 'Canon Alberic's Scrap-book', *The Collected Ghost Stories of M. R. James* (London: Edward Arnold, 1931), 18.

behaviour is expressive of another's point of view, are we not considering behaviour which is intentional, though it may be behaviour which is imitative of such non-intentional behaviour as verbal hesitancy or avoidance of direct statements? I think we need to make room for the idea that a narrator whose narrative is oriented to the point of view of a character may be incompletely aware—and in some cases entirely unaware—that this is so. Aspects of a person's style need not be intentional. And stylistic features of a narrative are attributable to a speaker or writer without our needing to pass judgement on the extent to which they are consciously cultivated. As we saw in Chapter 5, there is good evidence that we have only to think briefly of a person or certain sort of person to find ourselves, inadvertently, imitating their manner, attitudes, and even their intellectual competence.[18] This may happen as often with authors as with readers. But some special kinds of character-focused narration work only if we understand them as intentional. That is the case with M. R. James' ironic narration of the scene in the church; we shall see in the next chapter that an ironic effect is achieved only when it seems that an ironic effect has been intended.

Is the idea of narration which is oriented to a character's point of view one that admits of degrees? If we are in the grip of the idea that character-focused narration must be narration *from* the point of view of a character, our answer will be no: while, on this conception, a narrator may shift between points of view, he or she either has, at a given moment, that point of view, or does not. Freeing ourselves from this idea, there is no longer a barrier to thinking in terms of more or less. In this passage Strether is reflecting on the effect of Miss Gostrey's dress at dinner, and its relation to the dress of another lady:

Mrs Newsome's dress was never in any degree 'cut down', and she never wore round her throat a broad red velvet band: if she had, moreover, would it ever have served to carry on and complicate, as he now almost felt, his vision?[19]

---

[18] The idea that a narrator's activity may be, and often is, expressive of another's point of view is important for deciding when a narrator is 'self-effacing'. Critics (Lubbock, Chatman, and Sternberg among them), impressed with James' own valorization of seeing over showing, have convinced themselves that the Jamesian style effaces the narrator. But, as Richard Aczel points out, this is not a view that can reasonably be held when we shift our focus from what the narrator says (which certainly does contrast with the narratorial pronouncements of, say, Trollope) to the expressive aspects of his saying: 'it is precisely where it [the narration] fairly roars with lionish pride at its own dexterity that—irrespective of "explicit self-mention"—the narrator is at his most prominent' (Aczel 1998: 471).

[19] *The Ambassadors*, Book Second, 1. Göran Rossholm notes the need for degrees here (Rossholm 2004: 241).

The first part of the sentence can be considered a more or less straight-forward rendition of Strether's thought, but the second part, with its 'as he now almost felt', while not abandoning the influence of Strether's perspective entirely, is less thoroughly at one with it. The imitative account of orientation allows for this; one's behaviour can be more or less imitative of another's, more or less expressive of their point of view. I can imitate a person's whole manner of walking, or merely imitate their stride or their arm movements, while carrying a facial expression which manifests the pretended nature of the performance. In the passage quoted, James' narrator is limiting the thoroughness of his imitation. And in the following from Turgenev, the narrator's orientation to the points of view of characters is very qualified:

Bersenyev began again unfolding his views on the vocation of a professor, and on his own future career. He walked slowly beside Elena, moving awkwardly, awkwardly holding her arm, sometimes jostling his shoulder against her, and not once looking at her; but his talk flowed more easily, even if not perfectly freely; he spoke simply and genuinely, and his eyes, as they strayed slowly over the trunks of the trees, the sand of the path and the grass, were bright with the quiet ardour of generous emotions, while in his soothed voice there was heard the delight of a man who feels that he is succeeding in expressing himself to one very dear to him. Elena listened to him very attentively, and turning half towards him, did not take her eyes off his face, which had grown a little paler—off his eyes, which were soft and affectionate, though they avoided meeting her eyes. Her soul expanded; and something tender, holy, and good seemed half sinking into her heart, half springing up within it.[20]

On the one hand the narrator's descriptive terms are carefully chosen to reflect the assessments Bersenyev and Elena would themselves make of the scene's significance, but the fullness of the terms suggests a complacency the narrator is unlikely to share, and 'feels' and 'seems' further undermine the character's own points of view. At points like these talk of narrations which are 'according to' or 'oriented towards' the points of view of characters cease to supply the right images. James and Turgenev require us to think in terms of complex, multidimensional relations between the

[20] Turgenev, *On the Eve*, chap. 4. The two characters have distinct, indeed divergent perspectives, as we discover. As the passage develops, the narrator shifts from orientation to Bersenyev's point of view to orientation to that of Elena. But there is in addition, I think, a just discernible sense of orientation to a (supposed) point of view which the two of them would like to think they share.

narrator's point of view and that of a character—relations between which there may be (higher-order) relations of tension. These complexities will have to be dealt with elsewhere.

Another advantage of the present, admittedly simplifying, account is that it allows us to distinguish between narration which is oriented to the point of view of a character and narration which is merely coincident with that point of view. It often happens that a narrator and one or other of the principal characters seem to have very similar points of view.[21] Cecil Day-Lewis, writing as Nicholas Blake, was the author of a number of detective stories featuring Nigel Strangeways, a scholarly amateur sleuth. The narrator in these novels, an external one, seems to share a good deal by way of point of view with Strangeways, who incidentally was modelled on W. H. Auden. But there is not much temptation to say that the narration is oriented to Strangeways' point of view. The impression one gets instead is that Blake/Day-Lewis fashioned personas for his narrator and for his hero which turn out not to be so very different. We do not get the sense that the narrator is doing anything imitative of the style of Strangeways, any more than we would, without special reason, suppose, in the case of two very similar people, that each is imitating the other.

7.4. Focalization

I have used the label 'character-focused narration' for the topic of this chapter. Genette introduced a term which has subsequently taken on a life of its own: 'focalization'.[22] Narratologists are apt now to speak more of focalization than of point of view; we should ask whether the new term and their ways of using it reflect a conceptual innovation capable of accounting for things beyond the scope of the idea of character-focused narration as I have explained it. Genette, in introducing the terms, suggests it is merely an alternative to 'point of view', one which avoids a 'specifically visual connotation'.[23] Genette distinguishes between internal

---

[21] I say 'similar' rather than identical because, where the narrator is external, they cannot be said to be coincident in terms of knowledge. This, I think, indicates how little importance, overall, accrues to knowledge when it comes to assessing similarity of point of view.

[22] Genette 1981: 189. Genette protests about some of these extensions in Genette 1988: chap. 12.

[23] Genette acknowledges Brooks and Warren's earlier use of 'focus of narration' (Genette 1981: 186).

and external focalization. An *internally focalized* narrative is one where the narrator says only what a given character knows; I have suggested that an account of character-focused narration in terms of imitation and expression does a better explanatory job than does the idea of internally focalized narration. *Externally focalized* narratives are said to be ones where the narrator says less than the character knows.[24] This is unsatisfactory for reasons already given—what the narrator says about what the character knows tells us nothing much about the relationship between the narration and that character's point of view. Genette's examples—the novels of Dashiell Hammett, Hemingway's 'The Killers' and 'Hills Like White Elephants'—suggest that the category is intended to pick out narratives which focus our attention on the point of view of a character, raising questions in our minds about that character's motivation, without using the imitative and expressive techniques I have illustrated above in order to give the reader a feel for what that point of view is like. This is a genuine narrative category of some interest (though I will not investigate it here), but the use of the term 'focalization' for both this and character-focused narration suggests a closer affinity between the two than really exists. The two forms employ quite different techniques and produce different results. Once we abandon the idea that there is a neat formula in terms of 'quantity of information about a character's knowledge' that covers both, we can abandon the project of giving a unified account of them.

Focalization has been taken up by others whose treatments have made it more and more distant from our present concerns. According to some, we have focalization whenever someone tells us what someone else has seen; the seeing character is then the focalizer.[25] And the narrator may also focalize, as the older Pip focalizes the 'ideology' of *Great Expectations* (Rimmon-Kenan 1983: 82). According to Mieke Bal, any statement of a 'perceptible' fact involves focalization, with an external focalizer stipulated to be doing the perceiving (Bal 1997: 157). All seeing is focalization,

---

[24] Ibid. 189. Confusingly, Genette equates this with the narrative in which 'the hero performs in front of us without our ever being allowed to know his thoughts or feelings' (ibid. 190). A narrator may say less than the character knows while saying something of what he knows—in fact no narrator could claim to say *all* that a character knows.

[25] Bal 1997: 143; Rimmon-Kenan 1983: 72. Thus 'focalization', which Genette hoped would discourage an excessive emphasis on the visual, has been used to represent the idea that a character's point of view is largely or exclusively to be described in terms of what the character sees (Bal 1997: 142).

and so presumably are all forms of sensory and cognitive contact with anything. Seymour Chatman, in revolt against the overstretched use to which focalization has been put urges us to abandon the use of any single term—'focalization' or 'point of view'—in favour of two terms: 'slant' and 'filter', the first corresponding to the outlook of the narrator and the second to that of the relevantly highlighted character (Chatman 1990: chap. 9). I, to the contrary, see no disadvantage in retaining 'point of view', especially since that is exactly what the narrator and the character both have. We need a distinction here, and I have given it: the distinction between narrating from a point of view—always and necessarily the narrator's—and narration which is oriented to the point of view of a character.

Chatman has a reason, he thinks, for avoiding a single term like 'point of view', namely that narrators do not see the events they narrate (ibid. 142). Since narrators can be internal or external, the right thing to say here is that some do, as Watson sees much of what he relates, and some do not. We would then need further terms to discriminate seeing narrators from non-seeing ones. None of this is necessary. Point of view is a many-faceted notion, as I have explained, and no narrative highlights all or even much of a given agent's point of view; all we ever get is some aspect of it. In some cases, for some characters and for some narrators, that will be a visual aspect, in other cases it won't be. As long as we know whose point of view we are talking about, what function that agent is currently discharging (narrator? character?), and what aspect of that point of view is in question, we will not become confused.[26]

---

[26] Chatman makes another point: whether or not a narrator sees, the act of narration is not an act of seeing (Chatman 1990: 142). This is undeniable, but hard to see as relevant to the question whether vision is even an aspect of the narrator's point of view. A narrator's narration—certainly not an act of seeing—may tell us a good deal about what he sees or has seen, and in coming to know that we may come to know interesting things about his or her point of view. What a narrator sees may be as much a feature of point of view as what a character sees. But Chatman's discussion of this issue is puzzling, and I am not sure I follow it. For example, he slides between the claim that narration is not seeing and another claim, that the narrator does not get his or her information by seeing (see the passage 'It makes no sense to say that a story is told "through" the narrator's perception. . . . It is naïve, I think, to argue that this omniscient narrator "got" this information by witnessing it' (ibid.). So far as internal narrators like Watson are concerned, this latter claim is not always true. Anyhow, claims about the source of narration and claims about the act of narration should be kept separate. Slightly later, Chatman says that the narrator *does* sometimes see the events of the story, as the narrator of Conrad's *Heart of Darkness* sees (and hears) Marlow. But, says Chatman, the narrator sees these things 'in the discourse world' (ibid. 144). What sort of seeing this is and how it bears on the visual aspects of the narrator's point of view is unclear. For helpful comment on Chatman, see Levinson 1996.

7.5. Context Shifting

The imitative devices available to the narrator of a literary fiction are those that come via the use of language. It is not possible to list all the ways in which a narrator may use language to express aspects of a character's point of view; they are open ended and highly context-dependent. But there are some imitative devices of literary narration which are very prone to create an expressive effect. I will discuss two, the first one rather briefly.

Lauri Karttunen once argued that 'told' functions in two ways, depending on whether it takes a wh-complement, as in 'she told them where the money was', which requires that what she told was true, or takes instead a that-complement, as in 'she told them that the money was in the safe', which does not require truth-telling (Karttunen 1977). This has been doubted on the grounds that it makes sense to say

(1) John told the voters what he intended to do for them once elected, but, as usual, he was lying.   (Tsohatzidis 1993)

As Richard Holton points out, (1) is a rather 'literary' construction, though one we might occasionally, and self-consciously, use in conversation. Arguably (1) is not in any straightforward sense a counter-example to Karttunen's thesis, since, in its first part, the speaker is not describing how things are, or how she thinks they are, which is the standard mode of assertion. Instead, she is using words that suggest how things might be reported by someone taken in by John's lies, to whom it *seemed* that he was telling them what he would do for them; the speaker orients her report to the point of view of such a person. A rule like Karttunen's is good for standard modes of assertion, and it is not a criticism of the rule that fails in cases like (1), just as it is not a criticism of the claim that 'know' is factive to point to the acceptability of similarly literary constructions like 'Florence knew in her heart that the Soviet Union, for all its mistakes—clumsiness, inefficiency, defensiveness surely, rather than evil design—was essentially a beneficial force in the world'.[27]

---

[27] See Holton 1997. It has been suggested that the 'know' here is non-factive, as in 'I do not know that I will allow that' (Tsohatzidis 1997). Even allowing for a non-factive 'know', the clear force of the example, without which it would be lame, requires that 'know' here is meant to reflect a perspective, Florence's, according to which she factively knows this. The quotation is from Ian McEwan's *On*

A grammatically more complex form that orients us to an agent's point of view is free indirect discourse (FID).[28] If Beatrice, a character in a narrative, says or thinks

1. Tomorrow is Monday and I will still be in this dreadful place,

the narrator may choose to report (1) using FID:

2. Tomorrow was Monday and she would still be in this dreadful place.

To understand what is going on in such a case, note that the semantic values of some expressions depend on context. This is evidently the case with indexicals such as 'I', 'here', and 'now'. Normally these expressions are evaluated relative to the context of utterance; in (1), 'I' refers to Beatrice, because the context of utterance is one in which Beatrice is referring to herself as 'I'. But occasionally, evaluation needs to take place relative to another context, as with 'I am not here now', heard when I call your number and get your answering machine. I understand 'now' to refer to the present time—the time of my call—and not to the time at which you recorded the sentence.[29] Historians will sometimes shift the context of evaluation in ways that encourage us to imagine ourselves at the time and place of the action, as with this from Namier:

Dismal, humiliating failure has turned public opinion, and the House of Commons is resolved to cut losses and abandon the struggle; it is all over; Lord North's government has fallen; and the king is contemplating abdication.[30]

From this imagined perspective, failure is in the past and abdication at most in the future, while the resolve of the House and the King's contemplation are treated as present.

FID exploits this possibility for context-shifting, but shifts the context of evaluation for *some* expressions and not for others. In (2), the context of evaluation for tense and pronoun is shifted to the context of the narrator's utterance, while other indexicals must be evaluated with respect to the

---

Chesil Beach and was the subject of a brief controversy between the author and Natasha Walters, who took it as a general characterization of peace activists as 'hopeless naïfs' (*Guardian*, Mar.–Apr. 2007).

[28] Other terms for this include 'represented thought and speech' (Banfield 1982) and 'narrated monologue' (Cohn 1966).

[29] See Predelli 1998 for discussion of the broader implication of such cases.

[30] Namier 1962. Namier, presumably regarding the technique as an unfamiliar one, began 'Let us place ourselves in March 1782'.

context of Beatrice's utterance or thought. Thus, the use of 'tomorrow' is oriented to Beatrice's point of view, referring as it does to the day after her act of thinking reported in the sentence. But this tomorrow counts as past for the narrator, since the present time is taken to be that of the narrator's later utterance. And 'she' is not oriented to Beatrice's point of view; Beatrice does not refer to herself as 'she'.[31]

FID, I claim, is an efficient device of imitation and hence suitable for generating effects which are expressive of a character's point of view. This is contrary to the widespread opinion among critics who often suppose that the use of FID somehow 'displaces' the narrator.[32] Fortunately, Daniel Gunn has shown how this interpretation fails to make sense of the details of actual literary uses of FID, notably its imitative use in the hands of Jane Austen. In *Emma*, he notes, 'FID is best seen . . . as a kind of narratorial *mimicry*, analogous to the flexible imitations of others' discourse we all practice in informal speech and expository prose' (Gunn 2004: 35).[33]

Is there not a much more obvious and systematic (and hence more effective) form of imitation that narrators have available, namely the direct (word-for-word) reporting of speech (DRS)? It would be hard to claim that FID is valued because it is a powerful imitative/expressive device, if

---

[31] See Doron 1991. A variant of FID wherein pronouns, but not tenses, are evaluated relative to the narrator's context occurs in this passage from M. R. James where the narrator describes a character's despairing reactions. Up to this point the narrator has presented the events of the story as past with respect to his act of narration. But now he says: 'Doctors, he knows, would call him mad, policemen would laugh at him' ('Count Magnus'). Narration may count as FID without displaying all the characteristics mentioned above. In Jane Austen's *Northanger Abbey*, Catherine Moreland's utterance is reported this way: 'Miss Tilney, she was sure, would never put her into such a chamber as he [Henry Tilney] had described! She was not at all afraid' (ii. chap. 5). Here we have the shifting of tense and pronoun we associate with FID, with 'she was sure' replacing 'I am sure'. But there are no other indexicals to exhibit the full resources of FID. Our sense that this is FID comes, I think, from the naturalness of such an imagined extension of the narration as 'Nevertheless she hoped that tomorrow she would see such a chamber'.

[32] Views of this kind fall into two broad classes: those according to which the character's voice competes with and in some cases replaces that of the narrator, and views according to which FID constructions produce an objective, narrator-less discourse. See Gunn 2004 for critical discussion of these views.

[33] As Gunn points out, episodes of narratorial imitation through the use of FID in Jane Austen's *Emma* are matched by Emma's own use of it in relation to various other characters, as with her mimicry of Miss Bates: 'How would he bear to have Miss Bates belonging to him?—To have her haunting the Abbey, and thanking him all day long for his great kindness in marrying Jane?—"So very kind and obliging?—But he always had been such a very kind neighbour!" And then fly off, through half a sentence, to her mother's old petticoat. "Not that it was such a very old petticoat either—for still it would last a great while—and, indeed, she must thankfully say that their petticoats were all very strong" ' (Gunn 2004: 44).

there is a *more* powerful device for doing just this that is easily available at less processing cost than is required by FID; for the auditor of a statement in FID has to ascribe semantic values with respect to two distinct contexts instead of the one required for statements in DRS. But DRS is not a more powerful imitative device than FID. While FID is much less a *replication* of the character's speech/thought than is DRS, it is much more an imitation, at least in cases where DRS occurs in a written and not a spoken context.[34] The reason for this is that, in order to understand something as an imitation, we have to have a strong sense of the presence of the imitator, and the bare repetition, on the page, of a character's words gives us about as weak a sense of narratorial presence as we can get. With FID, on the other hand, we have the sense that it is the narrator speaking, though speaking in a way which is highly constrained by the words, the tone, the style of the character whose speech is represented: there is something theatrical about FID as a mode of reporting which makes it difficult not to think of the speaker as imitating another.[35] When Barkis says 'Barkis is willin' ', I might report this by saying 'Barkis said he is willing', or 'Barkis said "Barkis is willin' " ', neither of which strikes one as particularly imitative of his odd turn of phrase, though the second certainly draws attention to it.[36] If I say 'Barkis was willin' ', I have injected a distinct element of imitation into the report.

However, precise correlations between grammatical forms and degrees of imitative effect are hard to come by. It is sometimes the case that giving us the exact words of a character *does* achieve an imitative effect, when those words are placed in the right context. Towards the end of one of his stories, M. R. James' narrator gives what we may reasonably take to be the exact words spoken by the character, but not by the conventional method of DRS:

People still remembered last year at Belchamp St Paul how a strange gentleman came one evening in August years back; and how the next morning but one he was found dead, and there was an inquest; and the jury that viewed the body

---

[34] See Genette 1980: 169.

[35] Gunn writes: 'the continuing presence [in FID] of the narrator suggested by the third-person references is crucial, since the imitating voice inevitably reinflects and modifies the language it imitates' (Gunn 2004: 36). Genette argues that 'there is no place for imitation in narrative' (Genette 1988: 43). His argument is that narrative is either a description of events or a 'transcription' of speech; this exactly leaves out of account FID, though, as I go on to argue in the text immediately following, even transcription can sometimes count as imitative.   [36] Charles Dickens, *David Copperfield*, chap. 5.

fainted, seven of 'em did, and none of 'em would speak to what they see, and the verdict was visitation of God; and how the people 'as kept the 'ouse moved out that same week, and went away from that part. But they do not, I think, know that any glimmer of light has ever been thrown, or could be thrown, on the mystery.[37]

'Years back' and 'the jury that viewed the body' do not sound quite like the educated narrator we have been in contact with up to this point, and by the time aitches are dropping we realize that the narrator has taken on the persona of an artisan-witness recollecting events in his own community. With the next sentence ('But they do not . . .'), we are back with the educated voice of the narrator. By dropping, for a brief space, into the voice of the witness and thereby making salient the performance that he is engaging in, the narrator manages to emphasize the character's point of view in a way that simply displaying his words, as in DRS, would not achieve. Here, the purpose of the imitation is especially complex. It serves partly to ironize the perspective of the witness: the uneducated speech, compounded by the somewhat conventional emphasis in the exposition of the horrors, raises a slight doubt as to the veracity of the account. At the same time a vivid, eye-witness feel is given to the recounting of events which the narrator himself could not plausibly describe from a first-person perspective. These two effects are in tension with one another, and a very rational thinking through of the issues might result in each reducing the effect of the other. But James can count on our not responding so reflectively.

This example suggests that grammatical categories such as direct quotation, and FID are of limited usefulness in helping us to describe the landscape of narrative voice. Genette has said that 'in free indirect speech, the narrator takes on the speech of the character . . . in immediate speech, the narrator is obliterated and the character substitutes for him' (Genette 1981: 174). In fact, there is no such simple relation between categories of speech and narrative effects. The primary narrative distinction is that between character-focused and non-character-focused narration;

---

[37] 'Count Magnus', *The Collected Ghost Stories of M. R. James* (London: Edward Arnold, 1931), 119. Historians occasionally achieve an imitative effect, in this instance via what is ostensibly a piece of indirect reporting of speech: 'Mrs Venn, whose husband [was] a Trained Band captain . . . sat weeping and wringing her hands in a neighbour's shop. She had it for sure that the House of Commons was surrounded and her husband in danger to be slain' (Wedgewood 1958: 32).

grammatical categories do not track this distinction with any precision. And while ironic narration sometimes serves a character-focusing purpose, it does not regularly align with character-focused narration. In the passage from 'Canon Alberic's Scrap-book' in Section 3, we have character-focused narration with an element of irony; but the ironic presentation of a character's views can be so heavy-handed that it destroys any impression there otherwise might have been of orientation to the character's point of view. In this passage, George Eliot has her foot so hard on the irony pedal that her own point of view thoroughly occludes that of Mrs Glegg:

Mrs Glegg had both a front and a back parlour in her excellent home at St Ogg's, so that she had two points of view from which she could observe the weakness of her fellow beings, and reinforce her thankfulness for her own exceptional strength of mind. From her front windows she could look down the Tofton Road, leading out of St Ogg's, and note the growing tendency to 'gadding about' in the wives of men not retired from business, together with a practice of wearing woven cotton stockings, which opened a dreary prospect for the coming generation.[38]

In narrative, unsurprisingly, context is everything, and devices that promote the cause of character-focused narration in one context or with one degree of emphasis will not always do so where context or emphasis are altered.

7.6. Empathy

Expressive devices, such as FID, which are often used to orient the narration to a character's point of view, may also serve to encourage empathy between the audience and the character. This empathic contact may not amount to sympathy with the character, but it does give us a sense of how things are for that character. As Dorrit Cohn notes of an excoriatingly unsympathetic exercise in FID from Sartre, 'no matter how devastating the picture, the attempted empathy implied in this narrative situation is not entirely canceled, and the story leaves one with a feeling

---

[38] George Eliot, *The Mill on the Floss*, Book I, chap. 12. Monica Fludernick takes an entirely different view of this passage, saying that the narrator 'thoroughly espouses Mrs. Glegg's mind-set and opinion' (Fludernick 1991).

of having understood the type "from within" ' (Cohn 1966: 112). In this somewhat more gentle exercise in empathy through the expression of point of view, Jane Austen gives us a sense of what it is like for Emma to review her responsibility in the disastrous matchmaking she attempted between Harriet and Mr Elton:

How Harriet could ever have had the presumption to raise her thoughts to Mr Knightley!—How she could dare to fancy herself the chosen of such a man till actually assured of it!—But Harriet was less humble, had fewer scruples than formerly.—Her inferiority, whether of mind or situation, seemed little felt.—She had seemed more sensible of Mr Elton's being to stoop in marrying her, than she now seemed of Mr Knightley's—Alas! was not that her own doing, too? Who had been at pains to give Harriet notions of self-consequence but herself?—Who but herself had taught her, that she was to elevate herself if possible, and that her claims were great to a high worldly establishment?—If Harriet, from being humble, were grown vain, it was her doing too.   (*Emma*, vol. iii. chap. 11)

The first thing to note here—taking up again the issue of style—is that we are not required to think of this as a literal transcription, supposing there were such a thing, of Emma's thought processes. What we are given is a 'rational reconstruction' of those thoughts, so formulated that a certain (somewhat unwilling) shift of attention from Harriet's responsibility to Emma's own, is preserved in a way which enables us to feel, with Emma, the force of her own sense of guilt. It is Emma's style of thought that is imitated, and that is enough to make the narration expressive of her point of view.

The empathic effect of character-oriented narration is not always like this. It may happen that an exercise in character-oriented narration, such as the use of FID, has the effect of getting us to empathize, not with the character who is being imitated but with another character who may be the object of that first character's attention. And this has an important consequence: it is not universally true that character-oriented narration raises to salience the point of view of that character; it may have the effect of raising to salience the perspective of the other character, the one we empathize with. Here, Mr Elton proposes to Emma in the carriage:

declaring sentiments which must be already well known, hoping—fearing—adoring—ready to die if she refused him; but flattering himself that his ardent attachment and unequalled love and unexampled passion could not fail of having some effect, and in short, very much resolved on being seriously accepted as soon as possible.

In this passage, Austen exploits the freedom that FID provides in not requiring a merely mechanical transcription of the words uttered. We are certainly to think of the words used in the narration as corresponding (under the transformation wrought by FID) to words used by Mr Elton. But we are not to understand Mr Elton as uttering exactly the translation of this into direct speech. The narrator is giving us a more concentrated version of that speech, a speech where 'hoping', 'fearing', and 'adoring' might have occurred at somewhat different, more widely separated, places than they appear in the narrator's version. This helps to compensate for differences in the situations of Emma and the reader which would otherwise make empathic contact with her more difficult. Emma, after all, is confined in a closed carriage with a not entirely sober suitor and to her Mr Elton's speech would seem a rush of alarming words. The concentration of words provided by the exposition in FID goes some way to providing us with an imaginative surrogate for her situation, while at the same time preserving the contrast between Mr Elton's florid expressions of attachment and the rather business-like ending, suggesting as it does a certain calculation on his part. This sense of calculation is likely to come to us as a result of hearing the words in a certain way—a way we may think of as corresponding roughly to the way they are received by Emma herself—and drawing a conclusion much the same as the one Emma draws. We feel as Emma feels, not as Mr Elton feels.

7.7. Conclusion

Genette was right to insist that a narrator may orient the narration to the point of view of a character. But this distinction and the narratives that illustrate it say nothing in favour of placing narratives narrated by a character alongside narratives narrated in ways that are oriented to that character's point of view. Narrators always narrate from their own point of view; if they narrate according to the point of view of another that is an additional and independent fact about the narration. I have argued that a narrator who narrates according to another's point of view does so by behaving in ways which are expressive of that point of view, and that the means by which a narrator achieves this kind of expression is the imitation of the character's style of speech and thought. I have tried to show how this expressive account helps to make sense of some of the processes by which character-focused narration takes place, and to account for its production of ironic and empathic effects.

8

Irony: A Pretended Point of View

We have seen that narrators who orient their narrations according to the point of view of a character may do so with a degree of irony. Irony is crucial to a proper understanding of narration; this chapter and the next focus on it. This chapter offers a general characterization of what I will call *representational irony*, answers some objections which have been made against this formulation, and illustrates its use in narrative and conversation. The chapter following is a case study in ironic narration, which is not the same thing as the use of irony *in* narration, as we shall see. So as to add yet more complexity, I begin with another kind of irony.

8.1. Ironic Situations

Various kinds of things are called ironic, and we need to distinguish them. Here are some examples of *situational irony*:

Police Barrier:	The police car has crashed through the barrier on which is written 'POLICE: KEEP OUT'
Rust Control:	The anti-rust preparation cannot be used because the container has rusted shut.
Doomed Explorers:	The expedition members would have reached safety had they gone a further half mile; they camped where they did thinking they were much further from their base.

These are situations which involve a contrast between what is permitted or expected or hoped for or believed, and what is really the case. Not any such violation would be declared ironic; if the rust preparation had simply failed to work, that would not be an ironic situation. With *Rust Control* and *Police Barrier* the irony seems to be connected with the tightly knit causal structure of the situation: it is the very thing that the preparation is designed to prevent which prevents the preparation from working; the police end up frustrating their own aim of keeping vehicles beyond the barrier. With *Doomed Explorers* the irony seems connected with both the magnitude of the effect and the thin margin of error; it would seem less like irony if their error had merely made them a day late returning, or if the disaster had come about because they believed the goal to be in entirely the opposite direction. These differences between cases do not immediately suggest a way of bringing them together under a single specification of what it is for a situation to be ironic. I will not give such a specification here; I simply appeal to the intuitive notion.

What I have just given are representations of irony; descriptions of situations which are ironic. But representations of irony are not always ironic representations; none of mine was ironic, nor seemed so, as far as I can see. The irony of narrative point of view is, first of all, a matter of ironic representation. This is generally called verbal irony, but that is a bad name for it. Language is one form of representation, but not the only one and other forms can be ironic. There are ironic pictures, as with Cindy Sherman's *Untitled Film Still #6*, the subject of which is Sherman herself, adopting a ludicrous pose. With pictures, we need to be especially sensitive to the distinction between ironic representation (the picture is ironic) and representation of irony (the picture is of an ironic situation).[1] A picture of a rusty can of rust-prevention material is a picture of an ironic situation, but need not be an ironic picture. *Untitled Film Still #6*, on the other hand, is an ironic representation, but it is not a representation of an ironic situation.[2] To see the basis of these judgements we need a theory of representational irony.

---

[1] An account of the irony in some of Sherman's pictures is given by Biljana Scott, who adopts the Sperber–Wilson echoic theory of irony (Scott 2004). For criticism of the echoic theory, see Currie 2006.

[2] Not, at least, so far as I can see; it would, or might, be a representation of an ironic situation if Sherman had, for instance, been duped into posing as she did. Also, it is worth reporting that opinions vary as to the degree and kind of representational irony present in Sherman's picture; I give it as an example of a picture for which an ironic interpretation—one which accords it status as representational irony rather than as a representation of an ironic situation—is initially plausible and survives at least a first round of argument. I do not claim to have won the prize for best interpretation of this picture. See also below, pp. 152–3.

8.2. Representational Irony

As a place to start, note that only some kinds of representations can be ironic; perhaps it is ironic that last summer was very wet—we spent the whole previous winter saving water in preparation for drought and so neglected our flood defences. In that case the tree trunk's cross section, registering extra growth that summer and hence extra rainfall, represents something ironic. But tree trunks cannot be ironic representations. The only representations that can be ironic are artefactual ones, because irony of representation is a matter of performance; the maker does something in the act of representing that makes the representation ironic. What does the maker have to do? My answer is this: as exploiters of irony we engage in pretence. We pretend to congratulate, approve, admire, and, occasionally, to criticize and deplore.[3] This is as true of authors and narrators who may choose to sustain an ironic tone throughout a whole long work, as it is of casual contributors to a conversation.

If irony is pretence, not all pretending is ironic; I need to say something about the kind of pretence that irony involves. In the process, I will separate the pretence theory from some restrictive assumptions: that irony is essentially communicative, that it is essentially linguistic, that it is essentially critical.

That representational irony is a form of pretence is not universally acknowledged; it is more often explained as a case of saying one thing and meaning its opposite. Cicero says that, with irony, 'what you say is quite other than what you understand', and Quintilian calls it that 'in which something contrary to what is said is to be understood'—a view preserved in the dictionaries of Johnson and Webster.[4] Contemporary formulations

---

[3] For versions of the pretence theory of irony, see e.g. Clark and Gerrig 1984; Walton 1990; Kumon-Nakamura, Glucksberg, and Brown 1995 (for whom pretence is 'pragmatic insincerity'; this would make the echoic theory of Sperber and Wilson a pretence theory); Clark 1996; Recanati 2000, esp. 48. In a very brief discussion, Grice, going back on an earlier view, says that 'to be ironical is, among other things, to pretend' (Grice 1989: 54). Kendall Walton has long argued that pretence plays an important role in many aspects of linguistic and other behaviour. Steve Barker (2004) may be the most extreme advocate of pretence theory for linguistic phenomena; he holds that sentence meanings are not propositions but speech-act types, that compositionality require us to invoke pretence in order to explain how we get complex speech-act types from simple ones.

[4] Quintilian *Institutio Oratorica*, quot. Vlastos 1991: 21. Cicero, *De Oratore*, quot. Vlastos 1991: 28 n. 24. As John Ferrari points out, Vlastos toys briefly with the idea that irony is pretence (see Ferrari 2008: 3).

are similar: irony is 'the conveying of a truth by asserting its opposite'.[5] Reflecting on the irony of Socrates, Gregory Vlastos says that this idea has 'stood the test of time' (Vlastos 1991: 21).

For a theory that has lasted so long, this one explains very little.[6] Questions can be ironic, as with 'have you won the Nobel Prize yet?' What question, contrary in some way to the sense of the words spoken, is being asked? No question is really being asked; the speaker merely pretends to ask whether the conversation partner has won the Nobel Prize yet. It might be argued that questions, or some of them, have presuppositions, and it is the presupposition of the question that is being negated.[7] Perhaps the question presupposes that it is within the realm of possibilities worth discussing that I have won the prize, and that is what is being denied. What mileage is there in denying what everyone knows is false?[8] And take 'you sure know a lot', said to someone who does indeed know a lot but who is uncomfortably keen to impart what he knows; it would be a very feeble comment on his practices to be asserting that, really, he does not know much. Vlastos' own example of Socratic irony:

(1) teach me more gently admirable man, so that I won't run away from your school   (*Gorgias* 489d)

makes no sense if we understand Socrates really to be exhorting Callicles *not* to teach him more gently.[9]

I denied that the ironist who asks whether I have won the Nobel Prize is negating the presupposition that my having won is a live possibility. But the presupposition does play a role in creating the ironic effect. In pretending seriously to ask the question you are pretending to manifest a belief in the presupposition, and that is exactly what suggests a defective—very defective—point of view on your part. Earlier I asked, against the traditionalist, what the point would be of denying that my having won the Nobel Prize is a live possibility, given that every sensible person would deny it also. Turning the point against me, someone will ask what is the point of pretending to believe the presupposition, when everyone knows it is false? The answer is that pretence achieves things that straight-faced

---

[5] Ong 1978: 13. See also Livingston 2005: 149.   [6] Sperber and Wilson 1981.
[7] I am grateful here to Bence Nanay.   [8] See Sperber and Wilson 1995: 240.
[9] For criticism of Vlastos' treatment of Socratic irony, see Nehamas 1998. See also the excellent re-evaluation of Socratic irony from the point of view of the pretence theory in Ferrari 2008.

assertion or denial does not, or does not easily, or does not with the same lightness of effect. Pretending to be someone for whom that absurdity is a live possibility makes vivid—in a small and perhaps amusing way—how defective such a point of view is.[10] The point generalizes way beyond the strictly ironic. Telling you that cruelty is wrong will benefit you little; a vividly staged mimesis of cruelty may be more effective.

Since the traditional view according to which irony is saying one thing and meaning the opposite is badly wrong, its popularity over two millennia is a puzzle. Genoveva Marti suggested a solution: advocates of the traditional view locate irony in a contrast between (as we would now put it) semantic meaning and speaker's meaning. They are wrong; irony is not essentially a matter of saying one thing and meaning another. But, there is a contrast, not hard to confuse with that one, between the kinds of *effects* one intends from one's ironic utterance and the effects one would probably intend if one were speaking seriously. With (1), someone speaking in a serious, non-pretending way would be taken as intending to avoid humiliation at the other's hands by flattering him. In fact, we take Socrates to be intending something like the opposite effect: humiliating Callicles by giving voice, in pretend mode, to a perspective on Callicles' intellectual and rhetorical powers which is absurdly inflated. Perhaps this confusion explains why statements of the traditional theory often slip, unannounced, into what sound very much like versions of the pretence theory. Cicero remarks that Socrates was always 'pretending to need information and professing admiration for the wisdom of his companion'; Quintilian says that Socrates 'assumed the role of an ignorant man lost in wonder at the wisdom of others'. And Vlastos describes Socrates as 'casting himself as a pupil' of Callicles.[11]

Representational irony, as I noted, does not require language, and the pretence theory accommodates that easily enough. With Sherman's *Untitled Film Still #6* we have a picture which seems to invite a certain kind of attention: mildly erotic, perhaps with elements of pathos and

---

[10] See Walton 1990: 222.

[11] See Cicero, *De Oratore*, Book I. xxx; Quintilian, *Institutio Oratorica*, ix. 2. 44–53; Vlastos 1991: 26. There are hints of the pretence theory in other ancient formulations, such as this from the *Rhetoric to Alexander*, once attributed to Aristotle: '*Eironeia* is [a] saying something while pretending not to say it or [b] calling things by contrary names' (quot. Vlastos 1991: 26). [a] seems promising: better, anyway, than [b]. But it is not quite right; the ironist pretends to say something while *not* saying it.

drama thrown in; perhaps the picture was made, therefore, with
the intention that it be seen in this
way. Yet there are indications that
go against this hypothesis. There
is, first of all, the fact that the
picture is of and by Sherman herself. Taking this with facts about
Sherman's own high-profile artistic persona, it becomes unlikely,
to say the least, that the photograph is of the kind its appearance
most immediately suggests; it is
likely instead to constitute some
negative assessment of attempts to
generate or experience this sort
of erotic-pathetic-dramatic interest, and what is recorded by the
photograph itself is merely (part
of) a pretended act of produc-

Fig. 8.1. *Untitled Film Still #6*

ing a picture—indeed, that very picture—for this kind of attention.
None of this can be inferred directly from the photograph itself without
knowledge of external circumstances, but that is true of all legitimate
artistic interpretation.[12] In the light of what we know and may legitimately bring to the picture, it is reasonable for us to join in with the
pretence which we take to underlie the making of the picture, imagining that the shot was organized and taken with the intention that it
be appreciated as a certain kind of erotic photograph. In thus joining
in with the pretence we may vividly understand something about the
limitations of the perspective which would seriously motivate such an
activity.

Does irony at least require some external medium of representation:
words, pictures, or some other trace of representational activity? No;
the activity itself may provide all that is needed. I may stagger back in
mock-horrified distaste when confronted by an austerely elegant Sung vase,

---

[12] On the context-dependence of interpretation, see Walton 1970 and Currie 1993.

ironically expressing my rejection of your ludicrously demanding aesthetic standards.

Sometimes it is said that irony requires an audience, or at least the speaker's belief that there is an audience.[13] Sometimes it is said that ironic communication with an audience must be entirely non-deceptive.[14] Neither claim is true. Tories were very irritated by the irony of Defoe's *Shortest Way with Dissenters* and its argument for the extermination of Methodists. For 'it would not, on first reading, seem impossible that an extreme Tory could argue in this manner' (Booth 1983: 319). The communicative view might be reformulated so as to insist merely that the audience have to be given a fighting chance of getting it. This would not help. We can have irony which the audience is intended not to get; a defeated prisoner may have to keep the irony in his confession to himself. And there can be irony without any audience in fact or according to the speaker's belief. When I go out without my umbrella only to encounter heavy rain, my utterance of 'great' is an ironic comment on failure meant for me alone.

Representational irony is a form of expression.[15] In speaking or picturing or merely acting ironically one expresses, via an act of pretending, an attitude towards something. Expression may be communicative, as when a disgusted facial expression is intended to communicate one's disgust to others. But what is essential to irony is the expression, not the communication. That said, those interested in the role of irony in narrative will not go far wrong by thinking of irony as a communicative device; the author or narrator—or for that matter one character speaking to another character—generally engages in an ironic act for communicative purposes, aiming to express their attitude (often a negative one) concerning someone or something. Because it has a fundamentally expressive purpose, irony often conveys no factual information. Conversational irony is notable for merely recycling what we already know in the service of expression: 'I am looking forward to another day of rain' does not tell you anything about the British summer weather that you did not already know. But irony can serve a serious and sustained project of informing us about things—though

---

[13] See Clark and Gerrig 1984.   [14] Vlastos 1991: 27.
[15] Ironic utterances embed: 'If Albert is going to give us one of his delightful sermons I am leaving.' This raises problems familiar from the debate over expressivism. I cannot deal with these problems here; a good place to start is Blackburn 1984: chap. 6, sect. 2.

I take 'informing' in a broad sense which includes the telling of fictional stories as well as the narration of fact. Here (a case of non-fiction) John Julius Norwich describes the death of the Emperor Julian:

He is said to have been killed by St Mercurius, one of the Christian Army officers whom he had had executed, but whom the Virgin had temporarily resurrected for the purpose—a fact subsequently proved by his contemporary St Basil who, commanded in a dream to visit the martyr's tomb, there found the bloodstained lance.   (Norwich 1988: 98 n.)

Norwich merely pretends to state that St Basil proved that Julian was killed by St Mercurius, thereby expressing a view about the beliefs of Early Christians. But he also manages to give us some precise information about one of those beliefs.

The passage just quoted represents a momentary turn to irony in what is not, overall, an ironic narrative. We shall see that irony in narration can play a role that allows us to speak of the narration itself as ironic in tone. In such cases we have not merely the ironizing of a point of view but an ironic point of view. The next two sections say something about the relations between irony and point of view.

8.3. Points of View

The ironist's pretence often involves saying something absurd or at least rather obviously wrong. But, mere pretence of asserting obvious falsehoods does not amount to irony. As Dan Sperber points out, merely pretending to assert that $2 + 2 = 5$, that the moon is made of cheese, or a host of other 'patently uninformed or injudicious' things, would not count as saying anything ironical (Sperber 1984: 131). We need in addition the idea that the pretence draws attention to something we might call a *target*. Suppose A is known for his relentless uttering of wild falsehoods; seeing A coming towards us I say '$2 + 2 = 5$, the moon is made of green cheese . . . ', carrying on in this manner for some while. This is irony, because its target is A's extreme unreliability. I am pretending to offer confident but unreliable opinions in the service of expressing my doubts about someone who—so we know or believe—actually does offer confident but unreliable opinions.

In saying these things, I am not *merely* pretending to assert them. These things, if really asserted, are such that it would be natural for an onlooker to see them as expressive of a certain point of view, a point of view from which it would be natural and appropriate to say such things. The ironists's pretence is, at bottom, a matter of pretending to have a certain outlook, perspective, or point of view—in this case a very unreliable one indeed. The ironist pretends to have a restricted or otherwise defective view of the world, or some part of it. Socrates pretends to plead with Callicles not to be so rough with him intellectually; in doing so Socrates pretends to see Callicles as someone of fearsome intellect and rhetorical power: a defective point of view if ever there was one. In uttering the words 'Especially when one of those two is such a fanciful, troublesome creature!'[16] Emma Woodhouse pretends to agree with Mr Knightley's (unstated) opinion that she, Emma, is a troublesome creature, and in so doing pretends to adopt a perspective from which she, Emma, is seen as a troublesome creature—a perspective from which Emma thereby disassociates herself.

In many case of irony, the target and the point of view the ironist pretends to have are the same things. In order to draw attention to the defects of a point of view, the ironist will often pretend to have that very point of view, giving us a vivid illustration of how absurd it would be really to have that point of view—as with Socrates' ironic pleas to Callicles. But there are more complicated cases, where the ironist pretends to have one point of view in order to draw attention to the defects in some *other* point of view. When ironizing an unreliable speaker's point of view by saying '2 + 2 = 5' I am adopting a perspective considerably more unreliable than the one I am ironizing. And it can go in the opposite direction. Consider this exchange:

(2) *Mother*:   'Anyone would think I was an ogress, and the companion a martyr.'

Son: 'I think that might be a possible view of the position, Mother.'[17]

Here the son draws attention to the deficiencies of the mother's perspective by pretending to adopt a perspective which is slightly *less* absurd than hers, a

---

[16] Jane Austen, *Emma*, vol. i. chap. 1.
[17] Ivy Compton-Burnett, *Mother and Son* (London: Victor Gollancz, 1955).

perspective which at least acknowledges as a possibility that which from her own perspective is unbelievable. And when, in the face of the downpour, I exclaim, 'What lovely British weather', my target is not someone stupid enough to think that a downpour really is glorious weather; it is (something like) a general tendency to be positive about what is in fact the relentlessly dreary British climate.[18] Are there a priori constraints on the relations between the target point of view and the expressed point of view? I am not sure, but the following is not a bad rule of thumb: the expressed point of view must be relevantly similar to the target. In Compton-Burnett's exchange (2), the son pretends to have a certain perspective on his mother's behaviour—seeing it as possibly open to certain criticism. He pretends to have a way of looking at the world which dimly recognizes certain obligations to others that most of us see very clearly and the mother, apparently, not at all. His pretended perspective resembles hers much as the optical perspective of a very poorly sighted person resembles that of one who is wholly blind.[19]

So what matters is that the ironist's utterance be an indication that he or she is pretending to have a limited or otherwise defective perspective, point of view, or stance F, and in doing so puts us in mind of some perspective, point of view, or stance (which may be identical to F or merely resemble it) which is the target of the ironic comment.[20] Perspectives can be of many kinds, and on just about anything. But irony is, I think, limited by the requirement that it targets perspectives only of a certain kind: those to which we can apply a standard of reasonableness. It would not be irony to pretend to the most literal of limitations of point of view, blindness, even if in doing so I seek to draw attention to the blindness of another. Tendencies to believe or desire in certain ways, or to have certain emotional reactions are fair game, so far as irony is concerned, even in cases where no blame

[18] Ferrari discusses an example somewhat along these lines offered by Clark and Gerrig, who say that the pretence in such a case is the pretence of thinking that appalling weather is fine (Clark and Gerrig 1984: 122). Why, asks Ferrari, would anyone act out the perspective of someone as silly as this? For such a perspective is *so* absurd that no mileage can be got from ridiculing it (Ferrari 2008: 5). My suggestion is that the pretence is indeed the pretence of thinking that appalling weather is fine, but that the target of the ironic pretence is the less obviously absurd tendency to be positive about British weather.

[19] See Sperber and Wilson 1995: 228–9. As this example shows, such resemblance is highly context dependent; in the country of the blind a very poorly sighted person might put us in mind of someone with very good eyesight.

[20] Perhaps it would be more strictly true to say that the target is some person's really having that perspective, or some tendency on the part of a group of persons, or persons in general to have or be attracted to having that perspective.

attaches to the person whose perspective is being singled out. If Martians are less subject to emotional outbursts than we are, they may comment ironically on our failings by pretending to be as emotionally irrational as we are by collective nature, without thereby implying that any of us individually could do better. Perhaps they are wrong, and our style of emotional responding is the more sensible, or is as sensible as theirs, given our differing circumstances. In that case their ironic commentary would lack justification; the important point is that irony represents—and hence may misrepresent—its target as unreasonable in some way, or at least as falling short of some salient standard of reasonableness. Perhaps—returning to an earlier example—Emma is wrong to judge Mr Knightley's opinion of her to be so very mistaken. In that case Mr Knightley is not violating any reasonable norm; he is violating what Emma takes to be a norm of reasonable assessment. To that extent Emma's irony is defective, or would be were it not for the playful tone of her speech which seems to accommodate the possibility that it is she herself who is mistaken. Irony can become very complex.

8.4. Responding to Criticism

With this characterization in mind, we can answer some criticisms of the pretence theory. Imagine that Bill is prone to say of himself

(3) I am a very patient person.

In response to a display of temper from Bill, Judy says, ironically,

(4) Bill is such a patient person.

As Dan Sperber points out (Sperber 1984), Judy cannot be pretending to *be* Bill, since Bill would not say (4). This is no criticism of the pretence theory of irony as I understand it; the theory says that Judy pretends to be adopting a perspective in the service of expressing something about a suitably related perspective: the one occupied by Bill. In pretending to assert (4), Judy makes it plain that she is pretending to occupy a perspective according to which Bill is a patient person, and thereby draws attention to Bill's tendency to think exactly this about himself, though he would express it in other words. Perhaps Bill never actually says things like (3), though we all suspect that he thinks them. No matter—it is the perspective that is the target of Judy's ironic comment, not any particular utterance or formulation. Judy engages in a performance which makes it pretence that she does something—asserting that Bill is a patient person—and which we are thereby encouraged to imagine her doing. But the target of her performance is not any doing of that exact thing by Bill.

Another criticism offered by Sperber requires a bit more background. We need to distinguish between what the ironic pretender does, and what we might call the *pretence-content* of the doing—the part of the act which lies within the scope of the pretence. The pretence-content often corresponds closely to the performance itself. When I say, ironically, 'it is a lovely day', as we are lashed by rain, you are likely to imagine me seriously (and ludicrously) asserting exactly that, though you know that in fact I am not doing any such thing. Sometimes, pretence-content is related in more complex and subtle ways to the nature of the performance itself. This holds quite generally of pretence. A ballet dancer pretends to be a swan; does she pretend to be a dancing swan, a swan in a tutu? No; we are to imagine that she is a swan, but not that she is a dancing swan in a tutu, even though her dancing in a tutu is integral to the actions which constitute pretending to be a swan. Aspects of staging and make-up in theatre are often highly stylized, and we are not always intended to imagine that the character has a facial expression or is clothed in the garments corresponding to the clothing or the expression of the actor on stage.[21] Acts of pretence sometimes require from us a sophisticated imaginative response: one which picks and chooses between elements of the performance, and which sometimes adds further elements which are merely implied by the performance rather than being explicit in it.

Bearing this in mind, we can assess a further criticism due to Sperber. He claims that the pretence theory is inconsistent with there being such a thing as an ironic tone, because an utterance made using an ironic tone is an utterance which 'makes any pretence impossible. There is no audience, real or imaginary, that would fail to perceive the derogatory attitude and hence the ironic intent it conveys' (Sperber 1984: 135). Sperber might as well say that plays can never effectively take place on sets that are manifestly

---

[21] Artists have sometimes advocated a minimalist approach to staging exactly because this encourages the use of imagination in creative ways; see e.g. comments on Jarry in Carroll 1993.

artificial: after all, no audience would fail to realize the artifice of the situation. But the case of staged performance makes it plain that we easily bracket out elements of what we are given in a pretence. Just as a dancer in a tutu can pretend to be a swan without pretending to be a swan in a tutu, so an ironic utterance of P, using an ironic tone of voice, need not constitute a pretence of [seriously uttering P in an ironic tone of voice]. Instead, the ironist pretends, using an ironic tone of voice, [seriously to assert P].[22]

A word, parenthetically, about ironic tone. We may signal our irony with a tone of voice, but that tone is not always needed, even when we want our irony understood. Why is there such an irregular relationship between irony and ironic tone? The ironist pretends to a limited perspective: pretends to be saying or doing something that only someone who failed to see certain facts or values in a lively and sympathetic way would say or do. However, we cannot count on universal agreement about what is a limited perspective, and we do quite often come across people whose perspective really does seem to us to be limited in this way. So the mere fact that your utterance derives from (what seems to me to be) such a perspective is no guarantee that you are speaking ironically. That is why we sometimes need an ironic tone, and dispense with it most often when in the company of people who share, in some detail, our own perspectives and who we think of as sensitive to even subtle shifts of perspective.[23]

Attending to the precise delimitation of pretence-content answers yet another criticism of the pretence theory offered by Sperber. Consider the ironic

(5) Jones, this murderer, this thief, this crook, is indeed an honourable fellow.

Sperber says that there is no speaker who could seriously utter such a blatant contradiction, nor an audience which could assent to it (Sperber 1984: 133). One point to make is that Sperber is encouraging us to consider the wrong question. It is not relevant to ask whether there is such a speaker and such an audience. The relevant question is whether we can *pretend* that there is such a speaker and such an audience. We are able to pretend all sorts of absurd things, and often take delight in doing so; why cannot

---

[22] See Walton's remarks on pretence that is betrayed (Walton 1990: 381).
[23] Grice doubts that there is such a thing as an ironical tone, but regards a tone indicative of negative feeling as mandatory 'at least for the unsophisticated examples' (Grice 1989: 54).

we pretend this? Note also that imagining someone saying or thinking an absurdity is not always as difficult as imagining the absurdity being the case.

That said, there is room here also for the thought that irony weaves in and out of our behaviour in subtle ways. With some of the examples of FID discussed in the previous chapter, irony is an identifiable element within part of a single sentence, the rest of which functions in a non-ironic way. We might hear irony in (5) by splitting it into an ironic part,

(5a) Jones is indeed an honourable fellow,

and a part which provides information in the light of which the serious assertion of (5) would be ludicrous, namely

(5b) Jones is a murderer, a thief, and a crook.[24]

Which account of (5) is right? Do we imagine the serious utterance of an absurdity, namely (5) itself, or do we imagine the utterance of the not-intrinsically absurd (5a), made incongruous by the assumption of (5b) as background knowledge? The answer may depend on precise details of the context, the tone of the utterance, or it might be up to auditors to respond in their own different ways. All we need say is that any theory of irony based on pretence should acknowledge the possibility of very complex and hard-to-regiment relations between the totality of the performance and what constitutes the content of the pretence.

8.5. Pretence of Manner

The idea that irony involves some sort of match-by-resemblance between points of view explains why ironic utterances can take such a variety of forms: there are ironic assertions, questions, orders, and insults, as well as

---

[24] This account of the distinction between what is within the scope of the pretence and what is outside corresponds to the distinction made by Clark and Gerrig between depictive and other aspects of what they call 'demonstration'; they further separate these other aspects into supportive, annotative, and incidental aspects (Clark and Gerrig 1990: 678). Precedent for my approach above can be found in treatments of other linguistic phenomena. One plausible theory of epithets has it that they serve to create a duality of propositions associated with the utterance. Thus, one who says, 'The Dean said he would come to the meeting but the idiot forgot' can be said to have communicated both that (i) the Dean said he would come to the meeting but he forgot, and (ii) the Dean is an idiot; see Corazza 2005.

ironic gestures and facial expressions. Anything that serves to indicate that one is pretending to have a certain point of view will do. There are even ironic pretendings. Suppose Albert is an enthusiastic player of war games. Welcoming guests for lunch, I say:

(6) You must excuse Albert for the moment. He is outside fighting for his life.

In saying this I am not expressing reservations of any kind towards Albert's or anyone's belief that Albert is fighting for his life; no one, including Albert, believes that he is. Rather, my pretend assertion of (6) picks out for consideration Albert's wholeheartedly engrossed—and rather ridiculous—pretending that he is fighting for his life. With (6), I really am pretending to assert that Albert is fighting for his life; But I am also pretending to pretend to assert this *in a very engaged way*; I am pretending that my pretence is an enthusiastic, wholehearted joining in with Albert's own pretence.

Authors of fiction, whose utterances are pretended assertions made in the service of getting us to imagine various things, sometimes involve a similarly complex pretence. In *Persuasion*, Jane Austen introduces Anne Elliot by saying:

(7) [Sir Walter Elliot's] two other children were of very inferior value.

It is immediately apparent that this description does not correspond at all to how Austen expects us to imagine Anne, but rather to how we are to imagine that she and her sister are thought of by Sir Walter Elliot. Austen is pretending to assert things about someone called 'Anne Elliot', but her pretence is not straightforward; we are not to take the words she uses to correspond to how we should imagine Anne. Rather, Austen pretends to be pretending in a straightforward way, when in fact her pretence is ironic, targeted at Sir Walter's defective perspective on his children and their merits. So Austen's pretence is complex. She is pretending, as fiction writers do, to tell us something. In addition, she is pretending that her pretence is straightforward, when in fact it is not.

In these two cases (6 and 7) we have a *pretence of manner*. The speaker pretends to be pretending in a certain way, when in fact he or she is not pretending in that way, though he or she certainly is pretending. That pretence of manner can make for irony opens up the possibility that one can utter an assertoric sentence ironically, and at the same time really be asserting it.[25] Take the following example, put to me by Stephen Barker. You and I have just landed on a flight that touches down both in Melbourne and in Anchorage. Stepping off the plane there are evident signs—the ambient temperature, for example—that we are in Melbourne. Failing to think things through, you ask where we are. I say, in an ironic tone:

(8) Well, we are either in Melbourne or in Anchorage.

Does the pretence theory have to deny that I am asserting (8)? If it did, it might be in trouble; after all, (8) is true, I believe it, and I want to get you to believe it, because your believing it will help you see that we have, given the temperature, to be in Melbourne. But a pretence-based account of the irony in (8) can live with the assumption that I really am asserting (8). All that needs to be observed is that I am doing something *more* than asserting (8). My pretence in uttering (8) need not be the pretence that I am asserting it. I might be genuinely asserting it, yet pretending to have the kind of interest in it we normally have in disjunctions, namely its providing us with the basis for an inference, should further information come in, of the form A or B; not A; so B, and so getting us to a definite conclusion about where we are. I am pretending, in Frank Jackson's terms, that the disjunction is robust with respect to the falsity of each of its disjuncts.[26] My target is your being uncertain about the truth of the first disjunct, when a glance around would tell you that it is true.

These two examples help to resolve a general problem. Let us understand the phrase 'pretend to Φ-in-manner-Ψ' to refer to acts of pretending in which one really does Φ, but in which one pretends to do it in manner Ψ. So, pretending to Φ-in-manner-Ψ is quite distinct from pretending-to-Φ, which involves not really doing Φ. We might initially think of the class of pretendings with the capacity to generate irony as the class of pretendings-to-Φ, and therefore be sceptical of the idea that pretending is itself a potential value of the variable Φ. For what would it be to pretend

[25] That is, asserting P for the same audience as that for which the utterance is intended to count as ironic. Irony and lies may, unproblematically, coexist in the same performance, where one audience is supposed to see the point and another to be deceived. That is how it is with Frank Churchill, whose remark about the dangers of opening windows are meant to be taken seriously by Mr Woodhouse and ironically by Emma. That Frank expects Emma to be complicit in his deception of Mr Woodhouse is a significant indication of his character (see below, Sect. 6).
[26] See Jackson 1987: 22–3.

to pretend? Is that logically possible? If so, is it something that we are psychologically capable of? Answering 'no' to either of these last two questions suggests that pretence cannot be the target of irony. But we should not conclude this, whatever difficulty we may see in the notion of pretending to pretend. For irony can also be generated by the class of pretending-to-Φ-in-manner-Ψ, which does allow pretending to be a potential value of Φ without our having to countenance pretending to pretend.[27]

8.6. Ironic Narration

When Jane Austen tells us that Sir Walter Elliot's two other children were of very inferior value, she is being ironical. She is choosing to narrate in such a way as to imitate the perspective of Sir Walter himself, a perspective from which it would seem perfectly reasonable to say this, or at least to think it, and mean it. She is narrating ironically. But there is a difference between narrating ironically and what I shall call *ironic narration*, something we find in Austen, Meredith, Turgenev, and an array of later authors. Ironic narration will involve narrating ironically, but it will typically involve other things as well. A narrator may adopt, just for a moment, the pretence of another point of view, and do so in an ironical way, intending to highlight the defects of that point of view. This is a case of narrating ironically, but it does not automatically give their narration on overall ironical quality. Here is an example of narrating ironically from *Oliver Twist*, which I would not call an ironic narration. Dickens is speaking of the crowds forming in anticipation of the execution of Fagin:

From early in the evening until nearly midnight, little groups of two and three presented themselves at the lodge-gate, and inquired, with anxious faces, whether any reprieve had been received. These being answered in the negative, communicated the welcome intelligence to clusters in the street.   (*Oliver Twist*, chap. 52)

While 'anxious faces' gives us some reason to think that a reprieve would be welcome to the bystanders, it turns out that the anxiety is in fact in

---

[27] Compare this with the argument that, while Frankfurt's willing addict is not responsible for her drug taking, she is responsible for taking it willingly (see Fara 2008: 858–9).

the other direction.[28] Dickens is not pretending to share the point of view of those for whom news of a reprieve would be unwelcome because it would deprive them of a spectacle; he is pretending to have a perspective which treats the fact that many people prefer spectacles to reprieves as if it were entirely unremarkable—a preference merely to be noted rather than complained against. Here is one of those places where the point of view the speaker pretends to have is not the one which is the target of irony, but it is closely enough related to it to show us in what direction the target lies.

With this, and in many other places in the same novel, Dickens is using irony. But—and this is a matter of degree rather than of placement firmly on one side of a boundary—I hesitate to call his narrative style ironic. His use of irony is strategic, and deployed in the service of sharply illuminated moral principles which do not come close to being the targets of his irony. Besides, it is so easy to be ironic at his expense. To have something that is unambiguously an ironic narration we may need more than an accumulation of instances of representational irony. Ironic narration is narration from an ironic point of view, and mere use of irony as a device is not always a sign that such a point of view is in play; irony is used, sometimes, by un-ironic people. We are looking, rather, for narration which expresses a sustained, natural tendency to value, celebrate, and enact the suit of devices constitutive of irony, as well as those closely related to it. Recall the primary features of representational irony: it is a form of pretence which targets the defects in points of view, generally without any assertion of a contrary stance. Ironic narration is thus marked, as well as by the use of irony itself, by a general tendency to playfulness of expression, and avoidance of manifest commitment to theories or principles. We will see an example of narration which embodies these features in the next chapter. With an ironic narrator like Austen we find all these things, together with a narration frequently oriented to the point of view of a character, where the effect is to make vivid the defects of that character's point of view. The most sympathetically treated characters are not immune. In *Mansfield Park*, the narration orients ironically to Fanny Price's way of reflecting—a defective one, given all she has been through—on the comparison between Portsmouth and Mansfield Park: 'At Mansfield, no sounds of contention,

---

[28] See Sperber and Wilson 1995: 242 on irony and 'garden-path' utterances.

no raised voice, no abrupt bursts, no tread of violence, was ever heard; all proceeded in a regular course of cheerful orderliness; everybody had their due importance; everybody's feelings were consulted.'[29] And, when narrator's irony would be unseemly, Austen illustrates the value of an ironic turn of mind by putting it in the mouths of characters seen at their most meritorious, as with Elizabeth Bennet's comment on her own (real, warranted) happiness: 'I am the happiest creature in the world. Perhaps other people have said so before, but not one with such justice.'[30] The closeness in understanding between Emma and Mr Knightley, even at moments of disagreement, is indicated by the irony of their exchanges.[31] And irony requires the capacity to engage imaginatively with another's point of view even though one may think it defective; lack of this capacity is a frequent feature of those characters whose faults, great and small, arise from thinking everyone must see the world as they do.[32]

The next chapter, a study of how use of the elements of representational irony goes to create an ironic narration, will take us far from the world of Jane Austen.

[29] Jane Austen, *Mansfield Park*, vol. iii. chap. 8. Emma Woodhouse is a natural target for this kind of ironic orientation to point of view, and Austen makes full use of her right to the end, as with 'What had she to wish for? Nothing, but to grow more worthy of him, whose intentions and judgement had been ever so superior to her own. Nothing, but that the lessons of her past folly might teach her humility and circumspection in future' (*Emma*, vol. iii. chap. 18).

[30] *Pride and Prejudice*, vol. iii. chap. 38. See also Henry Tilney's remarks on reading *Udolpho* (*Northanger Abbey*, vol. i. chap. 14).

[31] *Emma*; see especially the exchange at the beginning of vol. i. chap. 12; see also above, this chapter, text to n. 16, and n. 25. Ironic behaviour sometimes obscures the ill nature of a character: see William Elliot's ironical remarks on Anne Elliot's insistence that she knows little Italian (*Persuasion*, chap. 20).

[32] With Catherine Morland, the lack results merely in a tendency to attribute overly creditable motives: 'With you, it is not, How is such a one likely to be influenced? . . . but, How should *I* be influenced, what would be *my* inducement in acting so and so?' (*Northanger Abbey*, vol. ii. chap. 1). While Austen makes play with the idea in trivial ways ('His [Mr Woodhouse's] own stomach could bear nothing rich, and he could never believe other people to be different from himself' (*Emma*, vol. i. chap. 2)), she clearly regarded breadth of imaginative understanding as crucial to virtuous conduct. It is notably possessed by Elinor Dashwood (see Stohr 2006 for discussion).

9

Dis-interpretation

This chapter deploys some of the ideas that have gone before: character-focused narration, ironic narration, and the distinction between the internal and external perspectives. The example chosen—Hitchcock's *The Birds* (1963)—will expand our discussion of the media where ironic expression is available to a narrative-maker; film has not yet had the attention it deserves, and I also consider the contribution of sound. I hope the discussion will do more than merely illustrate general points; if it goes well, it will contribute to a better understanding of that film's narrative style and genre. That will require a glance at things beyond the theoretical framework so far established.

My first item from *The Birds* is a piece of representational irony—a comparatively rare phenomenon in film. From there I will draw back to get a larger view, and draw attention to things in the film which, while they do not count as instances of irony proper, as I, perhaps rather narrowly, define it, are related to irony in ways that make the whole system of features count as one way of creating a narratorial point of view which does not merely use representational irony; through its imaginative recombination of the elements of irony, it displays what we might call an ironic sensibility. This will suggest that we ought to be wary of some of the ambitiously psychological readings to which the film has been subject. Interpreting *The Birds* has largely been a contest to see who can find the most meaning in it—or project the most meaning onto it.[1] My aim is not to add another layer of meaning. I hope to find less, much less, meaning in *The Birds* than anyone has found before. I make a suggestion about how, in the light of all this, we should reframe our understanding of some of Hitchcock's work. I comment, finally, on one aspect of the relations between fictions

---

[1] See e.g. Paglia 1998.

of the super- (or at least contra-) natural and those which retain an at least faux-scientific background.

9.1. Irony in Pictures

Before attending to the details of the film, I need to say something about representational irony in a pictorial medium, which cinema at least partly is; irony is more difficult to manage in a pictorial medium than in a linguistic one, and our judgements about what is and what is not an ironic narration in film must be keyed to standards different from those that prevail in literature. The depictive nature of cinematic representation means that a range of subtle representational modulations that are important for ironic effect are not available in cinema; it also makes it difficult to embody in the work itself a level of commentary on the events of the story, except by means of devices which are generally too heavy-handed to implement irony in an effective way. Here is an example a little like an earlier one from *Oliver Twist*; it is from *Middlemarch*: 'Mrs Bulstrode had a long-standing intimacy with Mrs Plymdale. They had nearly the same preferences in silks, patterns for underclothing, china-ware, and clergymen.'[2] Here we have the representation of situational irony: Mrs Bulstrode and Mrs Plymdale fail to live up to their professed values by (it is implied) speaking and thinking as often about patterns for underclothing as about clergymen. But there is also ironic representation; by excluding all commentary, the narrator manifests a pretence of narrating from a perspective which sees nothing wrong in treating preferences in underclothes and in clergymen roughly on a par. Eliot refrains from suggesting that there is anything deplorable in this attitude, or indeed anything at all in it worth remarking on; she merely notes that the comparable degree of attention these matters get. But Eliot has gone to the trouble of setting up her description so as to contrast underclothes and clergymen, and the effect of that is very salient. There is likely to be a reason for this construction, and that reason is likely to be that she wants us to understand the sensibilities of Mrs Bulstrode and Mrs Plymdale as deficient; by not commenting, she merely pretends to have a perspective

---

[2] George Eliot, *Middlemarch*, chap. 31.

which is blind to these deficiencies, thereby making vivid the shortcomings of that perspective.

An effect of comparable subtlety is hard to achieve in cinema. A little episode might be interpolated, with the two ladies turning from underclothes to clergymen in their conversation. But it is difficult to see what would be ironic about this qua representation; it seems better described as a straightforward representation of a situation which is deplorable, perhaps amusingly so, and one which is, perhaps, a situational irony—given the elasticity of that term it would be hard to disallow that description absolutely. It would not, I think, count as a representational irony. The lack of explicit commentary in Eliot's description is the key to the irony in her remarks on conversational topics, because it is easy to combine description and commentary in language, and so the absence of commentary is salient. But explicit commentary is simply not possible in film without resorting to essentially non-cinematic means like voice-over, and so one does not in this case notice the absence of commentary. When it is easy to interpolate commentary, one may easily make a point by refraining from commentary; where commentary is difficult or impossible, no such effect can be achieved.

In general, it is much more difficult for a film-maker to achieve something that will be understood as 'pretending to have a point of view' than it is for a writer. But this sort of pretence is central to ironic effect. So in the cinematic case, we have to look for those rare, sometimes ambiguous indications that representational irony is in play—though in film representation of ironic situations is frequent and unremarkable. It is against the background of this limited palette that we should judge the extent to which a film achieves an ironic tone.

9.2. Point of View Shots

Representational irony, I have said, need not involve language: I can express my contempt for a certain kind of movie by saying—while we are watching it—'What a great movie'; Or I might sit watching a movie of this kind and pull exaggeratedly emotional faces, manifestly pretending to be overwhelmed by the film's power. I can do it also by making a movie, and doing certain things in the making of that movie which will—like the ironical remark 'What a great movie!'—be acts of manifest pretending that a certain kind of moviemaking is valuable. I might even contrive, as a film-maker, to have a character who is watching events unfold, adopt the kind of exaggerated expression I just now mentioned in connection with the ironical viewer.

In *The Birds*, we have a great many point of view shots associated with Melanie Daniels, a San Francisco socialite whose arrival in Bodega Bay coincides with the beginning of the bird attacks. Several of these shots occur at a point where people sheltering in a restaurant watch in horror as petrol is accidentally ignited by a match during a bird attack; a man is killed in the explosion. The fire then moves along the stream of petrol, causing further destruction. As it moves, we are given a series of pairs of shots: one is of the progress of the flames, the other of Melanie's face as she watches.[3] Her face in these shots is both static and composed into an oddly exaggerated expression, each of the four images being a variation on the same artificial expression of shock. Often the function of reaction shots is to engage the viewer's emotions. These shots of Melanie's so *un*expressive face—a parody of emotion—are unlikely to contribute to making the viewer more involved with the scenes of mayhem than they would otherwise be. Why are these shots given to us? My claim is that these shots, by recording a face which fails, spectacularly, to pass the test of emotional verisimilitude, are an expression of the film-maker's ironic attitude to the project. The expression may signal, to someone who notices and reflects, that the standpoint of one who is thoroughly taken over by these events is here being ironized. These shots pretend to derive from an outlook which takes seriously the business of making a frightening movie, intending to instil in the audience an appropriate reaction of fear—but which, in reality, expresses an awareness of the deficiencies, or at least the limitations, of that outlook and purpose. They constitute a glimpse of a template the maker—Hitchcock—offers to the irony-sensitive viewer: this is a way you might, occasionally, want to view this film. Or, perhaps, this is a way of viewing you might want to bear in mind while viewing it.

---

[3] We do not see the blazing petrol from Melanie's point of view, but from closer and from lower down, so one might quarrel with the claim that these are PoV shots, though the speed of cutting makes this far from obvious. Deviation from what is strictly the protagonist's point of view is probably due to the fact that the moving flames look more impressive from a vantage point closer than Melanie's own would afford. Anyhow, I am content to treat them as PoV shots.

9.3. Ironic Narration

I do not claim that this episode—admittedly rather isolated within the larger context of the film's narration—takes us very far in understanding *The Birds*. I suggest it as the starting-point for an interpretive enterprise which spreads out conceptually from the sort of irony I have identified, to take in a variety of tropes of narration which are closely related to irony. Before I illustrate their appearance in the film, let me list the features I have in mind and their relations to irony.

First of all, irony is, I have said, a form of pretence, a form which substitutes a pretended assertion for a real one. So we might expect to see elsewhere in the narrative a foregrounding of ideas of play, pretending, and the unreal substituted for the real. Second, irony in narration, where it is expressive of some attitude towards the narration itself, draws attention to the act of narrative-making and hence to the boundary between story world and the real world within which the story world is embedded, something generally kept recessive in classical film-making. Third, irony, as a form of expressive pretence which avoids the direct representation of a claim or assertion, which is a way of avoiding *saying* anything, is naturally associated with a lack of earnestness, conviction, explanatory principles or theories, and overt didactic purpose. Let us see how these irony-related features are deployed in the film.

There is, first of all, the early establishment of the related themes of pretence and artifice. In the first scene we have Mitch pretending, within the highly artificial surroundings of a shop full of caged birds, to think that Melanie is a shop assistant, and Melanie pretending to be one; later, Melanie offers Mitch the wholly unbelievable pretence that she is in Bodega Bay to see Annie, an old girlfriend of Mitch. In between these incidents we have a shot of obviously artificial caged lovebirds leaning, absurdly, into the direction of turn in Melanie's car as she drives to Bodega Bay. The shot does nothing to advance the narrative and might be read as a proleptic comment on the sometimes unreal-looking effects served up during later scenes of bird attacks—a mechanical-looking seagull that pecks rhythmically at a fallen child during the birthday-party scene, or a child running with an obviously fake bird attached. In the context of the film's more dramatic scenes the artifice might be overlooked: the leaning birds in the car, observed at an entirely undramatic moment, prime us for these later defects. As if to underline this, the first bird attack—a single gull swoops at Melanie—is prefaced by an odd mirroring of this earlier movement; a full face shot in which Melanie's head leans leftwards, adopting another artificial and this time oddly bird-like pose of expectation.

Perhaps the most notable piece of artifice in the film is the use of sound; this, I will argue, functions partly to emphasize the activity of the narrative-maker by making us uncertain about where the boundary between the film world and the world of making lies.[4] Thus, the use of sound illustrates my second point about the unusual emphasis on the narrative-maker's intrusion into the world of the story. There is no score for *The Birds*, though long-time Hitchcock collaborator Bernard Hermann acted as a 'sound consultant' on the film. We have instead a series of electronically created noises, first heard during the credits and then during bird attacks and occasionally at other moments. These sounds, intended to invoke both the ideas of bird calls and flapping wings, are certainly bird-like (and are indeed mixed with genuine bird noises) but are not the sounds of real birds, possessing a disconcertingly hollow and mechanical tone.[5] The artificiality of the bird sounds is emphasized right at the start of the film during the credits sequence. The credits appear superimposed on starkly black and white images of birds in flight; at first the birds are moving uniformly to the right but later they come in from both directions. Notably, the bird sounds here are not associated with particular birds; we simply have a mass of birds and a mass of bird-like sound, and the two are not connected in any systematic way. Thus, the sound, no longer a way of tracking individual objects, becomes an object of attention for its own sake, giving further salience to its unusual qualities.

These sounds serve to make salient the artifice of the project in somewhat the way that a particularly mannered style of acting or a particularly unrealistic choice of stage set would do in the theatre. They also make salient the distinction between the internal and external perspectives, because the quality of the sound makes it unclear where the boundary lies. It is notable that the peculiarity of this sound does not seem to make any

---

[4] For a good introduction to the use of sound in *The Birds*, see Weis 1978.

[5] It has been suggested that the idea of seeing-in, thought to be explanatory of depiction, can be generalized across modalities to include hearing-in. Perhaps one hears birds in the mechanical sounds that go with the film.

impression on the world of the story: no one in the film seems to notice it, and certainly no one comments on the quality of the sounds, though other deviations of behaviour, like the chickens at the Brenner house being off their feed, are discussed at great length, and the lady ornithologist, whose opinions we shall hear again, would surely have detected even slight variations in bird tone. While it is to be understood that the birds make sounds which are heard by the characters, their odd quality seems to lie on our side of the divide between audience and film world. We may as a consequence feel less than usually confident about the placement of the boundary between what is happening in the story, and the activity that goes into creating the cinematic representations which make that story available to us.[6]

I said that ironic narration generally goes with a distancing from explanatory principles and didactic purpose. Earlier portrayals in film of humanity under threat such as *The Beast from 20,000 Fathoms* (Lourié, 1953) and *Them* (Douglas, 1954) tended to settle on didactically focused themes such as the threat from nuclear testing; more recent films in which humans are overwhelmed by various species have suggested, as a kind of underlying metaphysics, that the explanation for their events is a rectification of moral imbalance, itself the result of human beings' thoughtless and excessive exploitation of nature. In *The Birds*, such gestures at moral issues are relentlessly lampooned, first with the drunken-Irishman-from-Central-Casting's repeated and formulaic pronouncement that 'it's the end of the world'. Soon after, we have the conveniently dropped match which, during the filling station incident, puts paid to the curmudgeonly man who moments previously in the restaurant had been urging people to 'wipe them

---

[6] Hitchcock's use of sound in *The Birds* has interesting relations to a well-known scene in Tournier's *Cat People* (1942) where Alice (Jane Randolph) is walking a dark street, followed, presumably, by Irena (Simon Simone), who, we are led to believe, may change at any moment into a predatory panther. At the climax of the scene, when it seems most likely Alice will be attacked, we hear a loud and threatening hiss—which turns out to be the air-brakes of a bus stopping. In both these cases, we have film sound which aims to reproduce something like the sound of a given animal—a big cat, a bird—but where the sound is not quite verisimilar with its target, deliberately so. In the case of *Cat People*, we have been primed for big-cat noises and when we get the sound of the air-brakes of the bus stopping, we are momentarily confused into thinking that it is, in fact, the sound of a big cat; that it is, more exactly, such a sound within the world of the story. The sound is not quite like that of a big cat, not to us and not for the character who hears it, though Alice, primed as we are by big-cat thoughts, is as much taken in by the sound as we are at first. So the case of *Cat People* differs from the case of *The Birds* in this: that the mechanical quality of the sound penetrates into the world of *Cat People*; we can assume that the sound heard by Alice is qualitatively the same as the sound heard by us.

[the birds] off the face of the Earth'—a very cursory nod in the direction of nature's retributive power. The lady ornithologist in the restaurant who challenges Melanie's account of the attack begins a disquisition which will, it seems, take us down the exploitation-of-nature route according to which birds 'bring beauty into the world, whereas it is mankind who—'. At this point she is interrupted by a waitress calling a dinner order of 'three fried chicken': a surrogate authorial intervention expressing impatience with this windy way of thinking.[7] While people wonder throughout at the bird attacks, with emphasis (ornithologist again) on the scientific impossibility of avian planning or inter-species flocking, no explanation, scientific or otherwise, is elaborated at any point; as the radio broadcast moments from the end puts it: 'the reason for this does not seem clear as yet.' A scene between Melanie and Mitch on the morning after the first attack on the Brenner house during which they half-jokingly elaborate a theory of bird uprising against humanity was discarded. Indeed, the film is careful to leave it entirely unclear as to the extent of the bird attacks; the radio report describes events only in Sonoma County and a proposed final shot of the Golden Gate Bridge covered in birds was not filmed.[8] That there is no rationality, however malevolent or deranged, on the birds' part is shown by the fact that Mitch and the others are able to escape through a great mass of birds, now in a quiet phase between attacks, just as people might take advantage of a lull in a storm.[9] Contrasting with the film's theoretical and explanatory minimalism is its emphasis on particularity, as with Mitch's slow walk through the mass of birds just noted, but visible also in thematically irrelevant scenes such as the one inside the Bodega Bay Store/Post Office, with its distractingly massed stock of objects in brilliant blue and red.

One other thing makes for a sense of ironic narration in *The Birds*. Earlier I distinguished ironic representation from the representation of

---

[7] See O'Donnell 2006 for a useful analysis of this scene, though I am not attracted to his conclusion that *The Birds* 'portrays the formation of modern subjectivity as an attack on subjectivity, or more precisely, subjectivity under attack from itself' (O'Donnell 2006: 58). Evan Hunter, the scriptwriter, reports that while he and Hitchcock agreed that no explanation of the bird's behaviour should be offered, a scene should be included wherein characters wonder about the reasons for the attack—hence the discussion in the restaurant.

[8] A final scene of devastation as they drive through Bodega Bay after leaving the Brenner house was scripted and storyboarded, but also not filmed. Evidence of this sort—evidence of refraining from doing something, or from including it in the finished work once done—is discussed by Livingstone (2003), who focuses on *pentimenti*.

[9] In this much, at least, I am in agreement with Robin Wood, according to whom 'the birds . . . are a concrete embodiment of the arbitrary and unpredictable' (Wood 1989: 154).

irony; a picture or description of a situation may depict or describe it as ironic, without thereby being an example of representational irony—it may instead be a 'straight' description or depiction of the situation, but one which makes its situational irony evident. But, for all the distinctness of situational and representational irony, a tendency on the part of a narrator to describe situations in ways which make their irony evident seems to me a further indication of a narrative point of view which is itself ironic, exhibiting its ironic nature in this case by its manifest sensitivity to the irony of situations. This is all the more evident in fictional cases, where the narrative does not merely pick out the irony in a situation, but rather creates a situation which, we can often assume, was constructed so as to emphasize its irony.[10] And, with *The Birds* there is a basic and manifest irony in the plot: that Melanie Daniels, wild city girl, travels to Bodega Bay, apparently the quiet weekend retreat of San Francisco lawyer Mitch Brenner, with the purpose of delivering a pair of harmless lovebirds, only to find herself trapped in a bird-induced nightmare of destruction.[11] Here the representation of situational irony makes an *independent* contribution to a sense of ironic narration: a contribution independent of the extent to which that representation is expressively ironic.

9.4. The Birds and the Psyche: Internal vs External Perspective

The minimalism I have so far sought to identify in *The Birds* is explanatory minimalism. It is consistent with the acceptance of this idea that the film is highly contentful in other ways—psychological ways, for example. Interpretations of *The Birds* have, by and large, focused on exactly this sort of content, with many arguing that, while the causal role of the birds themselves in the film is unclear and perhaps unimportant, their symbolic role as indicators of psychical processes is highly significant. Explanations of

[10] To avoid yet more complication, I assume here that the irony of a situation is a feature of the situation itself and not an artefact of its representation. For a questioning of this assumption, see my (forthcoming).

[11] The love birds do remain harmless; indeed the characters take them with them in the car when they eventually depart the Brenner Farm at the end of the film.

this kind typically claim that the birds and their behaviour are symbolically related to the characters and events of the human world, serving thereby to illuminate psychical aspects of those characters and events. The result has been a large number of readings deriving from psychoanalysis or from other psychodynamic perspectives which have taken up the themes of female transgression, loss and anxiety, the gaze, sight and sightlessness, and other interpretive usual suspects.

These projects depend on taking what I will call the external perspective. Within the world of the story, the birds are not symbols for anything, and if they were—suppose it were part of the story that the inhabitants of Bodega Bay treated birds as religious symbols—that would not make them symbols in the sense relevant here. To say that the birds symbolize, say, Lydia's anxiety is to say that the birds bear an external relation to Lydia and her anxiety—a relation not accounted for by looking at what goes on in the story itself, but which is explained only in terms of meanings imposed on the birds from without. Thus, the film's foregrounding of the external perspective through its use of sound may be thought of as adding interpretive weight to the idea that the birds are, indeed, symbolic. One might also claim that a symbolic role for the birds is supported by the placement of incidents within the film which suggest exactly such an intention: Lydia's heavily emphasized hostility, the discussion between Mitch and Melanie at the children's party of the value of 'a mother's love', Lydia's final cradling of Melanie in the car, and a number of other scarcely resistible temptations to psychodynamic extravagance. Indeed, the basic irony of the plot—described a moment ago—makes this more appealing; a carefully constructed irony of plot ought to be a pointer, ought it not, to some deeper meaning?

I am not persuaded. I claim that the film's minimalism is not merely explanatory minimalism; it is minimalism at the level of interpretive significance. The birds have no meaning; they are only causes. The placement of indicators of psychodynamic significance—certainly deliberate—are better explained as more of the pretence exemplified in the petrol fire shots; a pretence that now encompasses a making as if to explore deep psychological themes. I grant that the web of relationships between the characters does play an at least modest role in achieving the film's artistic and entertainment goals. It helps sustain a story of human interaction that parallels the inexplicable avian attacks and gives a kind of groundedness and continuity to the narrative which would otherwise be a disconnected sequence of violent events. While, as is sometimes the case with Hitchcock, the characters are not especially rounded, sympathetic, or empathy-inducing, we need to experience the threat posed by the birds as one which disrupts, and may terminate, a set of human relations which have to be established quickly.[12] In such a situation, strong psychological markers are required, and psychoanalytically resonant themes will come easily to the film-maker, especially to this one. But it needs some special justification to convince us that these relationships are worth elaborating by reference to a symbolic or other non-causal role for the birds themselves. That special justification has not, so far as I know, been given. Standard practice has been merely to assert some symbolic role for the birds; but it is not sufficient simply to announce that the birds 'are the incarnation of a fundamental disorder in family relationships' or that 'the bird attacks function primarily as an extension of Lydia's hysterical fear of losing her son, Mitch'—statements often made as if it were obvious what value they add to our understanding of the film.[13]

I am puzzled by the idea that we have made interpretive progress when we have said that this thing is a symbol for that thing. But let me make a friendly suggestion about how symbol-hunting might, in certain circumstances, play a role in an activity which helps us understand or appreciate a film better. In my story this depends on the exploitation of two kinds of relationships. The first is an expressive relationship to which psychodynamic theories typically appeal when explaining aberrant or otherwise apparently irrational behaviour. The strategy is to say that the behaviour is expressive of some hidden, perhaps unacknowledged desire or psychological tension; thus, jealousy can be productive of behaviour

[12] The lack of sympathetic portrayal in *The Birds* contrasts markedly with that other treatment by Hitchcock of family dynamics (also, incidentally, in Sonoma county), *Shadow of a Doubt* (1943).

[13] Respectively, Zizek 1992: 99 and Horwitz 1986: 279. Having described the birds as an 'extension', Horwitz goes on to call them an 'expression of Lydia's jealousy' (p. 280). It is not clear whether any distinction between these two relationships is intended. Richard Allen has recently given a new twist to the psychodynamics of *The Birds*, invoking a less-familiar psychological authority, Harry Guntrip, whose version of object relations psychology Allen thinks might have had some influence on Evan Hunter, the scriptwriter. This theory emphasizes the desire for close relations with others rather than specifically sexual desires. Thus, 'the birds represent the defensive rage that issues from a sense of emotional isolation and abandonment'. They epitomize the 'dehumanized and unresponsive other that the humans in the film threaten to become on account of their sense of emotional isolation' (Allen 2002: 288).

which, while it does not constitute a rational response to the jealous person's situation, is explicable by reference to the jealous state—take Freud's own example of the child whose throwing out of the crockery is expressive of his desire to get rid of his baby brother.[14] Here there is supposed to be a causal, indeed psychologically causal, connection between the state and the behaviour, and one which, in some sense, makes the behaviour understandable as a response to the jealousy, without straightforwardly rationalizing it. In understanding this kind of connection, the subject herself may be able to intervene to change the behaviour; the connection is not supposed to be a brute causal one that one would seek to alter only by means of drugs or a surgical operation.

In this way, a psychological theory is put to work to extract from some piece of behaviour, perhaps verbal behaviour, an underlying need or desire of which the behaviour is then seen to be expressive, as Lydia's behaviour in *The Birds* is said to be expressive of her fear of Melanie and the potential she has to disrupt the family's relationships; this is the exploitation of the first kind of relationship. Then—this is the more tricky part—some association is found between the state of which this behaviour is expressive and the activities of agents—in this case the birds—which are said, variously, to 'epitomize', 'express', 'represent', or 'be the incarnation of' that state. But here the behaviour of the birds is supposed to be expressive of the state itself, in a way rather different from that in which the behaviour of the subject is expressive of it. While the behaviour of the subject can be thought of as *symptomatic* of the state, as Lydia's hostility is symptomatic of—that is, caused by—her jealousy and insecurity, the behaviour of the birds is more like a *causal analogue* of the state, in that the behaviour of the birds can be thought of as having a causal structure which in some relevant way—and of course only partially—parallels and reveals that of the state itself.[15] So, while it is true that one can learn something about the state from both sets of behaviours, what one learns is different as between the two cases. In the case of the subject's (Lydia's) behaviour, one learns from it, via whatever interpretive methods are sanctioned by the psychological theory in question, that the subject is in that state. In the case of the birds, one learns, from observing the causal

---

[14] Strachey 1953–75: xvii. 146–56.

[15] Again there is here a contrast between *The Birds* and *Cat People*, in which the panther is symptomatic of (as well, perhaps, as being a metaphorical representation of) Irena's state of mind.

structure of their behaviour, something about the causal structure of the psychological state.

We can take this a bit further. The behaviour of the birds might also be thought of as providing information, by way of metaphorical association, about the *phenomenology* of the state concerned: what it is like to be in that state, or what it is like to be in contact with someone who is in that state. It is difficult in any particular case to know which of these two options—causal structure and phenomenal structure—applies most aptly, and in some cases both sorts of information might be extracted. In the case we are considering, it would be legitimate to inquire whether both or either sorts of information could be extracted.

This way of understanding the idea of symbolic relations depends upon the dynamic character of narrative, and would be hard to implement within the static medium of, say, painting. While some paintings have an undeniably narrative element, the capacity of single depictive works to represent the details of causal interactions spread out in time is severely limited. The current proposal, if it works at all, will work for media rich in the capacity for the representation of the spatio-temporal particularity characteristic of narrative. Film is certainly one of these media, and that may partly explain the popularity of psychodynamic interpretative methods in film studies.[16]

How might this general characterization apply to the particular case of *The Birds*? In the scene at the Brenner home where Mitch, Melanie, Lydia, and Cathy sit anxiously expecting an attack from the birds, the house is suddenly invaded by a flock of small birds which have come down the chimney. General confusion ensues during which Mitch takes the lead in trying to get rid of the birds while Melanie hustles Lydia and Cathy outside into what seems, paradoxically, a safer environment. Here it is not unreasonable to wonder whether the frenzied, though in this case not particularly harmful, bird invasion gives us something to illuminate the psychical tensions implicit within the group. Similar relations may be explored in the case of the more dangerous attack on Melanie the next

---

[16] While psychodynamic accounts of *The Birds* do not put things this way, some at least seem to imply that there is much to be gained from exploring causal parallels between emotional states and bird attacks; see Smith 2000: 139: 'The images of Melanie moving along the wall in circling movements and of her curled up on the sofa "recoiling from nothing at all" heighten [the] sense of her being under attack from her own emotions rather than any external force.'

evening in the upstairs room, which might be thought to represent some projection of Lydia's ill-will towards her.

What should we think of this critical/interpretive project? While this approach is not one which it would be sensible to rule out a priori, it does seem to me that there is little value accruing from it in the particular case in hand. Once we have said that the two sets of tensions in the film—the interpersonal tensions and those created by the threat from the birds—have a generally mutually reinforcing effect on the attentional and emotional states of the audience, there is very little of interest to be said about detailed parallels between them. In particular, there is little to be learned about the causal structure of the emotional tensions among the characters from the causal structure of the birds' attacks. While it may sound promising to suggest that the birds 'symbolize' various psychical forces, any attempt to specify what might actually be learned from this falters at the first step. The behaviour of the birds, while apparently coordinated at the macro level, does not have a complex and systematic structure, elements of which or relationships within which could be seen as correlates for aspects of the relationships between the human characters; the scene of the sparrow attack at the Brenner house, which certainly occurs at a moment of significant tension between the characters, is especially chaotic, with the birds flying around in no coordinated pattern, doing nothing in particular. Nor can the birds' behaviour provide insight into the intra-psychical processes we are to understand Lydia and the other characters as undergoing. Attempts to see the causal processes here are revelatory of the causal processes connecting the psychic states of several at this time rather sedentary people are unpromising.

Perhaps the most highly structured episode of this kind is also in the Brenner House, on the following night, during which we see highly specified instances of individual birds attacking Melanie. Even here it is difficult to see credible similarities that would illuminate the causal structure of Melanie's or anyone else's states. Even more obviously, there is little that is really shared in common between the two cases from a phenomenological point of view. In what sense does Lydia's or Melanie's sense of anxiety and threat *feel like* being attacked by birds? Are there significant similarities between the effects of these characters' states on each other and the experience of being under attack from birds in ways portrayed in the film? Positive answers to these questions will seem very strained.

I have accepted, for the sake of the argument, that the first set of relations on which the method draws—interpretive relations between behaviour and underlying psychical states—are as real and as explanatory as is necessary to vindicate the method. To that extent my elaboration has been a sympathetic one. My claim is simply that no deeper understanding of the underlying states is arrived at through investigation of the second set of relations—those whereby the activities of the birds are said to express, manifest, or embody the psychical states of the characters. It is, however, notoriously difficult to prove a negative, and I may have failed to see ways in which interesting structural similarities could be pursued. I hope, at least, to have laid down a challenge to psychodynamically inclined critics who ought not, I suggest, to rest content with vague statements to the effect that this thing symbolizes that thing; such claims are interesting only if they lead to further illumination of the psychic processes involved, and I have suggested one way they could be shown to do that.

This should not lead us to deny that there are external relations between the birds and the human characters which have at least some interpretive significance. The behaviour of the birds and the psychological states of the humans may not have much in common or be mutually revealing of anything, but the rather different anxieties that these two groups induce are, at least, mutually reinforcing, maintaining the audience in a state of sustained tension that the birds could not themselves manage without wearing out their welcome. Things are arranged thus and so for reasons, and the reasons lie outside the causal structure of the pro-filmic world—that is certainly true. Beyond this rather banal observation, it is difficult to assert plausible and informative connections between the birds and the psychologies of the human characters.

If we accept my conclusions directly above, they strengthen the minimalist interpretation of *The Birds* already offered: the explanatory minimalism I have claimed to find is now matched by an absence of any serious symbolic role for the birds. Is that disappointing? Interpreters look for meaning—what else should interpreters do? But the task of interpretation is not to fill every space with meaning; it is to help us understand the meaning that is there, or which may be projected onto the work in such a way as to illuminate its qualities. Sometimes the best interpreters, like the best composers and authors, have simply to refrain, to accept that it is better to do nothing more. Good interpretation involves sensitivity to the point at which piling meaning on will not be an improvement.

9.5. Irony and Horror: The Tradition

My emphasis on the role of ironic pretence in Hitchcock's style, along with minimalism of content, suggests a way of seeing his work, or parts of it, as belonging to a certain micro-genre in British horror-narration which I find exemplified in the ghost stories of M. R. James.[17] While James is not short of admirers, few would claim that his work examines the deeper aspects of human relationships. Rather, his stories are celebrated for their miniaturist brilliance, economy of expression, unerring construction of tension and—above all—the maintenance of a cool irony which contrasts so effectively with the stories' horrifying content. While there are sometimes tensions between the human characters, it would entirely miss the point to suggest that the spectral and monstrous creatures described are 'expressions' or 'extensions' of these tensions and their psychological causes.

James' style contrasts with that of some of his contemporaries who were in a similar line of business, notably Algernon Blackwood. Blackwood's stories are marked by a fatal tendency to metaphysical explanation. In his most highly regarded tale, 'The Willows', the narrator is conveniently provided with a stolid but sometimes prescient companion who is able, somehow, to divine the causes of their strange experience and who expounds at length on the nature of the powerful beings they are up against and what they must do to defeat them.[18] Nothing could be further from

---

[17] James was writing in the first decades of the twentieth century; I do not know whether Hitchcock was influenced by him directly, though stories by James appear in some of the anthologies of horror stories (nominally) edited by Hitchcock around 1960. The project of comparing the two could easily go too far, but I note the following: the cinematic quality of some of James' stories (for example, 'The Haunted Dolls' House'); certain scenes from James, which could naturally be filmed by Hitchcock in a sympathetic style, as with the awkward but good-humoured exchange at the opening to 'Mr Humphrey and his Inheritance'; some of James' more sinister characters, who parallel Hitchcockian portrayals: compare Karswell from 'Casting the Runes' with Professor Jordan (Godfrey Tearle) from *The Thirty-Nine Steps* or Charles Tobin (Otto Kruger) from *Saboteur*. See also Ackroyd 2002.

[18] Algernon Blackwood, *The Willows, and Other Queer Tales* (1934). Another of Blackwood's annoying characters, John Silence, is given to similar expositions. Lovecraft is another exponent, while Vernon Lee (*Hauntings* (1890)) is an anti-theorist. In film, this theory/anti-theory divide is visible also, though plenty of material falls into an indeterminate middle ground. Nicolas Roeg's *Don't Look Now* (1973), another Du Maurier adaptation, is strongly marked by anti-theory leanings, and shares with

the method of James, whose narrative never gives way to theory.[19] His ghostly and monstrous beings wreak horrible revenge for ill-understood transgression and then disappear, with very little explanation provided and often not much that can be inferred. And the victims and other human characters are generally uncomprehendingly terrified, at best vaguely aware that they have strayed into territory they ought to have kept out of. Often the spectral beings involved show little rationality beyond a low malevolence, as with the creature whose blind pursuit of Professor Parkin up and down the coastal groins in 'Oh, Whistle, and I'll Come to You, My Lad' is so disturbing—a pattern of behaviour one may think of as closely mirrored in *The Birds*.

James understood that the ideas he developed in his stories needed very careful handling lest they should appear bathetic or absurd, which is what they are prone to do when the spotlight of theory is shone upon them; they retain their power only so long as they are held in narrative form via brief and vivid episodes of activity connected by passages that move (we, at least, know) steadily towards a disaster the characters are busy denying or ignoring, and understand very poorly.

At least in *The Birds*, Hitchcock follows a similar course.[20] His focus is on the local and the particular (we never know what is happening outside Bodega Bay), on human interactions that (just) manage to hold our attention without falling outside the mundane, on the frightful details of the birds increasingly violent and coordinated attacks, on (finally) the slow and fearful walk through the brute-causal mass of birds to the car. Hitchcock's method in this last scene is particularly instructive. All attention is focused on how Mitch slowly moves through the mass of birds, carefully planting footsteps so as not to disturb them, while the birds themselves, showing no inclination to attack *en masse*, are strangely unperturbed by his proximity, their reaction confined to one or two casual pecks at him

The Birds a tendency to focus on not always narratively relevant detail, as if deliberately expending time which could be put to explanatory use. Robert Wise's *The Haunting* (1963) employs the theorist's device of having on hand a scientist to interpret events; John Hough's *The Legend of Hell House* (1973) is, if anything, more tedious in this regard.

[19] Having written this, I was glad to find the following from James himself: that the best ghost stories leave the reader 'just a little in the dark as to the workings of their machinery. We do not want to see the bones of their theory about the supernatural' (quoted at Cox 1986: 32).

[20] *Psycho* is a different case, and gives way to heavy-handed psychological explanation. *The Birds* is in many ways not typical of Hitchcock's work but the emphasis on ironizing the very conventions the plot depends on is present in a number of films.

that help to maintain, without significantly raising, the tension. Mitch must start the engine without provoking the birds, and Melanie must be got into the car, walked between Mitch and his mother in a reprise of the final scene from *Notorious*. Together, these elements, the human interactions punctuated with inexplicable brutality, presented with mastery of pace and atmosphere, combined with surprising moments of irony which, in another's hands, would spoil the whole thing, provide a rich aesthetic and emotional experience that does not benefit from attempts to account for what is going on by reference to large themes: causal, symbolic, or of any other kind.

9.6. Science and the Supernatural

Finally, I will speculate shamelessly on a question raised by our discussion just now of what works and what does not work in certain kinds of narration. One general question of interest is this: to what extent are scientific attitudes and attitudes to the supernatural distinguished as parts of human cognitive structure? Is belief in the supernatural an inhabitant of the same mental space as belief in, say, the Higgs boson? Pascal Boyer notes that while people want explanations for certain kinds of things, their desire for explanation is very uneven: the fact that a roof collapses needs an explanation and we may get one in terms of the malevolence of witches (Boyer 2001). But those who proffer those sorts of explanations tend not to seek explanations for witchcraft itself, or for the particular powers that are manifested in witchcraft. The supernatural seems to enter the cognitive system with a handy set of instructions attached: use to explain but do not seek an explanation. And this tendency reaches down into our ordinary, unselfconsciously supernatural thinking, as when Olive Chancellor thinks of Verena Tallant as 'an exquisite whim of the creative force', something concerning which 'a few shades more or less of the inexplicable didn't matter'.[21] Of course, this explanation-blocking ordinance is not quite adhered to in the sort of systematic reflection we find in academic theology, which attempts to provide an explanatory basis of some kind for the will of God, divine intervention, and the malevolent actions of Satan. But Boyer

---

[21] Henry James, *The Bostonians*, chap. 15.

and, I think, other anthropological writers would class this highly refined version of the impetus to religion as going against the grain of people's natural inclinations in this field. And it is possible to believe that the theological tradition has not consistently covered itself in glory in its attempts at this sort of explanation—there is, surely, a marked contrast with the explanatory success of science.

Now, it is a stretch, I grant, from here to horror narratives in literature and in film. But there is something worth having a look at. We do not, on the whole, think of explanation as part of the package deal that supernatural horror offers us and I at least have asserted that attempts at such explanations sit badly with the genre. Science fiction horror on the other hand seems much more comfortable with the idea and in some cases it would appear more or less obligatory. Thus H. G. Wells' invisible man spends a good deal of time telling us about the mechanisms by which he managed to achieve invisibility—all done with at least a show of scientific respectability.[22] Of course, the explanations are bogus and may amount to little more than the strategic placement of impressive terminology. But the effort has been made, and the audience feels easier for it. Perhaps—just perhaps—this is explicable in terms of the distinct evolutionary histories of our receptivity to scientific and contra-scientific ideas.

[22] H. G. Wells, *The Invisible Man*, chap. 19.

10

Narrative and Character

Towards the end of his account of the reign of James II, in a passage marked 'His Character', Hume says:

His frugality of public money was remarkable, his industry exemplary, his application to naval affairs successful, his encouragement of trade judicious, his jealousy of national honour laudable. What then was wanting to make him an excellent sovereign? A due regard and affection to the religion and constitution of his country. Had he been possessed of this essential quality, even his middling talents, aided by so many virtues, would have rendered his reign honourable and happy.[1]

More recently, much historical writing has avoided issues of character by avoiding a focus on the individual. But where historians do consider the contribution of an individual to events, it is evidently difficult for them to abandon the notion of character altogether, though they do not now offer a confident summary in the style of Hume. Perhaps the idea of character continues to play a role in historical work because character is a vital determinant of events, and a historian who does without it is likely to fail. But recent work in social psychology has been unkind to the notions of character and personality, which have come increasingly to look like remnants of a superstitious past. Might enthusiasm for character also be something to do with the way in which narrative encourages us to frame the roles of individuals in terms of their characters?

The representational profile of narrative, with its emphasis on the particularity of causal histories and temporal relations, certainly makes it especially apt for the representation of experience, decision, and action,

---

[1] David Hume, *The History of England*, 6 vols (1754–62), vi. 520. While Hume talks here of 'essential qualities', his list of attributes often, as above, contains items that seem merely to summarize the subject's behaviour in rather circumscribed areas, as with application to naval affairs. Hume's appeal to Character is to that extent a more limited one than it would at first appear.

and their effects on the wider world. We make sense of people's actions by embedding an account of them within a wider narrative that emphasizes prior, rationalizing causes which look forward to intended, and often actual, effects. The narratives which have endured across time, culture, genre, and style are narratives of motive and action. Narratives encourage us to make sense of the world by telling of the ways in which mind controls it. Perhaps narrative encourages us to think of the mind as more structured, more orderly, more robustly in control of circumstance than it really is.

In this chapter, I try to show that character and narrative are made for each other, and I give a defence of character-focused literary criticism. In the next and final chapter I am more critical: I give a sympathetic hearing to the arguments sceptical of character as a psychological category. I do offer a defence of character as a narrative device but I also suggest a reason for distrusting the argument.

10.1. Preliminaries

We speak of the characters *in* a narrative, meaning the agents of its story. In this chapter, 'character' will usually refer to something else: an agent's distinctive psychological profile, if he or she has one. To say that a character 'has a character' sounds confusing and we ought to distinguish character as person and character as property of a person. A character (person) in a story may or may not have a very clearly drawn or interesting character (property), and there are stories with characters (persons) in them which we would not call narratives of character (property), by which I mean narratives which give some explanatory role to the notion of character (property). It is the idea of character as property, as inner source of action, something related to personality and temperament, which interests me here. I will write 'Character' when I am referring to this. I will use 'character' to denote things like Emma Woodhouse in *Emma*, Iago in *Othello*, and, though this is less common usage, James II in Hume's *History of England*. The first two of these have interesting Characters, or rather it is part of their respective stories that they do, which is the best one can say about the Character of a fictional person. Whether James II had a Character and if so of what sort is a matter for empirical investigation, though it is part of the story told in Hume's narrative that he does. Sometimes, rather than say 'the Character of a character', I shall talk, as I just did, about 'people' having Characters. Remember that these are often people who, like Emma and Iago, do not exist.

10.2. Some Claims about Character

Authors may describe the Characters of the people in their stories, but this does not make for a novel or drama or history of Character; for that we need Character to be represented as causally implicated in the actions and events of the story. Character is sometimes described, but often comes in part from what we are to infer from what is described: actions and events. In that case, stories of Character require us to work back and forth between behaviour, intention, and Character. We judge the behaviour to derive from a certain kind of intention, and the intention to be (or not to be) the expression of a certain Character trait. Much depends on the coherence of the overall picture: how plausible it is that the person acted on this intention may depend on our sense of their Character, which makes the having of such an intention more or less likely. And how plausible it is that they have this Character trait depends on what other traits we have attributed to them, and how well the trait in question fits with the sorts of intentions most likely to explain the behaviour. After lots of toing and froing, we settle into a relatively stable pattern of attributions, though surprising behaviour revealed late in the narrative can pull the rug from under us. A supposed capacity to dissemble one's character is thus a feature of many narratives, creating opportunities for surprise.

Gilbert Harman says that Character traits are 'relatively long-term stable dispositions to act in distinctive ways' (Harman 1999: 317). Should we find the dispositional account too strong and identify Character simply with the mere regularity of action instead? This would be untrue to the folk notion of character, for reasons familiar from the debate over causal laws. Assertions about Character are supposed to sustain counterfactuals. The person of Character would (probably) have acted this way if he or she had been in that situation; mere regularities of behaviour do not provide for this. And Character is supposed to explain action, while the fact that Smith regularly does X does nothing to explain his doing X on a particular occasion. Is a dispositional account of Character traits strong enough? Dispositions to action will serve to generate counterfactuals about intention/behaviour pairs, but they do not explain much; merely being disposed to break has limited power to explain why something broke; better would be a categorical basis for the disposition, as the crystalline structure of glass is the basis for the breakability of the tumbler. We might then see Character as the *basis* of our motivational-behavioural dispositions. But if someone wants to insist on the explanatory value of the disposition, and stick with the dispositional account of Character, the difference will not surface in the discussion here.[2]

We invoke Character most readily in contexts where praise or blame is likely; we explain the decision to rescue a child from a burning building in terms of Character, but do not appeal to Character to explain a choice from the menu, unless it is a very self-denying one. People may be of good or bad Character, and of strong or weak Character, but these distinctions are not symmetrical. Strong Characters may be good or bad, but weak ones are bad to some degree; we do not count someone as of weak but good Character if they are not up to the challenge of behaving badly. Weakness means susceptibility to temptation, and we do not think of goodness as tempting. Strong Character is a necessary but insufficient condition for being morally good.

The explanatory and evaluative use to which we put Character suggests that we regard Character traits as very unevenly distributed. We occasionally postulate a broadly human Character, when we reflect on general tendencies to warlike and other behaviours. But if everyone was assumed to have the same or very similar Character traits we could not explain differences in people's behaviour by appeal to Character, and we do offer such explanations. We choose our friends, we think, partly because of their Characters, and this would make no sense if Character did not distinguish people.

All this—frequently reflected in narratives of Character—is part of what we commonly take Character to be. I do not say it is all essential to the notion, but the more of it we chip away at, the less inclined we will be to think that Character is a useful notion.

---

[2] On the inadequacy of a dispositional account of Character traits, see Adams 2006: 121. Adams defends virtue ethics against the social psychological attack which I shall describe in the next chapter.

10.3. What Narrative does for Character

Narrative is suited to the representation of Character. It is able to represent richly individuated temporal and causal connections between motivation, decision, and circumstance in ways that other representational forms cannot match. It provides the space within which we can see a person's Character gradually revealed, and perhaps gradually changing in response to events and to the actions of others.

Why should we think narrative especially important for revealing Character when our real-life encounters with people offer the same opportunities? Because narrative provides an especially benign environment for Character-attribution. People in real life rarely act with the purpose of having their behaviour inform us about their Character; when they do, it is usually because they hope to misrepresent it. Even believers in the efficacy of Character agree that much behaviour is either Character neutral or contra-indicative; lots of behaviour, we accept, does not arise from Character, and when Character is called on it sometimes fails us. So the channels we have for getting information about Character are noisy, and inference to Character is difficult. Some of this can be said about the people in narratives; they generally do not act in order to display their Characters, except when they wish to mislead us about them. But there is a difference. The behaviour of a character in narrative is represented by the narrative, and the narrative is an artefact, intentionally crafted to be the representation that it is. If we are persuaded, or suspect, that the narrative is one of Character, behaviours which are represented in it can often be taken as a rational basis for inference to Character, simply because they *are* represented within it. A narrative is rich in indications of the maker's intentions, and anything a character is represented as doing in the narrative can be assumed to be so represented for a reason. Often it will be inferable that the reason is that the behaviour is expressive of Character (perhaps in some complex and ambiguous way). The mediating agency of the narrative-maker vastly increases the range of possible inferences from behaviour to Character.

Putting this in terms taken from Sperber and Wilson's relevance theory, we can say that a narrative of Character acts as an indication that the information it imparts is *Character-relevant* to our concerns—worth the processing cost of calculating what it implies about Character.[3] We like to make inferences to Character; as we shall see, we do so even when the evidence that supports the inference is very weak indeed. And narratives of Character help reduce the cognitive burdens of doing so by providing us with information of high Character-relevance.

Narratives have other ways of making the inferential task easier. They scaffold our inferential activities with strategically placed descriptions of Character that take us directly into motivational structure, as George Eliot's interventions allow us to read off Character traits for the people in *Middlemarch*. And when narrators want to be less direct in their indications, metonymy enables them to link descriptions of objects with the Characters of persons, as with Dickens' account of the 'hideous solidity' of the Podsnap family plate.[4] These descriptions create, through their verbal structures, implicatures that would be unavailable in other forms of representation. Narrators can choose how they use these devices, and many do so sparingly—some even mislead us with elements of strategically placed unreliability. But any coherent narrative, no matter how unobvious the inferences it warrants, allows for vastly more inferential connections between actions, events, and Character to be made than is ever legitimate when we are considering the actions and sufferings of real people. We know that the narrative is the product of an overarching intelligence that makes the connections for reasons; so, events that in the real world would be connected in a brute causal way will now also be connected by reason and rationality. The closest real-world approximation to this is the inferential practice of someone who thinks the world was produced and is sustained by an intelligible, rational deity whose aims can be inferred from events down to the level of transactions between individuals.[5]

Because narratives so enhance the relevance of the Character-indicating stimuli they provide, they can then afford significantly to raise the processing costs of these stimuli, introducing complex, overlapping plots, confusing twists, unreliable narration, and indications—as with writers like Henry

---

[3] Sperber and Wilson 1995. What I say here does not commit me to Sperber and Wilson's theory, for that theory claims, generally, that people are designed by evolution as seekers and detectors of relevance and that their communicative utterances, where they are not purely code-based, create a presumption of their own optimal relevance. These claims go well beyond anything I assert about narratives of Character.

[4] Charles Dickens, *Our Mutual Friend*, chap. 11. The example is discussed at Harvey 1965: 35–6.

[5] See above, Chap. 2, sect. 6.

James—that success in inference to motive and Character is to be judged by unusually high standards. In real life and real time, we may count ourselves as doing well if we gain (we think) some vague, working understanding of a person's Character. Within a narrative, we may expect to do much better; getting ourselves, within a space of hours, into the position of making confident evaluative judgements about a person's deepest motives.

10.4. What Character does for Narrative

Just as the intention-driven coherence of a narrative helps us to read the Characters of its people, so Character itself may add to the coherence of narrative, enriching the connections between its events. Narratives, we have seen, focus strongly on the particularity, the uniqueness, of events; but the mere recounting of one thing after another—even when they are causally connected—is not often of much interest. One step forward is to make the causal connections rationalizing ones; hence the focus in narrative on outcomes as the result, though not always the expected result, of intelligible motives. But, while introducing motive can make events understandable, motive by itself will leave them disconnected, for any two actions can follow from quite different motives. What is wanted is a unifying explanation for many instances of motive, and Character is just what we use to make coherent sense of a pattern of complex motivation.

While Character's unifying power lies partly in its capacity to discern explanatory patterns across distinct behaviours, there is also a forward-looking aspect to it. Character helps to create expectation, and to make salient what might happen.[6] Character can be used in many ways to form a landscape of expectation. With an otherwise somewhat disunified narrative such as *Middlemarch*, we have blocks of storytelling which are dominated, and united, by strongly emphasized Character-traits of a given individual, and which bear a high explanatory load. In each of these blocks the primary Character trait is negative. Fred Vincy's fecklessness, Casaubon's inability to face the failure of his project, Rosamund Lydgate's selfishness: all these traits work like constantly acting forces into the influence of

---

[6] As Harvey emphasizes, the greater temporal extent available in the novel makes this form more apt for subjunctive exploitation than is drama (Harvey 1965: 204–5).

which the other characters are pushed by circumstances.[7] They are the primary drivers of the action in their respective parts of the narrative. By being so, they throw into relief certain possible outcomes: the undesirable ones they make probable and the desirable ones they make unlikely. Fred's fecklessness reduces the fortunes of the Garth family, making it less probable that he and Mary will find happiness, Casaubon's self-deception makes less likely any salvage from the wreckage of his life's work, or any mutual comfort in his marriage; Rosamund's monstrous egocentrism puts in jeopardy Lydgate's project of medical renewal, as well as their marriage. Not all these outcomes occur, but all are made salient by Character.

Sometimes, a coalition of several interacting Characters gives a more systematic unity to narrative. As Bradley puts it, 'We see a number of human beings placed in certain circumstances, and we see, arising from the cooperation of their [C]haracters in these circumstances, certain actions' (Bradley 1905: 6).[8] Iago reads the Characters of those around him, sees their tensions and the consequent weaknesses in the ties between Othello and Desdemona, and exploits all this to bring about events the attractions of which are accountable only in terms of his own peculiar Character. He cannot do this without taking advantage of contingencies as they occur, notably with the episode of the handkerchief. Still, Character bears a lot of explanatory weight; Iago had his eye on the handkerchief and might have got it some other way, or, being of a creative Character, found some other device to further his plan. There is contingency in the scene where Desdemona responds to Othello's demands for the handkerchief by pressing Cassio's case; Character did not dictate that these events would co-occur. But this is contingency made significant by its revelation of Character. Desdemona's honest simplicity makes her unsuited to read the bleaker parts of motivation; she naturally interprets Othello's demands for the handkerchief as a device to distract her from pressing Cassio's suit, and will not be put off, adding unknowingly to the case against her. Iago's agency—his conscious pursuit of a goal made intelligible by his own Character—functions to affect the likelihoods of various possible outcomes at each stage, creating a landscape of probability which accounts

---

[7] In each block, other characters have distinctive Characters: Mary Garth, Dorothea Brook, and Dr Lydgate being the primary ones. But their actions are generally responses to problems posed by the Character-driven actions of the three characters named above.

[8] For more on Bradley, see this Chap., sect. 5.

for our sense that Desdemona is doomed. We understand that one thing happened and so caused another to happen. We also understand that, while this happening was highly contingent, the thing it caused would probably if not inevitably have happened anyway; some other cause would have supervened. And the mechanism of that is, once again, Character made efficacious through agency. A function of Character in plot is to increase the counterfactual robustness of the plot's events; Character turns outcomes which are otherwise unlikely, because they depend on accidents, into events with a dramatic inevitability.

Here is a final suggestion about the aid that Character gives to narrative, at least for the case of fictional narratives. It belongs to the psychological history of narrative, though I have no evidence for it beyond its plausibility. It starts with the thought that narratives which seek to engage us in the fortunes of their characters generally do so by making the external perspective—the perspective which sees the story as the product of an agent—recessive. According to this ambition we are to treat the narrative as a window into the actions and sufferings of certain people about whom we are to care a great deal, for caring about them requires us not to have a very conscious awareness of the unreality of their situations.[9] But it is not easy to bring off this effect; in particular it is not easy to avoid reminding the audience that the behaviour of the characters is dictated by an external agency, that of the narrative-maker. One way to improve the chances of avoiding it is to make more vivid the *self*-determination of the characters, or at any rate some of the most significant ones, thereby lowering the salience of external determination. I suggest that endowing characters with highly self-determining Character-traits is one way to do this, and this is in fact what has happened, within at least the western novelistic and theatrical tradition.

It is unlikely, of course, that narrative-makers have thought of it in quite this way, but the hypothesis does not entail that they have; rather, narratives according to which people possess Characters have done better, on average, at making the external perspective recessive, and so have tended to dominate the market, or a significant part of it, and their techniques have been preserved by imitation. But note that there is a

---

[9] This is phrased so as to avoid the idea that the narrative-as-window claim requires an illusory belief in the reality of the characters' situations.

cost to narrative-makers in this strategy, for there is sometimes a tension between maintenance of Character-driven behaviour and the needs of a plot. Trollope, for example, sometimes leaves us with the impression that the behaviour of his characters is dictated more by the need to keep the narrative on track than by consistent Character-traits. Thus, Ferdinand Lopez, who in *The Prime Minister* appears at first the coolly rational, firm-minded adventurer with a certain degree of dignity, and even courage, later on displays tendencies to irrational pursuit of goals, anger, and petty vengefulness which do not appear consistent with the earlier part. Trollope needs Lopes to behave in an outrageous way if he is to retain his readers, and so he gives us a shabby and tyrannical Lopes for the latter part.[10] In fact, the news coming in from social psychology, with its emphasis on situational determination of behaviour, is somewhat favourable to the realism of this depiction, and a case might be made for saying that the change in Lopes' behaviour is due to the changed circumstances of his marriage.[11] Since it does not occur to the reader that Trollope was motivated by a desire for realism of this sort—he almost certainly was not—we tend to see the changed pattern of behaviour as a narrative weakness.

In the next and final chapter, I will return to the question of what narrative-shaping values the idea of Character has when I consider the case for the unreality of Character.

10.5. Character and the Critic

Narrative and Character are, it would seem, made for each other. But Character-based criticism of narrative has for some time been an object of deep suspicion. L. C. Knights' *How Many Children had Lady Macbeth?* opened an attack which, for all its weakness, later generations have not tired of renewing.[12] A. C. Bradley's *Shakespearean Tragedy* was one of the more serious targets of this essay, though Bradley never asked the question

---

[10] In this I disagree with William Flesch, for whom Trollope has set himself a near impossible task in the late scene where Lopez asks Mr Wharton for money: 'to make Lopez consistent with his own dashing audacity even as he humiliates himself' (Flesch 2007: 151). On my account, Lopez has long since ceased to be dashing and audacious. See also below, n. 22.   [11] See below, Chap. 11, sect. 1.

[12] Knights 1933. On Bradley's influence, see Cook 1972. For a history of confusion about Bradley and the Macbeth children, see Britton 1961. For another defence of Bradleyism, see Bristol 2000.

of its title. Bradley is, in various ways, an imperfect critic: he declares ideas about motive or action 'impossible' when at most they would need a better defence than he has found; he is too inclined to see expressions of Shakespeare's own personality in the construction of the plays;[13] some of his Character summaries sound as if he were describing the recently deceased: '[The Queen] had a soft animal nature, and was very dull and very shallow' (Bradley 1905: 167); he will occasionally look further into the dramatic past for evidence of Character than most of us would think justified.[14] But Bradley did not neglect the plays, their dramatic structures or their poetry. He was alive to the differences (and trade-offs) between the realistic development of plot and dramatic and poetic effect; he was critical of writers whose speculations about Character took them into areas where the work itself offered no guidance. He reminds us that sometimes the best explanation for a character's action is that the drama requires it.[15] He even notes that 'the only way, if there is any way, that a conception of Hamlet's [C]haracter could be proved true, would be to show that it, and it alone explains all the relevant facts presented by the text of the drama' (Bradley 1905: 129).[16]

What reasons had Knights against Character-criticism, other than the bland observation that it should not be pursued at the expense of other aspects of the work? He conceded that Shakespeare had a 'remarkable power to make his men and women convincing', but insisted that they are abstractions 'from the total response in the mind of the reader or spectator, brought into being by written or spoken words'. We do not need telling—and nor did Bradley—that Shakespeare's characters are not real folk we could find out about from other sources which might supplement or even contradict the narrative. None of that stands in the way of the sensible view that we are to *imagine* Hamlet, Iago, and the rest as people—and not as peculiar entities constructed out of words or as existing in the mind of the spectator. In that case, the critic may surely attend to the

[13] See e.g. discussion of Lear in Bradley 1905: chap. 8.

[14] In an extended line of reasoning about Iago's character, Bradley concludes that Iago must have prodigious powers to dissimulate, since he had 'apparently never enjoyed . . . occasional explosions of the reality within him', this on the grounds that, in the play, Iago is so universally regarded as a decent man.   [15] As with the discussion of Ophelia; Bradley 1905: chap. 4.

[16] Bradley's arguments are not stated with the economy and rigour that would allow us to be sure that he always followed this dictum, but the explanation of the plays is certainly never far away in his studies of Character.

question of what *sort* of people we are to imagine them as, and that must be by reference to how we understand the Characters of real people—if Character is constitutive of human psychology. This is not special pleading on behalf of Character; if the story tells us that the characters sat at a table, we make sense of this by importing our real-world understanding of what tables are and how they are used.[17]

Knights is right to say that characters are abstractions: the personalities, thoughts, and feelings possessed by characters supervene on the representational content of the play or literary work as a whole. Character is fixed once all the representational features of the play are fixed, so Character has no independence from the play, and our imaginings about them must respect these limits.[18] This is not true of real people: our Characters (assuming we have them) are not fixed by any narrative. Knights put some emphasis on 'the mind of the reader', and we can accommodate this by tweaking supervenience: for a given interpreter at a time, once the facts (up to indeterminacy) concerning the representational content of the play are deemed to be fixed, the facts (up to indeterminacy) concerning the Characters of its persons are fixed also. So it is a constraint on any act of interpretation I engage in that I accept the following: once I know all I can know about what the play represents as holding true, I know everything relevant to deciding what the Characters of the play's people are. And two interpreters (or one interpreter at two times) can accept this constraint, while disagreeing (perhaps with her past self) about what the representational facts are.

This reasonable idea does little to limit the scope for Character speculation, once we realize that the work and its text are different things. The work itself reaches well beyond the text of the work, and issues on which the text is silent cannot be assumed to be issues left undecided by the work.[19] There is no answer given by *Macbeth* to the question 'how many children had Lady Macbeth?', but this is not simply because the text does not name the number. The text does not say that the number was

---

[17] Knights' essay exercised a powerful influence on Shakespeare scholarship for many years, becoming an orthodoxy that had to be acknowledged, however inconsistent with what the critic actually wanted to say. J. F. P. Pafford, in his 1963 Arden Shakespeare edition of *The Winter's Tale*, insists, with Knights, that characters are 'vehicles carrying ideas and themes' at the same time as telling us that 'we must assume that [Leontes] had a noble heart' despite the play showing us no sign of it (Pafford 1963: p. lxxii).

[18] For a formalization of this idea, using a proposal of David Lewis, see Currie 1990: chap. 4. My proposal allows us to *define* characters in terms of the representational properties of the narrative.

[19] On the distinction between work and text, see Currie 2004: chap. 1.

less than 100, but we can be certain that it was. The text has always to be taken in conjunction with a set of background assumptions, and any reasonably chosen set of assumptions will tell us that the number was less than 100.[20] As things stand, getting a precise figure would require a textual statement, since there is no particular number of children that a woman is overwhelmingly likely to have. But if human females were capable of having at most one child, and this was part of common knowledge in Shakespeare's society, there would be a strong argument for saying that the number was one (given the textual implication that the number was at least one). How many hands does Lady Macbeth have? A reasonable answer is 'two', despite the text not being explicit on the question.

Deciding what the appropriate background is may be difficult. It may even generate unresolvable disputes.[21] In such cases, we may have answers—more than one—that go beyond what the text itself tells us, where the choice between them can only be a matter of personal preference. And even with a single set of background assumptions, many questions, if they get answers at all, will get equivocal ones: Hamlet's motive was this, or it was that. Again, we will have many interpretive options, and no grounds for regarding any one as best. Deciding what questions are resolvable is hard, in some cases so hard that we are unlikely ever to be confident that we have reached the limits of rational debate. It is also hard to know whether resolving a given question will shed light on others, especially when we do not know what the answer is. In such an environment it is unhelpful to discourage Character-speculation; you never know when it will come in handy. That it should always be speculation we have reason to think *might* be settled by the work itself, and *might* in turn settle interesting questions is something we can all agree on. By such standards, Bradley does not do so badly.[22]

[20] For some ideas about what the appropriate background assumptions are, see Lewis 1978.

[21] On which, see Currie 1993.

[22] For other defences of the notion of Character in fiction and of critical focus on Character, see Harvey 1965 and Holloway 1960. In the text to this note I simplify in one important respect: I ignore what I have called the external perspective. Acknowledging the external perspective means that in working out the best explanation for a character's behaviour we may need to take into account certain facts external to the world of the story. Thus, we might decide that a certain piece of apparently out-of-Character behaviour is best explained in terms of the dramatic requirements constraining the author's construction, rather than by revising our notion of the character's Character. This does not affect the point I want to make against Knights (see above, Chapter 3).

11

Character Scepticism

Suppose the argument of Chapter 10 is right: the narrative mode is well suited to the presentation of Character, and Character is well suited to giving a narrative the kinds of engaging qualities that will help it succeed. We might still have a concern about narrative representations of Character; in fact we might, in the light of Chapter 10's results, have the concern to a greater degree than we otherwise would. The fit between narrative and Character tells us nothing about whether there is any such thing as Character. This would be of no moment if we had strong, independent reasons to believe in Character; I shall suggest that we do not. And if there is some reason to doubt the existence of Character, or to doubt well-entrenched assumptions about its role in our lives, then the question arises as to whether our belief in it is not founded on evidence but has something to do with the fit between narrative and Character: a fit that contributes to explaining our believing in Character without contributing to validating the belief. Then another question arises: if our beliefs about Character are badly flawed, what consequences follow for the value of narratives, even fictional ones, which embody those beliefs?

11.1. The Case against Character

Commenting on the debate provoked by Knights' essay, Michael Bristol notes that, while Knights himself thought discussion of the Characters of dramatic persons 'intellectually naïve', many recent critics hold that

notions of [C]haracter or unified subjectivity do not pertain even to actual persons, let alone to their representations in fictional texts . . . Any concern therefore with discovering the attitudes or assessing the praiseworthiness of a literary Character conceived as a distinct and autonomous individual is not just an egregious ontological blunder but an ideologically motivated . . . misrepresentation.[1]

These claims, deriving, apparently, from Lacanian psychoanalysis, do not come with any impressive evidence to support them. But there is evidence (of which the Lacanian critics are perhaps unaware) which suggests that our reliance on Character as an explanatory tool is misplaced.[2] The evidence is of three kinds. Evidence of the first two kinds is indirect, and is intended to undercut our confidence in our own, pre-scientific insight into the mind and its ways. Evidence of the third kind is intended to show that people do not behave as we would expect them to if the belief in a strongly determining role for Character were justified. If evidence of the third kind were conclusive, we would not need to consider the other two kinds of evidence. As usual, the evidence is not conclusive; there are ways, ranging from subtle reinterpretations of the idea of Character itself to downright denials that the experiments show us anything relevant about human behaviour in non-experimental situations, that people have found to defend the notion of Character from the evidence.[3] The extent to which these strategies are rational depends on what we—good Bayesians that we are—think about the prior probability of the hypothesis that human behaviour is significantly determined by Character. If we think the probability very high, we need correspondingly more direct evidence against this hypothesis to persuade us to give it up. It is therefore worth reminding ourselves of the reasons we have to place little faith in our ordinary, pre-scientific picture of the mind.

---

[1] Bristol 1994. For a sample of these arguments, see Cixous 1974. In reporting these views, Bristol rightly associates doubts about the notion of Character with doubts about the existence of 'distinct and autonomous individuals', for this association is certainly present in the literature he is summarizing. But I will not assume that rejection of Character leads inevitably to the rejection of the idea of the individual. As will be evident further on, I agree with Doris (2000) that scepticism about Character is compatible with the retention of a rich psychological account of individuals through such concepts as decision, memory, and responsibility. For sensible comment on the relation between fictional characters and real people, see Hochman 1985: 44, 62. See also Rosenberg 1992. Rosenberg argues that Dickens' characters 'do not so much re-create actual individuals as re-create our reactions to actual individuals' (ibid. 162). The best defence of psychological realism in narrative is Smith 1995.

[2] The work of Milgram and Zimbardo, which indicates alarming levels of willingness to co-operate in abusive behaviour, along with evidence of the apparent moral ordinariness of many people who have been active participants in genocide, forms the background to this research.

[3] Strategies of the first kind are well represented in the literature; I have heard the second strategy used in discussion.

First, there is a good deal of evidence that our insight into the mind generally is very limited. This is true, to a surprising degree, of our relation to the mind we can be expected to take most interest in and know most about—our own. I have already cited evidence which suggests that our minds are prone to capture by unconscious imitation: we start to think, and act, like the people around us—even like casually imagined Characters, as in the 'imagined professor' experiment.[4] Yet, people have little or no awareness of imitation as a force which shapes their own behaviour or that of others. Few people these days dispute the evidence for the role of smoking in the causation of lung cancer; here, opinion has tended to converge in line with the weight of evidence. By contrast, there is little general acceptance of the idea of a causal link between exposure to the representation of violence in the media as a child and aggressive behaviour in later life. Here, even educated opinion is divided by rhetorically embellished pictures of human motivation which, whatever their merits, are not derived from serious empirical study. In fact, the evidence for a causal connection (and not merely a correlation) between media violence and imitative aggression is quite strong.[5] In our risk-sensitive society one would expect even the hint of such a relationship to generate a powerful movement for legislative change. As Susan Hurley puts it, 'the disconnect between research results and public opinion on this topic is so striking that it has become an object of research interest in its own right' (Hurley 2004a: 169).

Lack of insight into the wellsprings of our own behaviour is common across the whole domain of the mental. People's reasons for their preferences often turn out to be confabulations. In one experiment, subjects were shown photographs of two women and asked to choose the one they found more attractive; they were then shown the photographs they preferred and were asked for the reasons for their choice. On some trials, however, they were shown the photograph of the person they had declared less attractive. Subjects noticed the switch only about a quarter of the time, but most of those who did not notice gave confident-sounding reasons for preferring this face, some of them manifestly inconsistent with their prior choice (Johansson, et al. 2005).

Evidence of this kind is not of any special relevance to the debate over Character. But it does suggest that we have little grounds on which to trust

---

[4] See above, Chap. 5.   [5] See Huesmann 2005 and Comstock 2005.

our folk-psychological theories—any more than we these days trust folk physics, which has been shown to be substantially at odds with scientifically informed theories of the interactions of bodies. The fact that Character is a well-entrenched element within folk-psychology cannot give us much reason to believe in it.[6]

Secondly, and with more specific relation to Character, there is experimental evidence that we tend to think that people's behaviour justifies attributions of Character when there is strong, independent reason to conclude that it does not. In an experiment, subjects heard people read out statements which the subjects knew had been prepared by others and which the readers were simply instructed to utter; the subjects were still inclined to rate speakers as having this or that Character-trait, according to the tone of what was said. We unjustifiably infer good Character from attractive appearance; we infer too quickly from observation of a person's behaviour in one situation to a general view of their Character, overestimating the likelihood that a person rated honest in one situation will retain that rating in another.[7] This sort of evidence does not show that we are wrong in attributing Character to people, but it shows how cautious we should be in endorsing the common, poorly evidenced, belief in Character.

The third kind of evidence is more directly a threat to belief in Character: it shows that people behave in ways which are strongly determined by circumstances. In a now-famous experiment, seminarians who had just carried out some test procedures were asked to go to another room where they would give a short talk on the parable of the Good Samaritan. One group was told that there was no hurry, another that they were slightly late. As the Seminarians went towards the room, a confederate faked a collapse. Those in the 'high-hurry' group were much more likely to ignore the apparently ill person in their path than were those in the low-hurry group (some, apparently, stepped over the fallen person).[8]

---

[6] One might argue for the reliability of folk psychology on the grounds that its evidential basis is introspection, a reliable and richly informative (though of course not infallible) source of knowledge. But see Schwitzgabel 2008, for a broad-ranging and philosophically motivated denial that introspection is either reliable or richly informative.

[7] For a summary of this evidence, see Doris 2000: chap. 5.

[8] See Darley and Bateson 1973. While 63 per cent helped in the low-hurry condition, only 10 per cent did so in the high-hurry condition. Owen Flanagan describes the experiment as 'mischievous' (Flanagan 1993: 301). I cannot see why it is wrong to confront those who propose to devote their lives to the good of others with some of the less-obvious difficulties that stand in the way of such an ambition.

Similarly, people who have just found a dime in a phone booth will be much more likely to help someone outside pick up spilled papers than someone who has not found the dime.[9] A slight urgency, or a tiny piece of luck can, it seems, make a great deal of difference to people's willingness to help—much more than we would expect if we thought that people are of distinct Characters, and that Character is a significant determinant of helping behaviour.[10] Thus, trivial aspects of the situation turn out to be highly predictive of behaviour. If people had a Character-based tendency to a certain degree of benevolent behaviour—a tendency that was robust under change of circumstance—we would not expect small situational differences to make such a big difference to behaviour.

I note one other piece of work, not generally cited in connection with scepticism about Character, because it indicates that behaviour is vulnerable to forces other than, and even more trivial than, minor change in circumstance; I referred to this work earlier on in another context.[11] Word-priming experiments expose subjects to words associated with some state or trait such as old age or politeness; the relevant words are mixed up with others so that subjects have no conscious idea that, together, these words cluster around a certain concept. John Bargh and colleagues exposed subjects in this way to words associated with rudeness or politeness. Subjects were then to seek out the experimenter in a hallway to get the next part of the test, where they would find the experimenter deep in conversation with a confederate. The aim was to see how long people would wait before interrupting the conversation, and in particular to see if there was any difference between the politeness-primed and rudeness-primed groups. There was a great deal of difference; while those in the rudeness-primed group tended to interrupt after five minutes, 80 per cent of the politeness-primed group never interrupted during the ten minutes the conversation ran. It looks as if behaviours we think indicative of Character are easily

---

[9] Isen and Levin 1972. See again Doris 2000: chap. 3.

[10] Kamtekar suggests that the kinds of experiments described above depend, for their Character-sceptical interpretation, on the unrealistic assumption that people with a given trait—helpfulness, for example—will always display that trait and will never be subject to irresolvable conflicts between demands for helpfulness (Kamtekar 2004: 74–5). What is striking in the experiment with seminarians is that awareness of a relatively trivial requirement of helpfulness to those conducting the experiment can so easily eclipse what we would naturally think of as a vastly greater responsibility—helpfulness towards someone who may be dying.   [11] See above, Chap. 5, sect. 4.

manipulated by slight alterations to the associations unconsciously present in the subject's mind.[12]

Belief in virtues as Character-traits goes along with, and is not always distinguishable from, belief in personality; we speak readily of personality traits such as warmth and coldness.[13] But our judgements here are as fragile as our judgements about Character. Researchers have wondered whether our ready use of a warmth–coldness scale for persons is metaphorical transfer from developmentally important experiences of physical closeness to caregivers, and hence subject to interference from irrelevant experience of temperature. A recent experiment showed that people are more likely to rate someone as 'warm' if they, the rater, have briefly held a cup of hot coffee moments before. The same experience makes people more likely to behave generously (Williams and Bargh 2008). I take it we agree that briefly holding a warm object is not a way to detect, or to acquire, the virtuous character trait of generosity.

11.2. Response

One defensive response to these attempts at revision appeals to a supposed demarcation between conceptual schemes or 'worlds' which the proposed revision ignores. Roger Scruton, expressing a debt to Kant, Husserl, and Wittgenstein, distinguishes 'the world of human experience from the world of scientific observation' (Scruton 1986: 4). These are not really, for Scruton, distinct worlds, but distinct 'ways of understanding the world'; or perhaps the distinction is best expressed as one between the surface and the depth of the world: 'as agents we belong to the surface of the world, and enter into immediate relation to it.'[14] While both ways of understanding are necessary, the way of science cannot persuade us to 'replace our most

[12] See Bargh, Chen, and Burrows 1996. Prejudice in favour of Character is probably sustained by other biases as well. Once the notion of Character takes hold, our general confirmation bias—our tendency to give weight to instances that support our beliefs—will make it hard to dislodge.

[13] One way to sharpen the Character/personality distinction is to say, with Peter Goldie, that Character traits are 'deeper' than personality traits, and are 'concerned with a person's moral worth' (Goldie 2004: 27).

[14] Ibid. 9. Scruton is not promoting an anti-scientific or subjectivist programme; he insists that the world of human experience, the *Lebenswelt*, is 'just as much a public object, and just as much susceptible to third-person description, as is the world of science' (ibid. 387).

basic, everyday concepts with anything better than themselves, for they have evolved precisely under the pressure of human circumstance and in answer to the needs of generations'. They are concepts which it is 'the duty of philosophy . . . to sustain and validate' (Scruton 1986: 9). Scruton does not apply this line of thinking to the present case—the case of Character—and might not choose to do so; the remarks I have quoted come from his discussion of the relations between sex as a phenomenon of the *Lebenswelt* and the science of sex. But it is a natural thought that the two-worlds (or surface/depth) view offers a way to cut off the debate with social psychology concerning virtue before it has a chance to unsettle our pre-scientific convictions. Others have subscribed to the thought that great literature reveals aspects of our mental lives that do not require scientific validation. Colin McGinn says that Shakespeare offers us

the human mind as we recognize it—as we experience it in the marketplace and at home. He is not informing us of facts about human nature of which we have no prior knowledge . . . he provides instead the shock of recognition—dramatically presenting human psychology as we humans experience it.   (McGinn 2006: 166)

I am not sympathetic to the two-worlds view. While bad inferences have been made from premises concerning what is called the sub-personal level to conclusions about how things are with persons, these inferences, or ones in the other direction, are not always invalid.[15] But we need not argue about the extent to which the two-worlds view can be defended; the debate over virtues engendered by social psychology is not one which involves any sort of crossing of levels that the two-worlds view would identify as problematic. In the case of research into Character and its role in human affairs, the relevant scientific description of the evidence lies within the resources of our folk-psychological description of the *Lebenswelt*. The experiments do not involve brain scans or surgical interventions; they involve, as we have seen, manipulating the social circumstances a person finds herself in and seeing how, in those circumstances, the subject responds to an opportunity to help someone. These are situations of just the kind which occur when people really face a choice between continuing the concerns of daily life and attending to an unexpected moral imperative.

---

[15] Some work on so-called 'neuroaesthetics' strikes me as an example of bad cross-level inference; for comment, see John Hyman, 'Art and Neuroscience' <http://www.interdisciplines.org/artcognition/papers/15>.

No doubt people have wondered, on observing such situations, quite what it is that makes people behave the way they do, and why human behaviour in such situations is as disappointing as it sometimes is. Both in terms of the question asked and the experimental set-up, the scientific approach to this issue is continuous with and understandable within the *Lebenswelt*, though the approach is somewhat more systematic and quantitative than one generally finds in casual conversation. That we are not moving beyond the realm of common understanding is underlined by the fact that researchers concerned to interpret these experiments have said that the primary determinant of behaviour is not the situation considered as something independent of the subject, but the situation *as the subject conceives it*.[16]

Nor is there anything globally revisionary about the approach taken or the results that follow; nothing in these experiments undercuts the idea that people have beliefs and desires on which they act, or that they have perceptions, feelings, and emotions. The idea of Character stands at some remove from more robust bits of mental furniture in the folk-psychological system, such as beliefs, desires, perceptions, and feelings. Character is said to be difficult to read, even, or especially, by the Character's owner; we are surprised by revelations of Character which overturn our previous conceptions of that person—a device drawn on time and time again in fiction. Disbelieving in Character is consistent with retaining much of the rest of moral psychology.

So we may treat the results of these experiments and their interpretation, not as invasion by an alien culture, but as a friendly attempt to render more effective a folk-psychological conversation which all competent participants can be expected to understand and respond to without having to learn a new conceptual scheme or abandon their common sense network of beliefs about human motivation. It would not do simply to say that our beliefs about Character are off-limits to critical inquiry because they 'answer to the needs of generations'.[17]

I will assume, from now on, that the challenge from Character-scepticism cannot be deflected by the 'two worlds' strategy, but must be confronted

---

[16] See Ross and Nisbett 1991: 12–13.

[17] Conversely, it is available to the philosophers to question, within this common framework, the conclusions drawn by social psychologists, as is done by Neera Badhwar, disputing the conclusion that mildly self-deceptive tendencies have a positive effect on well-being (Badhwar 2008).

head-on. One suggestion is that we abandon the notion of Character traits as dispositions highly insensitive to the situation the agent finds herself in, and put our faith in the existence of situation-dependent dispositions, something we might think of as either a slimmed-down version of Character or as a replacement for that now defunct notion.[18] Others have defended the more or less traditional notion of Character against the arguments drawn from social psychology.[19] I won't try to analyse the prospects for a defence, limited or total, of Character. Instead, I ask what the effect should be on our thinking about Character in narrative and about Character-based criticism, *if the best, most rational response to the evidence is to say that there is here a serious challenge to our ideas about the role of Character in real human affairs.* In fact, I will simplify by assuming that the evidence suggests that there is no such thing as Character. But it is worth noting that this issue does not cease to be a live one for the narrative theorist if some less-extreme response is called for. If we conclude that virtues and other Character traits exist, but turn out to be something rather different from what we first thought they were, or that virtue is simply a lot less important to understanding moral behaviour than we thought it was, then we ought to rethink the ways in which and the extent to which we credit literary representations with the power to give us insights into Character. In general, anyone who wants to claim anything at all about the relation between values in literature and the representation of Character and virtue ought to be intensely interested in the outcome of the empirical debate. If its results do not persuade us to abandon the idea of Character, they are likely to change it in some, perhaps subtle, way, and subtle variations in our understanding of Character translate into variations, perhaps subtle, perhaps not, in our understanding of what is valuable in the representation of Character.

---

[18] Perhaps the most extreme sceptic about Character is Gilbert Harman (Harman 1998–9). John Doris, whose *Lack of Character* I refer to a number of times, is a little more guarded in his conclusions, suggesting we might believe in Character traits that are highly circumstantially circumscribed (Doris 2000); this conclusion also seems problematic from the point of view of the narrative of Character, which so often presents Character as extremely robust under circumstantial change.

[19] Kamtekar argues that a virtue-ethicist's notion of Character is not committed, as Harman and others suppose, to the idea that people differ much in Character (Kamtekar 2004). I think we can ignore this point here, since narratives of Character do seem to thrive on the notion of Character *difference*. Kamtekar expresses some scepticism about our ordinary notion of Character. Some recent work in social psychology suggests evidence for the predictive role of Character-trait attributions; see e.g. Hogan 2005 on conscientiousness. I am grateful here to Lawrence Jost.

11.3. Simplifying the Problem

There are some lines of inquiry we might pursue here but which I will comment on only briefly. First, we might insist on the complexity with which Character is presented in the best of narratives, highlighting their emphasis on circumstance, weakness of will, and other contingencies that lessen the influence of Character; it would note their acknowledgement that, as *Middlemarch* has it, 'there is no creature whose inward being is so strong that it is not greatly determined by what lies outside it'; it would point to episodes such as the narrative of Fred Vincy, wherein other characters show a good deal of sensitivity to the role of the situation in moral choice: they recognize that Fred's best purposes depend on propitious circumstances, and go to some trouble to bring them about.[20] It would trace the sometimes uncritical reliance on Character as an explanatory notion in history, but also the regular suspicion which this notion attracted, as with Johnson's remark on the historian Robertson, who 'paints minds as Sir Joshua paints faces in a history-piece: he imagines an heroic countenance'.[21] All this is worth examining in depth, but in another place. Instead I will stick with the project of engineering a confrontation between extremes. It may have some heuristic value when we get to the messy details of particular narratives. And there is a good reason to simplify: I am defending the role of Character in narrative, so the strongest challenge to that position is the one to focus on. The strongest contrary position—the one with the greatest potential to undermine the value we place on narratives of Character—is the one that simply denies the existence of Character.

Second, it has been argued that questions of truth and falsity are irrelevant to the merits of literature, so there is no tension between the scepticism-inducing facts about Character (as I am assuming them to be) and the ways in

---

[20] Indeed, George Eliot suggests a version of the extended mind hypothesis: 'Even much stronger mortals than Fred Vincy hold half their rectitude in the mind of the being they love best' (*Middlemarch*, chap. 24).

[21] Boswell, *Life of Johnson*, World's Classics (Oxford University Press, 1980), 528, 1034, quot. Hargraves 2003: 30. Robertson was keen to emphasize the ways in which Character is itself the product of social forces, deploring what he saw as the flattening effect on the opposition between virtues and vices of the Feudal system; he also suggests that, in some cases, the effects of Character are those of the conscious putting-on of a role (ibid. 34–7). For very recent examples of historical explanation by reference to Character, see e.g. Christie 1970. But a good deal of contemporary historical writing, even where it focuses on an individual, makes little appeal to Character. An excellent example is David Abalufia's Character-deflating study of Emperor Frederick II (Abalufia 1988).

which Character is represented in literature.[22] The problem posed by doubts about the notion of Character strikes me as a *reductio ad absurdum* of the truth-value-is-irrelevant view. Assume that there is, in fact, overwhelming evidence for the non-existence of Character; would anyone then argue that this poses no problem for our traditional ways of understanding, engaging with, and appreciating the great narratives of Character we find in the nineteenth-century novel or the plays of Shakespeare? I would find such a claim surprising.[23] Anyhow, for present purposes I simply ignore the truth-value-is-irrelevant view and address only those people who feel, as I do, that fictional narratives of real value ought to have some significant relation to what is true, particularly in the domain of human psychology. Given this, I am willing to grant that there would be a loss of literary value consequent on the discovery that scepticism about Character is correct. The question that remains is this: what kinds of literary (or, more broadly, narrative) values, if any, would be preserved in this situation?

Third, it might be argued that even if our assumptions about Character are false, they play a role in our lives which is significant enough for us to value the part that literature plays in inducting us into the network of beliefs which help to make up what we think of as sensitivity to Character.[24] One form of this argument points out that, as a matter of fact, sensitivity to Character is itself taken to be a Character-trait, and a positive one, in which case manifest sensitivity to Character (or the appearance of it) will contribute to one's thriving independently of the facts about Character, as long as certain views about Character remain part of common belief. As long as all or most other people believe in Character it may be advantageous to believe in it yourself; otherwise you face exclusion from certain kinds of gossip, and gossip is a powerful form of social cement.[25] And, attending closely to narratives of Character may assist your public relations department; sounding like a good discriminator of Character will make you admired even when there is no Character to

---

[22] See Lamarque and Olsen 1996.

[23] Kendall Walton says, and I agree with him, that 'It just does not seem plausible that what is so wonderful aesthetically about much great poetry, for instance, has nothing at all to do with the insights we receive from it' (Walton 2008: 4). While something need not be strictly and precisely true in order to count as an insight, its claim to being an insight does depend on its relation to truth.

[24] Such a position might be attractive as a fallback for those who would like to hold that Character is an unassailable part of the *Lebenswelt* (see discussion of Scruton above). See also Richard Moran on the ways in which a false self-conception contributes to one's real psychological profile (Moran 2001: sect. 2.3).   [25] See Dunbar 1996.

discriminate. Or it might be said that, while the facts are wildly at variance with what we typically believe about Character, belief in Character is an important part of the folk-psychological package which holds us together as communities, and that systematic refusal to think or speak in terms of Character-traits would be in some way disastrous to our interpersonal relations. It is even possible that talking and thinking in terms of virtuous Character-traits—especially when the thought or talk is scaffolded around vivid narratives of right action—has a positive effect on people's behaviour, though the effect is independent of whether Character traits actually exist. All these arguments seem to me interesting, but all depend on empirical assumptions about motivation and interpersonal relations which are difficult to assess. I therefore take them no further. In the appendix to this chapter I do say something more about the possible advantages of believing in Character, taking up points about the evolution of signalling made in the appendices to Chapters 2 and 5.

Fourth, in defending the idea of Character-based narratives, I shall not be arguing that this is the only morally and aesthetically serious genre of narrative able to explore issues to do with choice and responsibility; I am arguing that it is one such genre, with, incidentally, the advantage of being exemplified by works of manifest authority and value.

Fifth, I will not be suggesting (nor, I think, is anyone else suggesting) that the prominence of Character in a narrative is in itself a merit in the work—that depends on how the work is developed and on how the theme of Character is balanced and connected with other themes such as contingency and the role of stable social forces. My claim will be only that the capacity of Character, in the right hands, to add value to a work is not destroyed by scepticism about the role that Character plays in the real world.

Sixth, I will assume that much of our system of broadly ethical thought would survive the undermining of the notion of Character, that we would retain such concepts as deliberation, intention, decision, responsibility, blame, guilt, and (just possibly) shame, applying them in many of the situations we now apply them in. This is denied by some ethicists, but the denial is controversial enough to justify ignoring it in order not to make a difficult issue even harder.[26]

---

[26] See again Doris 2000, esp. chaps 6 and 7, for what seems to me a sensible approach. On Character and the self in Greek literature and philosophy, see Williams 1993; on the role of Character in Williams'

11.4. The Role of Character in Narrative

With all these simplifying assumptions in place, we may now ask: what kinds of value may accrue to narrative in virtue of its representation of Character, assuming there is no such thing as Character? A natural answer is that Character is just like many other non-existents. The Greeks were wrong to believe in their gods—if that is what they did—and to believe that we have responsibilities to them.[27] Those Elizabethans who believed in demons that present themselves as the ghosts of loved ones were also wrong. But we do not deny the dramatic and narrative-shaping force of gods and ghosts in Homer and in *Hamlet*. And we saw in Chapter 10 that Character does have these dramatic and narrative-shaping qualities. Character vividly differentiates and gives continuity to the persons of the plot, while the idea of robustness of Character generates questions, expectations, and corresponding emotional responses of uncertainty, pleasure, and disappointment. Rosamund ignores Lydgate's pleas for economy, and doing so seems to be expressive, in her case, of a very robust Character trait. Will she soften as things get worse? The narrative maintains our interest through many chapters by posing this question, and generates a good deal of satisfying ill-will towards her as the answer becomes clear.

Can the case for Character be made out on the basis of these parallels alone? We need to distinguish between what is valuable as a plot-enabling device and what is valuable because it creates a pathway to the exploration of genuine human concerns. Gods and ghosts may justify their presence in a story merely by creating circumstances for the persons of the plot to respond to in interesting ways; these ways of responding need to match (perhaps under some partially distorting transformation) genuinely human ways of responding. That makes the question of the reality of Character an urgent one, and one with quite different implications for story-construction from the question whether gods and ghosts are real.

own ethical thinking and in particular in relation to his use of fictional examples—his own and those of others—see Mulhall 2007.

[27] Paul Veyne's (1988) does little to answer the question of its title, partly because the question submerges under issues concerning the relativity of truth itself.

The question then to be asked is whether narratives which ascribe an important role for Character in the determination of behaviour—a role which is significantly at variance with the facts—will lack a capacity to give us insight into human motivation. I do not think a general answer to this question is possible; everything depends on the specific other features of the narratives in question. No doubt there are narratives that give a role to Character that makes it hard to find in them psychological insight. But for a wide range of cases, this is not so. Narratives which emphasize motivation rarely place the whole of the explanatory burden on the notion of Character, even when Character plays an important role in them; they emphasize the details of specific occasions of choice, conflict, dilemma, and decision and provide, or allow us to reconstruct, a great deal concerning situation, motivation, temptation, and all those other things that make a crucial difference to the particulars of a case. In such narratives we may think of Character, not so much as a psychological-explanatory tool, but as a device for making vivid and coherent the interplay of these other, psychologically real factors. And the personalized conflict between Character-traits makes it possible for narratives to explore tensions between values without recourse to didactic commentary: Mary Garth's generosity makes it harder for Fred Vincy to take the uncomfortable path she exalts him to, while Lydgate's character embodies the potential for conflict between personal loyalty and social obligation. Combining these roles in one, Character is an organizing principle around which a novel like *Middlemarch* plays out its moments of emotional conflict, its trackings of growing disappointment and dawning hope, its depictions of moral compromise and confusion. These things would survive the abandonment of Character as a psychological-explanatory concept, as long as we retain a thinner moral psychology based on desire, deliberation, and responsibility.[28]

The point is general. Gradgrindian insistence on absolute representational realism, whether in carpet decoration, plot construction, the psychology of motivation, or anything else, is to be avoided. As Noël Carroll points out, there rarely was a crime less likely to succeed than that which forms

---

[28] Something like this point is made by Karen Chase in her excellent book on personality in nineteenth-century fiction (Chase 1984). Discussing the eccentric psychology which informed the construction of *Jane Eyre*, she argues that Brontë's conception of the sources of human action is best seen as a device to establish 'fixed markers within the fluidity of human psychological experience'; what is valuable in the work is not its account of 'the sources and ends of human behavior' but 'its powerful implicit presentation of certain emotional tensions and resolutions' (ibid. 58).

the basis for Hitchcock's *Vertigo* (Carroll 1997). So much could have gone wrong that, multiplying together all the improbabilities necessary for its success, no sensible criminal would have contemplated it. Still, this plot, just as it is, is a sound vehicle for the depiction of selfish and cruel desire; a highly unrealistic motivational context brings out, with dramatic force, a very real feature of human motivation. And Gombrich, commenting on the insistence of Vitruvius that the painter 'keep strictly to [architectural] forms which . . . would stand up in reality', notes his failure to see how the flimsiness and paradox of 'playful and grotesque fictitious structures . . . enhanced their character as decorative fiction' (Gombrich 1999: 24). Likewise, Character, properly balanced by fine distinctions as to circumstance and the contingency of a point of view, may illuminate rather than distort the details of motive.

11.5. Reflections

I will conclude with three comments, the last being an attempt to undermine the argument just given. First, the mutually reinforcing connections between Character and narrative which I have emphasized have some tendency to contribute to scepticism about Character. If Character and narrative are well suited to one another, with Character a powerful plot device for sustaining discourse about human interactions, and narrative a powerful medium for the elaboration of Character, a tendency to credulity about Character would not be surprising. While the extent to which life is lived 'as narrative' is often overstated, it is plausible that we tend to frame our experience in narrative terms, especially when reflecting on events of personal significance.[29] If we do, we are likely to bring to these reflections those narrative devices which we associate most closely with that form; Character is one of these. And, while it is difficult to know how this could be quantified, a good deal of our faith in the existence of Character seems to arise, not from our direct experience of persons, but from their literary and dramatic representation. I have heard it said that most of us know what we do know about nobility of Character, not from people of noble Character, who are rare and tend to move in other circles, but from such

---

[29] On lives as narratives, see above, Chap. 1, sect. 4.

representations of nobility as we receive from Shakespeare. It would be odd to argue that, while witches are admittedly rather elusive beings, we have good evidence of their natures and actions from *Macbeth*.

Secondly, the argument proposes, in effect, that we take Character out of the category 'realistic background for the narrative' and put it into the category 'significant aesthetic and dramatic device'. Could we do this without badly affecting our responses to the works concerned? In particular, will scepticism about Character have an empathy-blocking effect that would compromise a narrative's emotional power?[30] I will examine this question within the framework of a simulationist approach to empathy, so I ask whether Character is a simulable aspect of a person's mental economy. If it is not, and if empathy (in the relevant sense) is simulation, then Character does not matter one way or another for empathic engagement. If the sceptics are right and Character is not a real aspect of human psychology, then it is not simulable, because it is a principle of simulationist approaches to empathy that the ability to empathize with a person having some mental state or feature X depends on the ability really to have X.[31] We can, on this view, empathize with the decision-making of others because we have the capacity to make decisions ourselves, and this allows us to model their decision-making in our own minds. And we can empathize with their emotional reactions because we have the capacity to respond emotionally. A being who cannot make decisions or respond emotionally cannot simulate decision-making or emotional responding. In that case we can say: if we came truly to believe that there was no such thing as Character, this could not affect our empathic engagement with the people who inhabit a narrative of Character, because it would in that case never have been true that Character was made available by simulative methods.

Can this argument be turned against the Character-sceptics? Is it not obvious that one strong reason why we like narratives of Character is that they possess an enhanced capacity to generate empathy? In that case, Character must be simulable, in which case it must exist. I say that this argument must be wrong, for I say that Character, even if it did exist, would not be simulable. What is simulable is confined to short-term states

---

[30] I thank Stephen Barker for raising this issue.
[31] See my (forthcoming), for some elaboration and a brief survey of evidence.

and processes such as decisions, as well, perhaps, as emotional episodes and emotionally coloured attitudes such as hope and expectation. We allow that beliefs and desires are simulable, but all that commits us to is the capacity to simulate a piece of theoretical or practical reasoning that involves certain beliefs and (in the case of practical reasoning) desires. We simulate the having of a certain belief-desire as it shows up on a given occasion, not the long-term state of being disposed to behave in certain ways. Through engaging with a narrative's people, I may imagine myself in their situations, feeling by turns fearful, pugnacious, resigned, and aggrieved. While these states may be presented by the narrative as emblematic of the Characters of these people, it is not possible to identify my feeling aggrieved with the simulation of anything more extended than an episode of aggrievedness, and everyone grants the reality of these states, whatever their attitude to Character.

What may be true of narratives of Character is that they enhance empathy in other ways. Drawing on the earlier suggestion that Character functions as an effective organizing principle for the presentation of other mental states, we may hazard the following. By presenting a person's beliefs and desires, feelings and decisions within a Character-based representation of that person, the narrative may succeed in making those beliefs, desires, feelings, and decisions more vivid, enabling us to hone in more effectively on those simulable aspects of a mental economy. That way, the representation of Character enhances empathy even without the prospect of empathizing with Character.

Finally, a concern about trying to settle the issue in the way gestured at above. It may seem that I am trying to argue from the wrong side of an imaginative divide which, if crossed, would reveal the seriousness of a problem which I am not at the moment properly able to confront. While I am aware of, and indeed impressed by, the evidence for scepticism about Character, I have not yet got to the position of vividly imagining what it would be like thoroughly to disbelieve in Character. I am very prone to draw conclusions about people's Characters, to explain actions in terms of Character—indeed, some of the evidence I have cited suggests that we spontaneously draw conclusions about Character when those conclusions are entirely unsupported. Given this, it is unlikely that I can fully understand how narratives of Character would affect me if I thoroughly and whole-heartedly came to disbelieve in Character, instead of being inclined, as Hume was about induction, to abandon scepticism on leaving the study. Character might, as I have suggested, retain much or all of its appeal on account of its sturdy usefulness in unifying narratives and its capacity to provide vivid occasions for the playing out of ethical problems which themselves survive the demise of Character. It is also possible that a thoroughgoing reorientation that made us no longer prone to appeal to Character would make Character-based narratives seem to be either quaintly sentimental tracts or propaganda in support of a dangerously mistaken morality.

Appendix: Character and the Costs of Deception

I have put some emphasis on the tendency of people to make their decisions about co-operation and reciprocity on the basis of a person's known reliability in past exchanges. It is natural to frame this as a phenomenon of *Character* and the *recognition* of Character: defections and other forms of deception are the product of Character faults (or, alternatively, of the possession of negative Character traits) and testimony about deception leads us to form hypotheses about Character, something we think of as explanatory of the deception and predictive of future unreliability. We have now seen that serious doubts have been raised about the notion of Character, deriving from empirical studies of how people's behaviour varies across situations.

The hypothesis outlined in earlier appendices has the capacity to shed light on the following question: how is it that we have the apparently universal belief in the efficacy of Character, if that belief is false? Recall: the hypothesis is that narrative co-evolved with language because the narrative form kept testimony about people's behaviour (relatively) honest. And the value of this honest testimony was that it enabled people to target their own co-operative and altruistic behaviour towards those with good reputations.

Now doubts about the efficacy/existence of Character seem to undermine this hypothesis, because they undermine the assumption that people will do well by attending to testimony about a person's reliability in past situations and extrapolating from that to future and qualitatively different circumstances. However, it is possible to see the belief in Character as part of an effective mechanism for discouraging deception *without assuming that the belief in Character is true*. Suppose that unreliability is highly situation-dependent: a person who proves unreliable on one occasion may in fact not be very likely to be unreliable in another. But if people believe that acts of unreliability are revelatory of a person's Character and hence that they indicate that one should avoid pairing with that person for future collaborative or reciprocation-based activities, then perpetrators of unreliable acts will incur high costs, and will hence face strong disincentives to dishonest behaviour. That way, the belief in Character, even if it has no basis in fact or is a substantial exaggeration of the facts, pays for itself by helping to control the explosion of unreliability that goes with the emergence of complex language.

This explanation leaves us with the problem of explaining how a tendency to believe in Character could emerge and spread. After all, a single believer in Character gets no advantage, as long as there is no such thing, because no one person's attitudes can materially affect the cost of dishonesty. And that single believer will be at some disadvantage, because he or she will pass up opportunities for co-operation that others will take and benefit from. The problem would be solved if we thought that sensitivity to Character was sensitivity to something real, since a single person who can detect and respond to Character-based tendencies will be a better predictor of behaviour; but at this point we are trying to explain the emergence of a false belief in Character, so this solution is unavailable to us.

Problems like this arise in evolutionary theorizing from time to time.[32] One solution is to assume that the trait in question was at first adaptationally neutral and spread for non-adaptational reasons, acquiring a proper function only once it had spread. As indicated above, the trait in question here—the belief in Character—seems to be initially disadvantageous, so this sort of reasoning is also not available to us.[33] Another solution has it that the trait came as the by-product of some other, adaptive, trait, as the polar bear's unwontedly heavy coat was a consequence of its advantageously warm coat.[34] I will briefly develop a solution of this kind, though there will turn out to be important differences between this case and the case of the polar bear.

The solution depends on the claim that we have a tendency to believe that more of the world is explicable in terms of mental organization than is actually the case. We believe in supernatural agents which do not exist, as well as in complex and deep mental structures that mysteriously govern our action; we attribute rational motives and deliberations to animals which are not capable of them; we believe, of what are in fact the unintended consequences of actions, that they are the product of malevolence; we believe, of what are in fact the outcomes of lone decisions, such as the Kennedy assassination, that they are the product of vast conspiracies; we put down our own failings to the force of circumstance, but we regularly attribute the irksome behaviour of others to Character faults, finding reason to complain, not merely about people's decision-making, but about deep-seated traits indicative of the 'sorts of people they are'.[35] Where there is no mind, we manage still to see

---

[32] See Origgi and Sperber 2001: sect. 8.

[33] I have framed this as a hypothesis about 'the belief in Character', but its earlier manifestations might have been at a level that would not happily be described in terms of belief; we might talk instead of 'an instinctive tendency towards future distrust of those who have deceived or defected in the past'.

[34] See Jackson 1982.

[35] For some of the implications of this fault for our understanding of the difference between belief and imagination, see Currie and Jurideini 2004. For more recent work, see e.g. Rosset 2008 on adult

it; where there is some mind, we see more of it; where mind is disorganized, we see it as highly organized; where there is mind at the level of decision, we find mind at the higher level of Character.

We ought not to conclude from this that mind is an illusion; on the contrary, the best explanation for these excesses may be one that depends on the assumption that mind *is* real, and really understood. At some stage in our evolutionary past we learned the trick of reading minds, our own and those of others. Because minds actually do exist, and understanding them confers such power on the one who understands, we went on to develop a mind-reading capacity of enormous strength. And, powerful devices are sometimes not very discriminating. Perhaps our mind-reading capacity is like a crude house-destruction technology: a bigger wrecking ball gives you greater penetration but less careful targeting.

My hypothesis then is that belief in Character emerged, not as an independent trait that needed to spread through the population under its own steam, but as the result of an overshoot in our otherwise highly adaptive tendency to mind-read. Here we come to a crucial difference between this case and that of the polar bear's coat. Given the resources nature has to work with, I take it there was some inevitability in the polar bear ending up with a heavy coat; nature just could not engineer the weight of the coat down below a certain level. One puzzle about the overshoot in mind-reading tendencies is why, assuming it was non-adaptive, it was not corrected. Why did selection pressure not refine our mind-reading skills to the point where we became much better mind-detectors? There does not seem to be any reason why a mind-reading creature has to be a *profligate* mind-reader. Faced with such a question, it is natural to look for countervailing pressures which would explain the preservation in the population of the tendency to overshoot in mentalizing. That is what my current hypothesis amounts to: if belief in Character came into the population as a consequence of a highly adaptive but overshooting tendency to read mind into the world, its spread to fixation is explained. The fact that its excesses were preserved is then explained in terms of the incidental advantage it conferred on us which I have outlined above: providing a disincentive to cheating which dampened the explosion of unreliability set off by the development of complex language.

bias towards seeing intention in all behaviours and Kelemen and Rosset 2009, where it is argued that 'despite exposure to the causal explanations characterizing contemporary science, adults maintain certain scientifically unwarranted teleological ideas very explicitly'.

12

In Conclusion

Narrative is a form of representation; one with special features and a special role in our individual and collective lives. As a vehicle of thought and of communication it may have co-evolved with language, serving to dampen the explosion of unreliability that language, with its low-cost signals, unleashed on the social world. Narratives are artefactual representations which emphasize the causal and temporal connectedness of particular things, especially agents; they are exquisitely suited to the representation of motive and action. As well as representing minds and their transactions with the world, narratives depend for their capacity to represent on a special mind–world transaction: the communication of intention; their representational contents depend on what their makers manage to convey about their intentions to represent.

Narratives also have an expressive aspect which need not, though it sometimes does, depend on intention. By being expressive they manage not merely to tell a story but to situate the audience in relation to that story, drawing often on the reader's or viewer's natural inclinations but sometimes prescribing ways of responding to stories that conflict with those inclinations. Cases of conflict range from those perspective-enhancing tales we celebrate for their enlargement of understanding, through uncomfortable cases where we suspect that emotional responses are being elicited to inflate the narrative's sense of significance, to those narratives with an unredeemed appeal to the worst of motives. While narrators have many ways to frame our responses to their stories, a good deal of what they do is managed through pretence or imitation, the former being the basis of ironic narration and the latter the basis of narration which is oriented to (but not narration from) the point of view of a character. Another significant weapon in the narrator's armoury is the provision of distinctive—perhaps unrealistically distinctive—Characters to the persons of the plot; they are endowed with salient and robust principles of action, helping to achieve a sense that the world of the story is autonomous from its maker as well as satisfying a more or less universal desire for order, coherence, and the mental mastery of circumstance.

Bibliography

Abalufia, D. (1988) *Frederick II: A Mediaeval Emperor*. London: Allen Lane.

Abbott, H. Porter (2002) *Narrative*. Cambridge: Cambridge University Press.

Ackroyd, P. (2002) *Albion: The Origins of the English Imagination*. London: Chatto and Windus.

Aczel, R. (1998) 'Hearing Voices in Narrative Texts', *New Literary History*, 29: 467–500.

Adams, R. M. (2006) *A Theory of Virtue: Excellence in Being for the Good*. Oxford: Oxford University Press.

Alexander, R. (1987) *The Biology of Moral Systems*. New York: De Gruyter.

Allen, R. (2002) 'Avian Metaphor in *The Birds*'. In S. Gottlieb and C. Brookhouse (eds) *Framing Hitchcock: Selected Essays from the Hitchcock Annual*. Detroit, Mich.: Wayne State University Press.

Auerbach, E. (1953) *Mimesis: The Representation of Reality in Western Literature*. Princeton, N.J.: Princeton University Press.

Bach, K. (1994) 'Conversational Impliciture', *Mind and Language*, 9: 124–62.

——(2000) 'Quantification, Qualification and Context: A Reply to Stanley and Szabo', *Mind and Language*, 15: 262–83.

——(2005) 'Context *ex machina*'. In Z. G. Szabo (ed.) *Semantics versus Pragmatics*. Oxford: Oxford University Press.

Badhwar, N. (2008) 'Is Realism Really Bad for You?', *Journal of Philosophy*, 105: 85–107.

Bal, M. (1997) *Narratology*. 2nd edn. Toronto: University of Toronto Press.

Balcetis, E., and R. Dale (2005) 'An Exploration of Social Modulation of Syntactic Priming'. In *Proceedings of the Twenty-seventh Cognitive Science Society*. Mahwah, N.J.: Lawrence Erlbaum: 184–9.

Banfield, A. (1982) *Unspeakable Sentences: Narration and Representation in the Language of Fiction*. London: Routledge and Kegan Paul.

Bargh, J., M. Chen, and L. Burrows (1996) 'The Automaticity of Social Behaviour: Direct Effects of Trait Concept and Stereotype Activation on Action', *Journal of Personality and Social Psychology*, 71: 230–44.

Barker, S. (2004) *Renewing Meaning: A Speech-act Theoretic Approach*. Oxford: Oxford University Press.

Barrett, J., (1998) 'Cognitive Constraints on Hindu Concepts of the Divine', *Journal for the Scientific Study of Religion*, 37: 608–19.

Barrett, J., and F. Keil (1996) 'Conceptualizing a Non-natural Entity: Anthropo-morphism in God Concepts', *Cognitive Psychology*, 31: 219–47.

Bayley, J. (1995) 'Sleepwalk into Popularity', review of John Sutherland, *The Life of Sir Walter Scott: A Critical Biography*, *Times Higher Education Supplement*, 5 Apr.

Beach, J. W. (1918) *The Method of Henry James*. New Haven, Conn.: Yale University Press.

Beardsley, M. (1981) *Aesthetics*. Indianapolis, Ind.: Hackett Publishing Company.

Biesele, M. (1993) *Women Like Meat: The Folklore and Foraging Ideology of the Kalahari Ju/'hoan*. Bloomington, Ind.: Indiana University Press.

Blackburn, S. (1984) *Spreading the Word*. Oxford: Oxford University Press.

Block, N. (2005) Review of Alva Noë, *Action in Perception*, *Journal of Philosophy*, 102: 259–72.

Bloom, P. (1996) 'Intention, History, and Artefact Concepts', *Cognition*, 60: 1–29.

Boghossian, P., and J. D. Velleman (1989) 'Colour as a Secondary Quality', *Mind*, 98: 81–103.

Booth, Wayne C. (1974) *The Rhetoric of Irony*. Chicago: University of Chicago Press.

—— (1983) *The Rhetoric of Fiction*, 2nd edn. Chicago: University of Chicago Press.

—— (1988) *The Company We Keep*. Berkeley, Calif.: University of California Press.

Bower, G., and D. Morrow (1990) 'Mental Models in Narrative Comprehension', *Science*, 247: 44–8.

Boyer, P. (2001) *Religion Explained*. London: Heinemann.

Bradley, A. C. (1905) *Shakespearean Tragedy: Lectures on Hamlet, Othello, King Lear, Macbeth*. 2nd edn, London: Macmillan.

Bremond, C. (1964) 'Le Message narratif', *Communications*, 4: 4–32.

Bristol, M. (1994) Reviews of Christy Desmet, *Reading Shakespeare's Characters: Rhetoric, Ethics, and Identity* and Bert O. States, *Hamlet and the Concept of Character*, *Shakespeare Quarterly*, 45: 226–31.

—— (2000) 'How Many Children Did She Have?' In J. Joughin (ed.) *Philosophical Shakespeares*. London: Routledge.

Britton, J. (1961) 'Bradley and those Children of Macbeth', *Shakespeare Quarterly*, 349–51.

Brooks, C., and W. P. Warren (1946) *Understanding Fiction*. New York: F. S. Crofts and Co.

Brownell, H. H., et al. (1990) 'Appreciation of Metaphoric Alternative Word Meanings by Left and Right Brain-damaged Patients', *Neuropsychologia*, 28: 375–83.

Bruner, J. (1990) *Acts of Meaning*. Cambridge, Mass.: Harvard University Press.

Butterfield, H. (1957) *George III and the Historians*. London: Macmillan.

Byrne, A. (1993) 'Truth in Fiction: The Story Continued', *Australasian Journal of Philosophy*, 71: 24–35.

Calvin, W. H. (2002) *A Brain for All Seasons: Human Evolution and Abrupt Climate Change*. Chicago: University of Chicago Press.

Cameron, J. M. (1875) *Illustrations to Tennyson's Idylls of the King and other Poems*. London: Messrs. King and Co.

Campbell, J. (1994) *Past, Space and Self.*. Cambridge, Mass.: MIT Press.

—— (2007) 'An Interventionist Approach to Causation in Psychology'. In Alison Gopnik and Laura Schulz (eds) *Causal Learning: Psychology, Philosophy and Computation*. Oxford: Oxford University Press.

Carroll, N. (1990) *The Philosophy of Horror: Or, Paradoxes of the Heart*. London: Routledge.

—— (1993) 'Historical Narratives and the Philosophy of Art', *Journal of Aesthetics and Art Criticism*, 51: 313–26.

—— (1997) 'Vertigo and the Pathologies of Romantic Love'. In David Baggett and William A. Drumin (eds) *Hitchcock and Philosophy: Dial M for Metaphysics*. Chicago: Open Court.

—— (2001a) 'On the Narrative Connection'. In Willie van Peer and Symour Chatman (eds) *Perspectives on Narrative Perspective*. Albany, N.Y.: State University of New York Press.

—— (2001b) 'Art, Narrative and Moral Understanding'. In N. Carroll, *Beyond Aesthetics*. Cambridge: Cambridge University Press.

—— (2006) 'Introduction to Part IV: Film Narrative/Narration'. In N. Carroll and J. Choi (eds) *Philosophy of Film and Motion Pictures: An Anthology*. Oxford: Blackwell.

Carston, R. (2002) *Thoughts and Utterances*. Oxford: Blackwell.

Carver, C., R. Ganellen, W. Froming, and W. Chambers (1983) 'Modelling: An Analysis in Terms of Category Accessibility', *Journal of Experimental Social Psychology*, 19: 403–21.

Chartrand, T. L., and J. A. Bargh (1999) 'The Chameleon Effect: The Perception–Behavior Link and Social Interaction', *Journal of Personality and Social Psychology*, 76: 893–910.

Chase, K. (1984) *Eros and Psyche: The Representation of Personality in Charlotte Brontë, Charles Dickens and George Eliot*. New York and London: Methuen.

Chatman, S. (1990) *Coming to Terms*. Ithaca, N.Y. and London: Cornell University Press.

Chen, C. K. (2008) 'On Having a Point of View: Belief, Action, and Egocentric States', *Journal of Philosophy*: 240–58.

Cheney, D. L., and R. M. Seyfarth (1990) *How Monkeys See the World*. Chicago: University of Chicago Press.

Christie, I. (1970) *Myth and Reality in Late Eighteenth-century British Politics and other Essays*. London: Macmillan.

Cixous, H. (1974) 'The Character of Character', *New Literary History*, 5: 383–402.

Clark, H. H. (1996) *Using Language*. Cambridge: Cambridge University Press.

——and R. J. Gerrig (1984) 'On the Pretense Theory of Irony', *Journal of Experimental Psychology: General*, 113: 121–6.

———— (1990) 'Quotations as Demonstrations', *Language*, 66: 764–805.

Cohan, S. (1983) 'Figures beyond the Text: A Theory of Readable Character in the Novel', *Novel*, 17: 5–27.

Cohen, E. (2003) 'The Inexplicable: Some Thoughts after Kant'. In Berys Gaut and Paisley Livingstone (eds) *The Creation of Art*. Cambridge: Cambridge University Press.

Cohn, D. (1966) 'Narrated Monologue: Definition of a Fictional Style', *Comparative Literature*, 18: 97–112.

—— (1978) *Transparent Minds: Narrative Modes for Presenting Consciousness in Fiction*. Princeton, N.J.: Princeton University Press.

Cohn, D. (1999) 'The Second Author of *Death in Venice*'. In *The Distinction of Fiction*, Baltimore, Md.: Johns Hopkins University Press.

Colston, H., and R Gibbs (2002) 'Are Irony and Metaphor Understood Differently?' *Metaphor and Symbol*, 17: 57–80.

Comstock, G. (2005) 'Media Violence and Aggression, Properly Considered'. In S. Hurley and N. Chater (eds) *Perspectives on Imitation*, ii. *Imitation, Human Development and Culture*. Cambridge, Mass.: MIT Press.

Cooke, K. (1972) *A. C. Bradley and his Influence in Twentieth-century Shakespeare Criticism*. Oxford: Clarendon Press.

Corazza, E. (2005) 'On Epithets Qua Attributive Anaphors', *Journal of Linguistics*, 41: 1–32.

Cox, M. (1986) Introduction, *The Ghost Stories of M. R. James*. Oxford: Oxford University Press.

Culler, J. (1980) 'Fabula and Sjuzhet in the Analysis of Narrative: Some American Discussions', *Poetics Today*, 1: 27–37.

Currie, G. (1990) *The Nature of Fiction*. New York: Cambridge University Press.

—— (1993) 'Objectivity and Interpretation', *Mind*, 102: 413–28.

—— (1995) *Image and Mind: Film, Philosophy, and Cognitive Science*. Cambridge: Cambridge University Press.

—— (2002) 'Desire in Imagination'. In T. Gendler (eds) *Conceivability and Possibility*. Oxford: Oxford University Press.

—— (2004) *Arts and Minds*. Oxford: Oxford University Press.

—— (2006) 'Why Irony is Pretence'. In S. Nichols (ed.) *The Architecture of the Imagination*. Oxford: Oxford University Press.

—— (2008) 'Pictures of King Arthur: Photography and the Power of Narrative'. In S. Walden (ed.) *Photography and Philosophy: Essays on the Pencil of Nature*. Malden, Mass.: Blackwell.

—— (forthcoming) 'Empathy for Objects'. In A. Coplan and P. Goldie (eds) *Empathy: Philosophical and Psychological Perspectives*. Oxford: Oxford University Press.

—— and I. Ravenscroft (2002) *Recreative Minds*. Oxford: Oxford University Press.

—— and J. Juridieni (2003) 'Art and Delusion', *Monist*, 86: 556–78.

—— —— (2004) 'Narrative and Coherence', *Mind and Language*, 19: 409–27.

Dancy, J. (1995) 'New Truths in Proust?', *Modern Language Review*, 90: 18–28.

Danto, A. C. (1978) 'Freudian Explanations and the Language of the Unconscious'. In J. H. Smith (ed.) *Psychoanalysis and Language*. New Haven, Conn.: Yale University Press.

—— (1984) 'Defective Affinities: "Primitivism" in Twentieth-century Art', *Nation*, 239: 590–2.

Darley, J., and C. Bateson (1973) 'From Jerusalem to Jericho: A Study of Situational and Dispositional Variables in Helping Behaviour', *Journal of Personality and Social Psychology*, 27: 100–8.

Dawkins, M., and T. Guilford (2003) 'The Corruption of Honest Signalling', *Animal Behaviour*, 41: 865–73.

Dijksterhuis, A. (2005) 'Why We are Social Animals'. In S. Hurley and N. Chater (eds) *Perspectives on Imitation*, ii. *Imitation, Human Development and Culture*. Cambridge, Mass.: MIT Press.

—— and A. van Knippenberg (1998) 'The Relation between Perception and Behavior, or How to Win a Game of Trivial Pursuit', *Journal of Personal and Social Psychology*, 74: 865–77.

—— H. Aarts, J. Barg, and A. van Knippenberg (2000) 'On the Relation between Associative Strength and Automatic Behaviour', *Journal of Experimental Social Psychology*, 36: 531–44.

Doris, J. (2000) *Lack of Character*. Cambridge: Cambridge University Press.

Doron, E. (1991) 'Point of View as a Factor of Content'. In S. M. Moore and A. Z. Wyner (eds) *Proceedings of SALT 1*. Ithaca, N.Y.: CLC Publications.

Dowe, P. (2000) *Physical Causation*. Cambridge: Cambridge University Press.

Dretske, F. (1988) *Explaining Behavior*. Cambridge, Mass.: MIT Press.

Dunbar, R. (1996) *Grooming, Gossip and the Evolution of Language*. London: Faber and Faber.

Eilan, N., C. Hoerl, T. McCormack, and J. Roessler (eds) (2005) *Joint Attention: Communication and other Minds: Issues in Philosophy and Psychology*. Oxford: Oxford University Press.

Fabb, N. (2002) *Language and Literary Structure: The Linguistic Analysis of Form in Verse and Narrative*. Cambridge: Cambridge University Press.

Fara, M. (2008) 'Masked Abilities and Compatibilism', *Mind*, 117: 843–65.

Ferrari, G. (2008) 'Socratic Irony as Pretence', *Oxford Studies in Ancient Philosophy*, 34: 49–81.

Fivush, R. (1994) 'Constructing Narrative, Emotion and Gender in Parent–Child Conversations about the Past'. In U. Neisser and R. Fivush (eds) *The Remembering Self: Construction and Accuracy of the Life Narrative*. New York: Cambridge University Press.

Flanegan, O. (1993) *Varieties of Moral Personality*. Cambridge, Mass.: Harvard University Press.

Flesch, W. (2007) *Comeuppance: Costly Signaling, Altruistic Punishment, and Other Biological Components of Fiction*. Cambridge, Mass.: Harvard University Press.

Fludernik, M. (1991) 'Subversive Irony: Reflectorization, Trustworthy Narration and Dead-pan Narrative in *The Mill on The Floss*', *Real*, 8: 157–82.

—— (1993) *The Fictions of Language and the Languages of Fiction*. London and New York: Routledge.

Fodor, J. (1984) *The Modularity of Mind*. Cambridge Mass.: Bradford Books.

Forster, E. M. (1927) *Aspects of the Novel*. London: Edward Arnold.

Frank, R. (2001) 'Cooperation through Emotional Commitment'. In Randolph M. Nesse (ed.) *Evolution and the Capacity for Commitment*. New York: Russell Sage Foundation Publications.

Freud, S. (1985) 'The Uncanny'. In A Dickson (ed.) *The Pelican Freud Library*, xiv. Harmondsworth: Penguin. First pub. 1919.

Friedman, N. (1955) 'Point of View in Fiction: The Development of a Critical Concept', *PMLA* 70: 1160–84.

Funkhouser, E., and S. Spaulding (2009) 'Imagination and other Scripts', *Philosophical Studies*, 143: 291–314.

Gaut, B., and P. Livingstone (eds) (2003) *The Creation of Art*. Cambridge: Cambridge University Press.

Gendler, T. S. (2000) 'The Puzzle of Imaginative Resistance', *Journal of Philosophy*, 97: 55–81.

—— (2003) 'On the Relation between Pretence and Belief'. In M. Kieran and D. M. Lopes (eds) *Imagination, Philosophy and the Arts*. London: Routledge.

—— (2006a) 'Imaginative Contagion', *Metaphilosophy*, 37: 183–203.

—— (2006b) 'Imaginative Resistance Revisited'. In S. Nichols (ed.) *The Architecture of the Imagination*. Oxford: Oxford University Press.

—— (2008a) 'Alief in Action (and Reaction)', *Mind and Language*, 23: 552–85.

—— (2008b) 'Alief and Belief', *Journal of Philosophy*, 105: 634–63.

Genette, G. (1980) *Narrative Discourse*. Ithaca, N.Y. and London: Cornell University Press. Trans. of a portion of *Figures III*. First pub. 1970.

—— (1988) *Narrative Discourse Revisited*. Ithaca, N.Y. and London: Cornell University Press. Trans. of *Nouveau discours du recit*. First pub. 1983.

Gibbs, R. (1994) *The Poetics of Mind: Figurative Thought, Language, and Understanding*. Cambridge: Cambridge University Press.

—— (1999) *Intentions in the Experience of Meaning*. Cambridge: Cambridge University Press.

—— (2000) 'Metarepresentations as Staged Communicative Acts'. In D. Sperber (ed.) *Metarepresentations: A Multidisciplinary Perspective*. Oxford: Oxford University Press.

Gibson, James J. (1979) *The Ecological Approach to Visual Perception*. Boston: Houghton Mifflin.

Gibson, John (2007) *Fiction and the Weave of Life*. Oxford: Oxford University Press.

Gluckman, M. (1963) 'Gossip and Scandal', *Current Anthropology*, 4: 307–16.

Godfrey-Smith, P. (1996) *Complexity and the Function of Mind in Nature*. Cambridge: Cambridge University Press.

Goldie, P. (2003) 'Narrative, Emotion and Perspective'. In Matthew Kieran and Dominic McIver Lopes (eds) *Imagination, Philosophy and the Arts*. London: Routledge.

—— (2004) *On Personality (Thinking in Action)*. London: Routledge.

Gombrich, E. H. (1999) *The Uses of Images: Studies in the Social Function of Art and Visual Communication*. London: Phaidon.

Goodman, N. (1981) 'Twisted Tales: Story, Study and Symphony'. In W. J. T. Mitchell (ed.) *On Narrative*. Chicago: University of Chicago Press.

Green. M. (2007) *Self-Expression*. Oxford: Oxford University Press.

Greimas, A. (1977) 'Elements of a Narrative Grammar', *Diacritics*, 7: 23–40.

Grice, H. P. (1957) 'Meaning', *Philosophical Review*, 66: 377–88. Repr. in H. P. Grice, *Studies in the Way of Words*. Cambridge, Mass.: Harvard University Press, 1989.

—— (1989) *Studies in the Way of Words*. Cambridge, Mass.: Harvard University Press.

Gunn, D. (2004) 'Free Indirect Discourse and Narrative Authority in *Emma*', *Narrative*, 12: 35–54.

Haack, S. (1993) *Evidence and Inquiry: Towards Reconstruction in Epistemology*. Oxford: Basil Blackwell.

Halliwell, S. (2002) *The Aesthetics of Mimesis: Ancient Texts and Modern Problems*. Princeton, N.J.: Princeton University Press.

Happé, F. (1993) 'Communicative Competence and the Theory of Mind in Autism: A Test of Relevance Theory', *Cognition*, 48: 101–19.

—— (1995) 'Understanding Minds and Metaphors: Insights from the Study of Figurative Language in Autism', *Metaphor and Symbol*, 10: 275–95.

Hargraves, N. (2003) 'Revelation of Character in Eighteenth-century Historiography and William Robertson's *History of the Reign of Charles V*', *Eighteenth-century Life*, 27: 23–48.

Harman, G. (1999) 'Moral Philosophy Meets Social Psychology: Virtue Ethics and the Fundamental Attribution Error', *Proceedings of the Aristotelian Society*, 99: 315–31.

—— (2000) 'The Nonexistence of Character Traits', *Proceedings of the Aristotelian Society*, 100: 223–6.

Harold, J. (2005) 'Infected by Evil', *Philosophical Explorations*, 8: 173–87.

Harris, P., and S. Want (2005) 'On Learning What Not to Do: The Emergence of Selective Tool Use in Young Children'. In S. Hurley and N. Chater (eds) *Perspectives on Imitation*, ii. *Imitation, Human Development and Culture*. Cambridge, Mass.: MIT Press, 2005.

Harvey, W. J. (1965) *Character and the Novel*. London: Chatto and Windus.

Heal, J. (2003) *Mind, Reason and Imagination*. Cambridge: Cambridge University Press.

Herrnstein-Smith, B. (1981) 'Narrative Versions, Narrative Theories'. In W. Mitchell (ed.), *On Narrative*. Chicago: University of Chicago Press.

Hetherington, S. (2001) *Good Knowledge, Bad Knowledge: On Two Dogmas of Epistemology*. Oxford: Oxford University Press.

Hobson, P. (2005) 'What Puts the Jointness into Joint Attention?' In N. Eilan, et al. (eds) *Joint Attention: Communication and Other Minds: Issues in Philosophy and Psychology*. Oxford: Oxford University Press.

—— and A. Lee (1999) 'Imitation and Identification in Autism', *Journal of Child Psychology and Psychiatry*, 40: 649–59.

Hochman, B. (1985) *Character in Literature*. Ithaca, N.Y. and London: Cornell University Press.

Hoerl, C., and T. McCormack (2005) 'Joint Reminiscing as Joint Attention to the Past'. In N. Eilan, et al. (eds) *Joint Attention: Communication and other Minds: Issues in Philosophy and Psychology*. Oxford: Oxford University Press.

Hogan, R. (2005) 'In Defense of Personality Measurement: New Wine for Old Whiners', *Human Performance*, 18: 331–41.

Holloway, J. (1960) *The Charted Mirror*. London: Routledge.

Holton, R. (1997) 'Some Telling Examples: A Reply to Tsohatzidis', *Journal of Pragmatics*, 28: 625–8.

Hopkins, R. (1998) *Picture, Image and Experience*. Cambridge: Cambridge University Press.

Horwitz, M. (1986) '*The Birds*: A Mother's Love'. In M. Deutelbaum and L. Poages (eds) *A Hitchcock Reader*. Ames, Ia.: Iowa State University Press.

Hough G. (1970) 'Narrative and Dialogue in Jane Austen', *Critical Quarterly*, 12: 201–29.

Huesmann, L. R. (2005) 'Imitation and the Effects of Observing Media Violence on Behaviour'. In S. Hurley and N. Chater (eds) *Perspectives on Imitation*, ii. *Imitation, Human Development and Culture*. Cambridge, Mass.: MIT Press.

Hugenberg, K., and G. V. Bodenhausen (2003) 'Facing Prejudice: Implicit Prejudice and the Perception of Facial Threat', *Psychological Science*, 14: 640.

Hume, D. (1985) 'On the Standard of Taste'. Repr. in D. Hume, *Essays: Moral, Political and Legal*. Indianapolis, Ind.: Liberty Fund. First pub. 1757.

Hurley, S. L. (2004a) 'Active Perception and Perceiving Action: The Shared Circuits Hypothesis'. In T. S. Gendler and J. Hawthorne (eds) *Perceptual Experience*. New York: Oxford University Press.

—— (2004b) 'Imitation, Media Violence and Freedom of Speech', *Philosophical Studies*, 117: 165–218.

—— and N. Chater (eds) (2005) *Perspectives on Imitation*, ii. *Imitation, Human Development and Culture*. Cambridge, Mass.: MIT Press.

Ignatieff, Michael (1998) *Isaiah Berlin: A Life*. London: Chatto and Windus.

Iseminger, G. (1992) 'An Intentional Demonstration?' In G. Iseminger (ed.) *Intention and Interpretation*. Philadelphia, Pa.: Temple University Press.

Isen, A., and P. Levin (1972) 'Effect of Feeling Good on Helping: Cookies and Kindness', *Journal of Personality and Social Psychology*, 21: 384–8.

Iser, W. (1989) *Prospecting: From Reader Response to Literary Anthropology*. Baltimore, Md.: Johns Hopkins University Press.

Jackson, F. (1982) 'Epiphenomenal Qualia', *Philosophical Quarterly*, 32: 127–36.

—— (1987) *Conditionals*. Oxford: Blackwell.

Jancke, R. (1929) *Das Wesen der Ironie: Eine Strukturanalyse ihrer Erscheinungsformen*. Leipzig: Johann Ambrosius Barth.

Johansson, P., L. Hall, S. Sikstromand, and A. Olsson (2005) 'Choice Blindness: On the Failure to Detect Mismatches between Intention and Outcome in a Simple Decision Task', *Science*, 310: 116–19.

Jolly, R (1997) Review of S. Teahan, *The Rhetorical Logic of Henry James*, *Review of English Studies*, 98, 555–6.

Jones, K. (1996) 'Trust as an Affective Attitude', *Ethics*, 107: 4–25.

Kahneman, D., and A. Tversky (1981) 'The Framing of Decisions and the Psychology of Choice', *Science*, 30: 453–8.

Kamtekar, R (2004) 'Situation and Virtue Ethics on the Content of our Characters', *Ethics*, 114: 458–91.

Kania, A. (2002) 'The Illusion of Realism in Film', *British Journal of Aesthetics*, 42: 243–58.

Karttunen, L. (1977) 'Syntax and Semantics of Questions', *Linguistics and Philosophy*, 1: 3–44.

Keil, F., M. Greif, and R. Kerner (2007) 'A World Apart: How Concepts of the Constructed World are Different in Representation and in Development'. In E. Margolis and S. Laurence (eds) *Creations of the Mind*. Oxford: Oxford University Press.

Kelemen, D., and S. Carey (2007) 'The Essence of Artefacts: Developing the Design Stance'. In E. Margolis and S. Laurence (eds) *Creations of the Mind*. Oxford: Oxford University Press.

——and E. Rosset (2009) 'The Human Function Compunction: Teleological Explanation in Adults', *Cognition*, 111: 138–43.

Kermode, F. (1981) 'Secrets and Narrative Sequence'. In W. J. T. Mitchell (ed.) *On Narrative*. Chicago: University of Chicago Press.

Kinkead-Weekes, M. (1962) Introduction, Everyman Library edn of *Pamela*. London: Dent and Son.

Knights, L. C. (1933) *How Many Children had Lady Macbeth? An Essay in the Theory and Practice of Shakespeare Criticism*. Cambridge: Minority Press.

Krauss, L. (2007) *The Physics of Star Trek*. Revised. New York: Basic Books.

Kreuz, R., and S. Glucksberg (1989) 'How to be Sarcastic: The Echoic Reminder Theory of Verbal Irony', *Journal of Experimental Psychology: General*, 118: 374–86.

Kumon-Nakamura, S., S. Glucksberg, and M. Brown (1985) 'How about Another Piece of Pie: The Allusional Pretense Theory of Discourse Irony', *Journal of Experimental Psychology*, 124: 3–21.

Lachmann, M., S. Számadó, and C. Bergstrom (2001) 'Cost and Conflict in Animal Signals and Human Language', *Proceedings of the National Academy of Sciences*, 98: 13189–94.

Lamarque, P. (1996) *Fictional Points of View*. Ithaca, N.Y. and London: Cornell University Press, 1996.

——(2004) 'On Not Expecting Too Much of Narrative', *Mind and Language*, 17: 393–408.

——(2007) 'Aesthetics and Literature: A Problematic Relation?', *Philosophical Studies*, 135: 27–40.

——and S. H. Olsen (1996) *Truth, Fiction, and Literature: A Philosophical Perspective*. Oxford: Clarendon Press.

Le Poidevin, R. (2007) *The Images of Time*. Oxford: Oxford University Press.

Levinson, J. (1996) 'Film Music and Narrative Agency'. In D. Bordwell and N. Carroll (eds) *Post-theory: Reconstructing Film Studies*. Madison, Wis.: University of Wisconsin Press. Page refs are to the repr. in J. Levinson, *Contemplating Art*. Oxford: Oxford University Press, 2006.

——(2002) 'Hypothetical Intentionalism'. In M. Kraus (ed.) *On the Single Right Interpretation*. University Park, Pa.: Pennsylvania State University Press.

Levinson, S. (2000) *Presumptive Meaning: The Theory of Generalised Conversational Implicatures*. Cambridge, Mass.: MIT Press.

Lewis, D. K. (1975) 'Languages and Language'. In K. Gunderson (ed.) *Minnesota Studies in the Philosophy of Science*, 8: 3–35. Repr. in D. K. Lewis, *Philosophical Papers*, i. Oxford: Oxford University Press, 1983.

——(1976) 'The Paradoxes of Time Travel', *American Philosophical Quarterly*, 13: 145–52.

——(1978) 'Truth in Fiction', *American Philosophical Quarterly*, 15: 37–46. Repr. in D. K. Lewis, *Philosophical Papers*, i. Oxford: Oxford University Press, 1983.

——(1982) 'Logic for Equivocators', *Nous*, 16: 431–41.

——(1986) 'Causal Explanation'. Repr. in D. K. Lewis, *Philosophical Papers*, ii. Oxford: Oxford University Press, 1986.

Livingston, P. (2003) *Pentimento*. In B. Gaut and P. Livingstone (eds) *The Creation of Art*. Cambridge: Cambridge University Press.

——(2005) *Art and Intention*. Oxford: Oxford University Press.

Lopes, D. M. (1996) *Understanding Pictures*. Oxford: Oxford University Press.

Lubbock, P. (1921) *The Craft of Fiction*. London: Jonathan Cape.

McGinn, C. (2006) *Shakespeare's Philosophy*. New York: HarperCollins.

McHale, B. (1978) 'Free Indirect Discourse: A Survey of Recent Accounts', *Poetics and the Theory of Literature*, 3: 249–87.

MacIntyre, A. (1981) *After Virtue*. London: Duckworth.

Maynard, P. (2003) 'Drawing as Drawn: An Approach to Creation in an Art'. In B. Gaut and P. Livingstone (eds) (2003) *The Creation of Art*. Cambridge: Cambridge University Press.

Meltzoff, A. (1985) 'Immediate and Deferred Imitation in Fourteen- and Twenty-four-month-old Infants', *Child Development*, 56: 62–72.

——(1988) 'Infant Imitation and Memory: Nine-month-olds in Immediate and Deferred Tests', *Child Development*, 59: 217–25.

——(1990) 'Foundations for Developing a Concept of Self: The Role of Imitation in Relating Self to other and the Value of Social Mirroring, Social Modelling, and Self Practice in Infancy'. In D. Cicchetti and M. Beeghly (eds) *The Self in Transition: Infancy to Childhood*. Chicago: University of Chicago Press.

Misak, C. (2008) 'Experience, Narrative, and Ethical Deliberation', *Ethics*, 118: 614–32.

Mithen, S. (2005) *The Singing Neanderthals: The Origins of Music, Language, Mind and Body*. London: Weidenfeld and Nicolson.

Moore, A. (1997) *Points of View*. Oxford: Oxford University Press.

Moran, R. (1989) 'Seeing and Believing: Metaphor, Image and Force', *Critical Inquiry*, 16: 87–112.

——(1994) 'The Expression of Feeling in Imagination', *Philosophical Review*, 103: 75–106.

——(2001) *Authority and Estrangement: An Essay on Self-knowledge*. Princeton, N.J.: Princeton University Press.

Morrow, D., G. Gower, and S. Greenspan (1989) 'Updating Situation Models during Narrative Comprehension', *Journal of Memory and Language*, 28: 292–312.

Muecke, D. C. (1969) *The Compass of Irony*. London: Methuen.

Mulhall, S. (2007) 'The Mortality of the Soul: Bernard Williams's Character(s)'. In A. Crary (ed.) *Wittgenstein and the Moral Life: Essays in Honour of Cora Diamond*. Cambridge, Mass.: MIT Press.

Nagel, T. (1979) *Mortal Questions*. Cambridge: Cambridge University Press.

Namier, L. B. (1929) *The Structure of Politics at the Accession of George III*. 2 vols. London: Macmillan.

Namier, L. B. (1962) *Crossroads of Power: Essays on Eighteenth-century England*. London: Hamish Hamilton.

Nehamas, A. (1998) *The Art of Living*. Los Angeles, Calif.: University of California Press.

Neumann, R., and F. Strack (2000) 'Mood Contagion: The Automatic Transfer of Mood between Persons', *Journal of Personality and Social Psychology*, 79: 211–23.

Noë, A. (2004) *Action in Perception*. Cambridge, Mass.: MIT Press.

Nolan, D. (2007) 'A Consistent Reading of Sylvan's Box', *Philosophical Quarterly*, 57: 667–73.

Norwich, J. J. (1988) *Byzantium: The Early Centuries*. Harmondsworth: Penguin.

Nosek, B. A. (2007) 'Implicit–Explicit Relations', *Current Directions in Psychological Science*, 16: 65.

Nowak, M. A., and K. Sigmund (1998) 'Evolution of Indirect Reciprocity by Image Scoring', *Nature*, 393: 573–6.

O'Donnell, P. (2006) 'James's Birdcage/Hitchcock's Birds', *Arizona Quarterly*, 62: 45–62.

Ong, W. J. (1978) 'From Mimesis to Irony: The Distancing of Voice', *Bulletin of the Midwest Modern Language Association*, 9: 1–24.

Origgi, G., and D. Sperber (2000) 'Evolution, Communication, and the Proper Function of Language'. In Peter Carruthers and Andrew Chamberlain (eds), *Evolution and the Human Mind: Language, Modularity and Social Cognition*. Cambridge: Cambridge University Press.

Pafford, J. F. P. (ed.) (1963) *The Winter's Tale*. Arden Shakespeare. London: Methuen.

Paglia, C. (1998) *The Birds*. BFI Film Classics. London: British Film Institute.

Papineau, D. (2005) 'Social Leaning and the Baldwin Effect'. In A Zilhao (ed.) *Rationality and Evolution*. London: Routledge.

Parsons, G., and A. Carlson (2008) *Functional Beauty*. Oxford: Oxford University Press.

Patel, A. (2007) *Music, Language, and the Brain*. New York: Oxford University Press.

Peacocke, C. (2005) 'Joint Attention: Its Nature, Reflexivity, and Relation to Common Knowledge'. In N. Eilan, et al. (eds) *Joint Attention: Communication and Other Minds: Issues in Philosophy and Psychology*. Oxford: Oxford University Press.

Pearl, J. (2000) *Causality: Models, Reasoning, and Inference*. Cambridge: Cambridge University Press.

Phelan, J. (2001) 'Why Narrators can be Focalizers'. In W. van Peer and S. Chatman (eds) *New Perspectives on Narrative Perspective*. Albany, N.Y.: State University of New York Press.

Pilkington, A. (2000) *Poetic Effects: A Relevance Theory Perspective*. Amsterdam: John Benjamins.

Plumb, J. H. (1956) *The First Four Georges*. London: Batsford.

Ponech, T. (2006) 'External Realism about Cinematic Motion', *British Journal of Aesthetics*, 46: 349–68.

Predelli, S. (2005) *Contexts: Meaning, Truth, and the Use of Language*. Oxford: Oxford University Press.

Priest, G. (1997) 'Sylvan's Box: A Short Story and Ten Morals', *Notre Dame Journal of Formal Logic*, 38: 573–82.

Prince, G. (1998) 'Revisiting Narrativity'. In W. Grünzweig and A. Solbach (eds) *Grenzüberschreitungen: Narratologie im Kontext*. Tübingen: Gunter Narr.

Recanati, F. (2000) *Oratio Obliqua, Oratio Recta: An Essay in Metarepresentation*. Cambridge, Mass.: MIT Press.

—— (2001) 'Literal/Nonliteral', *Midwest Studies in Philosophy*, 25: 264–74.

Richie, D. (1972) *Focus on Rashomon*. New York: Prentice-Hall.

Rimmon-Kenan, S. (1983) *Narrative Fiction*. London: Routledge.

Roberts, G. (2001) *The History and Narrative Reader*. London: Routledge.

Robinson, J. (1985) 'Style and Personality in the Literary Work', *Philosophical Review*, 94: 227–47.

Roessler, J. (2005) 'Joint Attention and the Problem of other Minds'. In N. Eilan, et al. (eds) *Joint Attention: Communication and Other Minds: Issues in Philosophy and Psychology*. Oxford: Oxford University Press.

Rosenberg, B. (1992) 'Character and Contradiction in Dickens', *Nineteenth-century Literature*, 47: 145–63.

Ross, D. (1976) 'Who's Talking? How Characters Become Narrators in Fiction', *Modern Language Notes*, 91: 1222–42.

Ross, L., and R. E. Nisbett (1991) *The Person and the Situation*. Philadelphia, Pa.: Temple University Press.

Rosset E. (2008) 'It's No Accident: Our Bias for Intentional Explanations', *Cognition*, 108: 771–80.

Rossholm, G. (2004) *To Be and Not to Be*. Berne: Peter Lang.

Sainsbury, M. (2009) *Fiction and Fictionalism*. London: Routledge.

Sartre, Jean-Paul (2004) *The Imaginary*. London: Routledge. 1st (French) edn.: 1940.

Sass, L. (1994) *The Paradoxes of Delusion*. Ithaca, N.Y. and London: Cornell University Press.

Scholes, R., and R. Kellogg (1966) *The Nature of Narrative*. New York: Oxford University Press.

Scott, B. (2004) 'Picturing Irony: The Subversive Power of Photography', *Visual Communication*, 3: 31–59.

Scruton, R. (1986) *Sexual Desire: A Philosophical Investigation*. London: Weidenfeld and Nicholson.

Schwitzgabel, E. (2008) 'The Unreliability of Naïve Introspection', *Philosophical Review*, 2008: 245–443.

Smith, Adam (1979) *The Theory of the Moral Sentiments*. Oxford: Oxford University Press. First pub. 1759.

Smith, M. (1995) *Engaging Characters*. Oxford: Clarendon Press.

Smith, S. (2000) *Hitchcock: Suspense, Humour and Tone*. London: British Film Institute.

Sosa, E., and M. Tooley (eds) (1993) *Causation*. Oxford: Oxford University Press.

Sperber, D. (1984) 'Verbal Irony: Pretense or Echoic Mention?', *Journal of Experimental Psychology: General*, 113: 130–6.

—— (2007) 'Seedless Grapes: Nature and Culture'. In E. Margolis and S. Laurence (eds) *Creations of the Mind: Theories of Artifacts and their Representation*. Oxford: Oxford University Press.

—— and D. Wilson (1981) 'Irony and the Use-mention Distinction'. In P. Cole (ed.) *Radical Pragmatics*. New York: Academic Press.

—— —— (1995) *Relevance: Communication and Cognition*. 2nd edn. Oxford: Blackwell.

—— —— (2002) 'Pragmatics, Modularity and Mind-reading', *Mind and Language*, 17: 3–23.

St Clair, W. (2004) *The Reading Nation in the Romantic Period*. Cambridge: Cambridge University Press.

Stanzel, F. K. (1971) 'Narrative Situations in the Novel'. English trans. of *Die typischen Erzahlsituationen im Roman*. 1st pub. 1955. Bloomington, Ind.: Indiana University Press.

Sterelny, K. (2003) *Thought in a Hostile World*. Oxford: Blackwell.

Sternberg, M. (1982) 'Proteus in Quotation-land: Mimesis and the Forms of Reported Discourse', *Poetics Today*, 107–56.

Stohr, K. (2006) 'Practical Wisdom and Moral Imagination in Sense and Sensibility', *Philosophy and Literature*, 30: 378–94.

Strachey, J. (ed.) (1953–75) *The Standard Edition of the Complete Psychological Works of Sigmund Freud*. 24 vols. London: Hogarth Press.

Strawson, G. (2004) 'Against Narrativity', *Ratio* NS 17: 428–52.

Sugiyama, M. (2001) 'Food, Foragers, and Folklore: The Role of Narrative in Human Subsistence', *Evolution and Human Behavior*, 22: 221–40.

Tanner, M. (1994) 'Morals in Fiction and Fictional Morality', *Proceedings of the Aristotelian Society*, suppl. vol. 68: 51–66.

Tarde, G. (1903) *The Laws of Imitation*, trans. E. C. Parsons. New York: Henry, Holt and Co.

Taylor, M. J. H. (1982) 'A Note on the First Narrator of *The Turn of the Screw*', *American Literature*, 53: 717–22.

Thomasson, A. (2003) 'Speaking of Fictional Characters', *Dialectica*, 57: 207–26.

—— (2007) 'Artifacts and Human Concepts'. In E. Margolis and S. Laurence (eds) *Creations of the Mind: Theories of Artifacts and their Representations*. Oxford: Oxford University Press.

Tilford, J. E. (1958) 'James the Old Intruder', *Modern Fiction Studies*, 4: 157–64.

Tomalin, Claire (2002) *Samuel Pepys: The Unequalled Self*. London: Penguin.

Tomasello, M. (2000) *The Cultural Origins of Human Cognition*. Cambridge, Mass.: Harvard University Press.

Trivers, R. L. (1985) *Social Evolution*. Menlo Park, Calif.: Benjamin Cummings.

Tsohatzidis, S. (1993) 'Speaking of Truth-telling: The View from Wh-complements', *Journal of Pragmatics*, 19: 271–9.

—— (1997) 'More Telling Examples: A Response to Holton', *Journal of Pragmatics*, 28: 629–36.

Turner, R. N., R. Forrester, B. Mulhern, and R. J. Crisp (2005) 'Impairment of Executive Abilities Following a Social Category Prime', *Current Research in Social Psychology*, 11: 29–38.

van Baaren, R. B., R. W. Holland, B. Steenaert, and A. van Knippenberg (2003) 'Mimicry for Money: Behavioral Consequences of Imitation', *Journal of Experimental Social Psychology*, 39: 393–8.

Velleman, J. D. (2003) 'Narrative Explanation', *Philosophical Review*, 112: 1–25.

Vermazen, B. (1986) 'Expression as Expression', *Pacific Philosophical Quarterly*, 67: 196–224.

Vermeule, B. (2006) 'Gossip and Literary Narrative', *Philosophy and Literature*, 30: 102–17.

Veyne, P. (1988) *Did the Greeks Believe in their Myths?* Chicago: Chicago University Press.

Vlastos, G. (1991) *Socrates: Ironist and Moral Philosopher*. Cambridge: Cambridge University Press.

Walton, K. L. (1970) 'Categories of Art', *Philosophical Review*, 79: 334–67.

—— (1973) 'Pictures and Make-believe', *Philosophical Review*, 82: 283–319.

—— (1978) 'Fearing Fictions', *Journal of Philosophy*, 75: 5–27.

—— (1984) 'Transparent Pictures: On the Nature of Photographic Realism', *Critical Inquiry*, 11: 246–77.

—— (1990) *Mimesis as Make-believe*. Cambridge, Mass.: Harvard University Press.

—— (1994) 'Morals in Fiction and Fictional Morality', *Proceedings of the Aristotelian Society*, suppl. vol. 68: 27–50.

—— (1997) 'On Pictures and Photographs: Objections Answered'. In R. Allen and M. Smith (eds) *Film Theory and Philosophy*. New York: Oxford University Press.

—— (2008) *Marvelous Images: On Values and the Arts*. Oxford: Oxford University Press.

—— (forthcoming) 'Fictionality and Imagination: Mind the Gap'. In K. L. Walton, *In Other Shoes: Music, Metaphor, Empathy, Existence* (New York: Oxford University Press).

Watt, I. (1960) 'The First Paragraph of *The Ambassadors*', *Essays in Criticism*, 10: 250–74.

Weatherson, B. (2004) 'Morality, Fiction, and Possibility', *Philosophers' Imprint*, 4: 1–27.

Wedgewood, C. V. (1958) *The King's Peace*. London: Collins.

Weis, E. (1978) 'The Sound of One Wing Flapping', *Film Comment*, 14.

White, H. (1981) 'The Value of Narrativity and the Representation of Reality'. In W. J. T. Mitchell (ed.) *On Narrative*. Chicago: Chicago University Press.

Williams, B. (1993) *Shame and Necessity*. Los Angeles, Calif.: University of California Press.

Williams, L., and J. A. Bargh (2008) 'Experiencing Physical Warmth Promotes Interpersonal Warmth', *Science*, 322: 606–7.

Wilson, D., and D. Sperber (1992) 'On Verbal Irony', *Lingua*, 87: 53–76.

Wilson, G. (1986) *Narration in Light*. Baltimore, Md.: Johns Hopkins University Press.

—— (2003) 'The Transfiguration of Classical Hollywood Norms'. In B. Gaut and P. Livingstone (eds) *The Creation of Art*. Cambridge: Cambridge University Press.

—— (2007) 'Elusive Narrators in Literature and Film', *Philosophical Studies*, 135: 73–88.

Wollheim, R. (1980) 'Seeing-as, Seeing-in, and Pictorial Perception'. In R. Wollheim, *Art and its Objects*. 2nd edn. Cambridge: Cambridge University Press.

Wood, R. (1989) *Hitchcock's Films Revisited*. New York, Columbia University Press.

Wynn, T. (2002) 'Archaeology and Cognitive Evolution', *Behavioral and Brain Sciences*, 25: 389–438.

Yablo, S. (2002) 'Coulda, Woulda, Shoulda'. In T. S. Gendler and J. Hawthorne (eds) *Conceivability and Possibility*. New York: Oxford University Press.

Zahavi, A. (1975) 'Mate Selection: A Selection for a Handicap', *Journal of Theoretical Biology*, 53: 205–14.

Zizek, S. (1992) *Looking Awry: An Introduction to Jacques Lacan through Popular Culture*. Cambridge, Mass.: MIT Press.

Index

Abbott, H. Porter 33n
Abulafia, D. 208n
achieved meaning 25–6
Ackroyd, P. 182n
Aczel, R. 134n
Aliefs 103n
Allen, R. 177n
Ambassadors, The 88n, 124–8, 131–2, 134
Anna Karenina 25, 71–2, 78
Annals of Saint Gall, 41
Aristotle 29
Atonement 67n
Auerbach, E. vi, 41n
Austen, J. 33, 86, 106, 141, 156, 162, 164–6

Baaren, R. B. van, 100n
Bach, K. 14n, 15n, 16n
Bal, M. 88n, 137
Balcetis, E. 100n
Baldwin effect 47–8
Banfield, A. 140n
Bargh, J., 203–4
Barker, S. 150n, 163
Barrett, J. 36n
Bateson, C. 203n
Bayley, J. 86n
Beach, J. W. 126–7
Beast from 20,000 Fathoms, The 173
Bicycle Thieves 31
Biesele, M. 44n
Birds, The 167–85
Blackburn, S. 154n
Blackwood, A. 182–3
Bleak House 99
Block, N. 4n
Blow Up 57
Booth, W. 70n, 87n, 154
Bostonians, The 184
Boswell, J. 75, 208n
Boyer P. 47n, 184
Bremond, C. 34n
Bristol, M. 195n, 199–200
Britton, J. 195n

Bruner, J. 24n, 43n
Butterfield, H. 36n
Byrne, A. 9n

Calvin, W. H. 2n
Cameron, J. M. 20
Campbell, J. 29n
Carlson, A. 2n
Carroll, N. 27n, 34n, 40n, 43n, 82n, 98n, 99, 159n, 212–3
Carston, R. 7n, 10n, 15n, 16n, 18n
Carver, C. 103n
Cat People 173n, 178n
causal structure 179–81
Chartrand, T. L. 100n
Chase, K. 212n
Chatman, S. 49n, 77n, 88n, 134n, 138
Chen, C. K. 89n
Christie, I. 208n
Cicero 151–3
Cixous, H. 200n
Clark, H. H. 150n, 154n, 157n, 161n
code model of language 14–15,
Cohn, D. 70–1, 141n, 144–5
collapse 63–4
Compton-Burnett, I. 59, 156
Comstock, G 201
Conditionals 81
Cooke, K. 195n
Corazza, E. 161n
corpora 8–9,
Cox, M. 183n
Currie, G. 12n, 20n, 56n, 67n, 80n, 82n, 110n, 111n, 118n, 149n, 154n, 197n, 198n, 217n

Dancy, J 118n
Danto, A. C. 126n
Darley, J. 202n
David Copperfield 142n
Day-Lewis, C. 136
Death in Venice 71–2
Dijksterhuis, A. 100–3
Don't Look Now 182n

Doris, J. 200n, 202n, 203n, 207n, 210n
Doron, E. 141n
Double Indemnity 58
Dowe, P. 29n
Dracula 66–7, 77
Dreams 23
Dretske, F. 5n, 6n
Duck Amuck 63
Dunbar, R. 44n, 209n

egocentric states 89
Eilan, N. 96n
Emma 12, 28–9, 120, 141, 145–6, 156, 158, 163n, 166, 187
emotion
    in *The Birds*, 170
    cost of, 120
    faking of 108
    flexibility of 115–7
    and framework 98–9
    shared 98
Epithalamion 17–8
Eyeless in Gaza 31–2

Fabb, N. 18n
Fara, M. 164n
Ferrari, G. 151n, 157n
First Four Georges, The 12
Fivush, R. 96
Flanagan, O. 202n
Flesch, W. 45n
Fludernik, M. 145n
Fodor, J. 3n
Forster, E. M. 30
free indirect discourse 140–3, 145–6
Freud, S. 56n, 178
Friedman, N. 88n

Gendler, T. S. 103n, 110n, 111
Genette, G. 33, 72–3, 88n, 123–8, 136–7, 142–3, 146
Gerrig, R. J. 150n, 154n, 157n, 161n
Gibbs, R. 6n, 18n
Gibson, J. J. 4,
Gluckman, M. 44n
Glucksberg, S. 150n
Godfrey-Smith, P. 116n
Goldie, P. 49n, 204n,
Gombrich, E. H. 213
Goodman, N. 35n, 50–2

Gorgias 151
Great Expectations 137
Green. M. 91
Greimas, A. 34n
Grice, H. P. 10n, 13n, 16, 18n, 23, 150n, 160n
Gunn, D. 123n, 141–2

Haack, S. 34
Halliwell, S. 123n
Hamlet 52, 71–2, 84, 196, 198, 211
Hargraves, N. 208n
Harman, G. 188, 207n
Harold, J. 100n
Harris, P. 101n
Harvey, W. J. 191n, 192n, 198n
Haunting, The 183n
Hauntings, 182n
Headmistress, The 84
Heal, J. 117n
Heart of Darkness, The 138n
Herrnstein-Smith, B. 33n
Hetherington, S. 34
History of the Franks, 41n
Hitchcock, A. 170–184
Hobson, P. 98n, 100n
Hochman, B. 200n
Hoerl, C. 96
Holloway, J. 198n
Holton, R. 139
Homer 211
Huesmann, L. R. 201n
Horwitz, M. 177n
Hume, D. vi, 41–2, 110n, 186–7
Hurley, S. 100n, 101n, 112n, 201

Idylls of the King 20
If on a Winter's Night Traveller 57
Ignatieff, M. 75
indicators 5
intentions, communicative 6–7, 16
    and evidence 57–8
    in film 18–21,
    limits of, in narrative 62
Invisible Man, The 185
Iseminger, G. 11n
Isen, A. 203n
Iser, W. 43n

Jackson, F. 163, 217n
James, H. 67, 88n, 106, 123, 126–7, 132, 135, 184, 192
James, M. R. 22, 58, 107, 133, 141n, 143, 182–4
Jane Eyre 212n
Johansson, P. 201
Jones, C. 63
Jones, K. 98n
Juridieni, J. 217n

Kahneman, D. 87–8
Kamtekar, R, 203n, 207n
Kania, A. 82n
Karttunen, L. 139
Kelemen, D. 2n, 218n
Keil, F. 2n, 36n
Kellogg, R. 28n
Kermode, F. 27
Kinkead-Weekes, M. 61n
Knights, L. C. 195–8
Knippenberg, A. van 102–4
Kumon-Nakamura S. 150n

Lacan, J. 200
Lachmann, M. 45n
Lamarque, P. 17–8, 33–4, 49n, 209n
Last Supper, The 60
Last Year at Marienbad 49, 53
Lebenswelt 205–6
Lee, A. 100n
Lee, V. 182n
Legend of Hell House, The 183n
Letter to Three Wives 68n
Levin, P 203n
Levinson, J. 25n, 77n, 92n, 93n, 138n
Levinson, S. 15n
Lewis, D. K. 40, 68n, 91n, 115n, 119, 197n, 198n
Little Dorrit 99
Livingston, P. 174n
Lonely are the Brave 55–6
Luck of Barry Lyndon, The 67

Macbeth, 195–8
MacIntyre, A. 110n
Mackie, J. L. 40
McCormack, T. 96
McGinn, C. 205
Manon Lescaut 72–3

Mansfield Park 110, 165–6
Marti, G. 152
media violence 201
Meltzoff, A. 100n, 101n
Memento 75n
memory 23
Middlemarch 68, 168, 191–3, 208, 212
Mill on the Floss, The 144
Mr Beluncle 109, 113–5
Mr Sardonicus 63n
Mithen, S. 94n
Moby Dick 124
Moore, A. 89n
Moran, R. 110n, 209n

Namier, L. B. 33–4, 140
narrative
    categorical and gradational concepts of 34
    characters in 4–5
    embedding of 71–2
    exemplary 35, 37
    extension of 73
    of disconnected events 38–9, 192
    improbable 56–8
    inconsistency in, 9–10, 112–3
    lives as 24–5
    and language evolution 15, 43–8
    orientation to 92, 124–7
    questions in 82–4
    thematic unity in 39
    and time 52–4, 118–9, 140–1
    truth in a 12
narrators
    and knowledge 67–8
    effaced 76–85
    internal and external 66–9
    in non-fiction 74–5
    unreliable 67, 92–3, 113n, 191
Nehamas, A. 151n
Neumann, R. 100n
New Nightmare 63
Noises Off 72
Nolan, D. 113n
Noë, A. 4n
Northanger Abbey 141n, 166n
Norwich, J. J. 155
Notorious 184

O'Donnell, P. 174n
Oliver Twist 56, 164

Olsen, S. H. 209n
On the Eve 135
One Thousand and One Nights 73–4
Ong, W. J. 151
Othello 193–4
Our Mutual Friend 109n

Pafford, J.F.P. 197n
Paglia, C. 167n
Pamela 61–2
Parsons, G. 2n
Passion, A 63n
Patel, A. 94n
Peacocke, C. 97n
Pearl, J. 29n
Personality 204
Persuasion 162, 166n
Phelan, J. 88n
phenomenological structure 179–81
photography 19–20, 82, 153
Pilkington, A. 18n
Poe, E. A. 107n
Poidevin, R. le 38n
point of view 88–93
    cinematic 169–70
    imitation of 130–3
    and irony 155–8, 164–6
    orientation to 125–7, 129, 134–6
pragmatics 3, 13–18, 190–1
Pride and Prejudice 166n
priming experiments 203
Proust, M. 90, 118–21
Plumb, J. H. 37
Predelli, S. 140n
Priest, G. 10n, 113
Prime Minister, The 195
Prince, G. 34n
Psycho, 183n

Quintilian 150n, 152n

Rashomon 73, 118–21
Ravenscroft, I. 111n
Recanti, F. 150n
relevance 18, 41, 190–1
Republic, The 123
Resnais, A. 49
Rimmon-Kenan, S. 137
Richie, D. 118n
Richardson, S, 11, 61–2

Rosenberg, B. 200n
Rosencrantz and Guildenstern are Dead 63
Ross, D. 206n
Rosset E. 217n
Rossholm, G. 134n

Saboteur 182n
Sainsbury, M. 5n, 111n
St Clair, W. 86n
Tomalin, C. 75
Sartre, J.-P. 88n, 144
science fiction viii, 116, 185
Scholes, R. 28n
Scruton, R. 204–7
Sept Péchés capitaux, Les 39
Scott, B. 149n
Scott, W. 86
Sherman, C. 149, 152–3
Shadow of a Doubt 177n
Shortest Way with Dissenters 154
simulation 214–6
Six Characters in Search of an Author 63
Smith, A. 100
Smith, S. 179n
Spenser, E. 17–18
Sperber, D. 3n, 4, 7n, 14n, 18n, 61n, 94,
    149n, 151n, 155, 157n, 158–61, 165n,
    190–1, 217
Sterelny, K. 101n
Sternberg, M. 134n
Strachey, J. 178n
Strack, F. 100n
Strawson, G. 24–5, 34n
*Structure of Politics at the Accession of George
    III, The* 33
Sugiyama, M. 44n
supernatural, the 21–3, 119, 182–5
symbols 177–82

Tanner, M. 112n
Tarde, G. 100–1
Tennyson, A. 20
tense 78–9
Them 173
Thomasson, A. 2n, 4n
Tilford, J. E. 125n
Tomasello, M. 100n
Trollope, A. 106, 134n, 195
Tsohatzidis, S. 139
Turn of the Screw, The 67, 73
Tversky, A 87–8

Unpleasantness at the Bellona Club, The 129
Usual Suspects, The 73

Velleman, J. D. 29–32
Vermazen, B. 91n
Vermeule, B. 47n
Vertigo 212–3
Veyne, P. 211
virtues 61, 110, 114, 189n, 205–6
Vitruvius 213
Vlastos, G. 151–3, 154n

Want, S. 101n
Waugh, E. 109–10
Walton, K. L. 56n, 59–60, 82, 110n, 111n, 150n, 152n, 160n, 209n
Watt, I. 88n, 131–2
Wedgewood, C. V. 143n

Weis, E. 172n
Wetherson, B. 110n, 111n, 113, 121n
what is said and what is implicated 10n, 14–6
White, H. 24n, 41n
Williams, B. 210n
Williams, L. 204
Wilson, D. 3n, 7n, 14n, 18n, 61n, 94, 149n, 151n, 157n, 165n, 190–1
Wilson, G. 59n, 76–85, 132n
Wood, R. 174n
Wynn, T. 2n

Yablo, S. 121n

Zahavi, A. 45n
Zizek, S. 177n